DEVELOPMENT OF HAPPINESS IN THE CONTEMPORARY WORLD

Studies in Critical Social Sciences Book Series

Haymarket Books is proud to be working with Brill Academic Publishers (www.brill.nl) to republish the *Studies in Critical Social Sciences* book series in paperback editions. This peer-reviewed book series offers insights into our current reality by exploring the content and consequences of power relationships under capitalism, and by considering the spaces of opposition and resistance to these changes that have been defining our new age. Our full catalog of *SCSS* volumes can be viewed at https://www.haymarketbooks.org/series_collections/4-studies-in-critical-social-sciences.

DEVELOPMENT OF HAPPINESS IN THE CONTEMPORARY WORLD

From GDP to Doughnut Economics

EDITED BY
MELTEM İNCE YENILMEZ
BURCU TÜRKCAN
GÜL HUYUGÜZEL KIŞLA
EYLÜL KABAKÇI GÜNAY

Haymarket Books
Chicago, IL

First published in 2025 by Brill Academic Publishers, The Netherlands
© 2025 Koninklijke Brill NV, Leiden, The Netherlands

Published in paperback in 2026 by
Haymarket Books
P.O. Box 180165
Chicago, IL 60618
773-583-7884
www.haymarketbooks.org

ISBN: 979-8-88890-800-6

Distributed to the trade in the US through Consortium Book Sales and
Distribution (www.cbsd.com) and internationally through Ingram Publisher
Services International (www.ingramcontent.com).

This book was published with the generous support of Lannan Foundation,
Wallace Action Fund, and the Marguerite Casey Foundation.

Special discounts are available for bulk purchases by organizations and
institutions. Please call 773-583-7884 or email info@haymarketbooks.org for more
information.

Cover design by Jamie Kerry and Ragina Johnson.

Printed in the United States.

Library of Congress Cataloging-in-Publication data is available.

Contents

Preface

The pursuit of happiness is still both a timeless goal and an urgent necessity in a world that is changing quickly due to environmental upheaval, technological advancement, and significant societal shifts. Although GDP (Gross Domestic Product) and other traditional measures have long been used as stand-ins for progress, they are unable to adequately represent the complexity of human well-being. The shortcomings of GDP as a gauge of society achievement have become apparent as societal issues become more complex, calling for a change to frameworks that place a higher priority on holistic well-being.

Development of Happiness in the Contemporary World: From GDP to Doughnut Economics presents a comprehensive investigation of happiness from the perspectives of political science, economics, psychology, sociology, and environmental studies. With its critical analysis and useful advice, this book shows how happiness may influence economic planning, public policy, and international collaboration for a more just and sustainable future. rst part of the book explores the relationship between happiness and money. The complex relationships between income, consumption, and subjective well-being are examined in chapters like Financial Frameworks and Contentment and Happiness and Income: Understanding the Complex Relationship. Readers are urged to reevaluate the significance of material riches in attaining life pleasure as these conversations highlight the complex reality that, although financial security is crucial, the marginal effects of cash on happiness fade.

Building on this framework, later sections explore the relationship between politics and happiness, including chapters such as The Quest for Global Peace: Happiness as a Crucial Element in International Relations and Political Systems and Their Effects on Happiness. At this point, the focus switches to the systemic mechanisms that influence communal well-being, such as public policy, governance, and international diplomacy. These talks support inclusive and fair policies that foster pleasure and peace as essential components of society advancement in addition to economic success.

The book goes into deeper detail about the societal and psychological aspects of happiness. According to Flow Theory, the book examines both external and internal elements that impact well-being, such as mental health, community involvement, and the transformational potential of physical activity, in chapters like Mind Matters: Exploring the Psychology of Happiness and Sociological Understanding of Happiness. Individual experiences and societal trends are combined in these parts to highlight how human flourishing is a community endeavour.

These topics are brought together in the last chapter, Behind the Global Crises: Ways Out of Pandemic and Environmental Disasters for a Sustainable Future, which addresses the twin crises of public health and environmental degradation. The chapter considers a balanced strategy for development, one that ensures social justice and everyone's well-being while respecting planetary boundaries, using Doughnut Economics as a guiding framework.

The goal of this book is to rethink how we quantify and accomplish progress in the modern world. It asks readers to imagine a day when pleasure is not just a personal aim but also a primary objective of global growth by fusing empirical data with imaginative frameworks. In the quest for a more peaceful, equitable, and sustainable society, may this work act as a call to reconsider priorities and spur revolutionary action.

Acknowledgements

Words cannot express how grateful I am to my mother, father, mother-in-law and father-in-law for all of the sacrifices that they have made on my behalf and whose love and guidance are with me in whatever I pursue. They are the ultimate role models. I wish to thank my sisters. I have no words to describe the meaning of your love and support. Most importantly, I owe my deepest gratitude to my loving and supportive husband, Özgür, and my wonderful beloved son, Bryan Poyraz who provides unending inspiration and is such a good boy who always cheers me up. You are the best thing that is still happening to me. Last but not least, I am so grateful to my dear teacher, colleague and more than a relative, Prof. Dr. M. Hulusi Demir, whose supportive approach and encouragement have guided me throughout the process.

Meltem İnce Yenilmez

There is no path to happiness. Happiness is the path itself. The most important thing is to enjoy the journey that we have been gifted. I am grateful to be a daughter of a lovely family, a wife of a supportive man, and a mother of three gorgeous kids during my journey. I am happy to share all my wonderful moments with them. I dedicate this book to my late father Mustafa Uğuş, my beloved mother Nesrin Uğuş, my dear husband Mehmet Türkcan and my sweet kids Azra Türkcan, Mustafa Türkcan and Ahmet Türkcan.

Burcu Türkcan

I would like to thank my wonderful parents for instilling in me the values of hard work, perseverance and integrity. Their belief in my potential has been the driving force behind my achievements. I am deeply grateful to my loving husband and son for their unconditional love and support. Their unwavering support and love have been the foundation of my journey. Finally, I would like to thank my friends who have filled my life with laughter, joy and inspiration. To the readers, I hope this book brings you hopes and dreams and reminds you that the journey is as important as the destination.

Gül Huyugüzel Kışla

This book represents the culmination of a shared vision and collaborative effort to explore the intricate connections between political strategies and economic realities, and I am deeply grateful to everyone who contributed to its realization. I am profoundly grateful to my esteemed co-editors and contributors of this book for their rigorous research and thought-provoking chapters. Their efforts have enriched this volume, making it a comprehensive and meaningful exploration of happiness in the context of policy and economic discourse. A special note of gratitude goes to the individuals and their institutions that supported this endeavour. Their encouragement and resources have provided the foundation for this interdisciplinary inquiry. This book stands as a testament to the power of collaboration, driven by a shared commitment to advancing understanding in this critical field. I hope that the insights within will contribute meaningfully to the ongoing dialogue on happiness and its place in shaping political and economic realities.

Eylül Kabakçı Günay

Tables and Figures

Tables

Figures

Notes on Contributors

Nermin AKARÇAY
(orcid.org/0000-0002-4827-6837) was born in Lüleburgaz in 1982 and studied at Lüleburgaz Anatolian High School between 1993–2000. Dr. Akarçay graduated from Istanbul University, Faculty of Economics, Department of Finance in 2004 then she completed her master's degree in Economic Theory at Marmara University in 2009. In 2020, Dr. Akarçay completed her doctorate in Business Administration at Istanbul Gelişim University. She also completed another doctorate in economics at Istanbul University, Department of Economics in 2024. Dr Akarçay has been working as a lecturer at Tekirdağ Namık Kemal University, Vocational School of Social Sciences, Department of Maritime and Port Management since 2009. Nermin AKARÇAY works in the field of maritime and economy.

Merve ÖZCAN ALTAN
(orcid.org/0009-0006-4777-5622) is a PhD candidate at Ege University, Department of Economics. Her undergraduate and graduate degrees are from Bogazici University and the London School of Economics and Political Science, respectively. She has former experience in the private sector and think-tanks. Her research areas are gender economics, economic development, regional economics and spatial econometrics. She is currently a Research Assistant at Celal Bayar University, Department of Economics.

Barış ÇAĞIRKAN
(orcid.org/0000-0002-0013-1831) completed his undergraduate studies in Sociology at Afyon Kocatepe University in 2012. In the same year, he was awarded the 1416 YLSY scholarship by the Turkish Ministry of National Education, which enabled him to continue his education in the United Kingdom. Dr. Çağırkan pursued language studies in London, followed by pre-sessional training at Richard Taunton Sixth Form College, and completed his Master's degree in Sociology and Social Policy at the University of Southampton in 2015, with a thesis titled *The Perception of Belonging of the Turkish Community Living in the UK within the Mainstream British Society*. Upon returning to Turkey in 2015, he began working as a research assistant in the Sociology Department at Bitlis Eren University. In 2016, he commenced his doctoral studies in Sociology at Gazi University, completing it in 2020. Dr. Çağırkan, who is fluent in English, has numerous publications in respected journals, as well as national and international articles, books, and book chapters related to his field.

Arif BAĞBAŞLIOĞLU
(orcid.org/0000-0002-8603-5014) is an Associate Professor in the Department
of International Relations at the Faculty of Economics and Administrative
Sciences, Izmir Democracy University, Turkey. His field of study is international relations—international security, European security and international
organizations. He graduated from The Department of International Relations,
Gazi University, Ankara/Turkey in 2002 and he completed his M.Sc. degree
in The Department of International Relations at the same university in 2004.
His master thesis is on "US intervention in Afghanistan and the evaluation
of its legal dimensions". He received his PhD degree from The Department of
International Relations, Gazi University, Turkey in 2011. His PhD dissertation is
on NATO's Enlargement and Balkans. He worked in the Turkish Partnership for
Peace (PfP) Training Centre from November 2005 to January 2009 as an international relations specialist and as a course director. He was a postdoctoral
fellow at the University of Ottawa between Sept 2012 and Sept 2013. Between
January 2009 and February 2019, he worked as a research assistant and faculty member at Kırşehir Ahi Evran University. Between February 2019 and
November 2023, he worked as a faculty member and head of the Department
of International Relations (English) at Çanakkale Onsekiz Mart University,
Faculty of Political Sciences. He has written for several academic publications
and contributed conference papers on NATO's partnership policy, international security, European security, peace research, and conflict resolution.

Necmettin ÇELİK
(orcid.org/0000-0003-0139-7778) is an Associate Professor at Izmir Kâtip
Çelebi University, Department of Economics. He teaches Regional Economics,
Defense and Security Economics, and Conflict Economics. His main areas of
interest are regional development and the economics of terrorism.

Gözde ERSÖZ
(orcid.org/ 0000-0002-4848-1929) is an Associate Professor at the Department
of Physical Education and Sports Teacher Education at Marmara University
who specializes in sport management, behaviour science in sport, sport and
exercise psychology. Dr. Ersöz has published 30 research articles and 6 book
chapters and presented more than 100 papers at a scientific congress. Dr. Ersöz
is the co-editor of the Journal of Sport and Social Sciences and The Journal
of Eurasia Sport Sciences Medicine. She also serves on the editorial board of
many journals published in the fields of Sports and Exercise Psychology, Sport
Sciences and Recreation. Dr. Ersöz has served on the committees and boards

of institutions and organizations such as the Turkish National Paralympic Committee, the Basketball Federation, the Triathlon Federation, the Exercise and Sports Psychology Association, the Sports Sciences Association, and the Sports and Physical Activity Association for Women.

Eylül KABAKÇI GÜNAY
(orcid.org/0000-0001-5547-4316) holds bachelor's, master's and PhD degrees in economics from Anadolu University. Dr. Kabakçı Günay's areas of research are Economic growth, development economics and international economics. Throughout her career, Dr. Kabakçı Günay took part in various international and national projects, participated in seminars and gave lectures in diversified areas of economics. Dr. Kabakçı Günay serves as an Associate Professor at Izmir Democracy University.

Gökmen KANTAR
(orcid.org/0000-0001-5120-110X) is an associate professor of political science, political communication, political discourse analysis, political history and politics at Tekirdağ Namık Kemal University, Department of Political Science and Public Administration. Dr. Kantar gave lectures as a visiting student in the field of political science at Esenyurt University Social Sciences Institute between 2018–2019 and 2019–2020 at Maltepe University. Since 2017, Dr. Kantar has been working as a visiting associate professor at Tekirdağ Namık Kemal University in Turkey. She is a political scientist focusing on political language, ideology, intercultural communication, social policy, democracy, feminism and modernization. Dr. Kantar has twelve international and two national books published by international publishing houses. The book on cyberfeminism, women and the state has been published in 2024. In addition to his thirty national and international articles, Dr. Kantar has nearly 20 international oral presentations.

Gül HUYUGÜZEL KIŞLA
(orcid.org/0000-0002-0901-2038) is an Associate Professor in the Department of Economics, at Ege University, Turkey. She completed her undergraduate study, MA and PhD in Economics at Ege University. She worked at Yaşar University from 2007 to 2009. Afterwards, she joined Ege University as an academic staff. She has been working at the same university since 2009. Currently, her primary research interests are macro-finance, labour productivity and currency crises.

Özge KOZAL
(orcid.org/0000-0002-5542-6290) is a Lecturer and Research Assistant at the Department of Economics, Ege University. She graduated with honours from Ege University, Department of Economics in 2012 and completed her PhD in 2019 with a thesis titled "The 200-Year History of Industrialization in Turkey: Continuities and Transformations." During her doctoral studies, she was a Visiting Researcher at the University of Groningen from 2017 to 2018. She currently teaches courses on the Turkish economy, economic development, and sustainable human development. Her research interests include economic development, political economy, industrialization, and ecological/circular economy.

Begüm YURTERI KÖSEDAĞLI
(orcid.org/0000-0002-3828-2598) is an Assistant Professor at the Department of Economics of Ege University. Her scientific areas are Spatial Econometrics, Panel and Time-Series Analysis and Financial Markets. She visited the University of Illinois at Urbana-Champaign as a visiting fellow between September 2015 and March 2016, benefiting the TÜBİTAK PhD Research Scholarship. She has written in the International Journal of Finance and Economics, Financial Innovation, and Tourism Analysis besides national and international book chapters and presented at various referred congresses and symposiums.

Burcu TÜRKCAN
(orcid.org/0000-0002-7494-5897) is an Associate Professor in the division of Economic Policy in the Department of Economics at Ege University. She got her bachelor's degree in Economics from Ege University in 2005. Then, she got her master's degree in Economics from the same university in 2008. She started the Economics PhD program in the same year. She conducted some of her research at the University of Turin as a scholar of the Scientific and Technological Research Council of Turkey. She got her PhD degree in 2012 at Ege University. Currently, she gives lectures on economic complexity theory, network economics, tourism economics and statistics at both undergraduate and graduate levels. Her current research interests include economic policy, regional economics, economic complexity and tourism economics.

Ulviye TÜFEKÇİ YAMAN
(orcid.org/0000-0003-3299-9448) completed her undergraduate education at Karadeniz Technical University, Department of Labour Economics and Industrial Relations, and her MA and PhD at Bursa Uludağ University, Department of Labour Economics and Industrial Relations. Between 2013–2022, she

worked as a research assistant at Bursa Uludag University. She is currently working as an asst. prof. at the same institution.

Meltem İNCE YENILMEZ

(orcid.org/0000-0002-4689-3196) is a professor at the Department of Economics at Izmir Democracy University who specializes in the economics of gender, labour economics and social work. Prof. İnce-Yenilmez was a Visiting Researcher at the University of California, Berkeley between 2014–2015; was at Georg-Universität-Gottingen at summer school in 2015–2016; was Visiting Researcher at Lund University, was a Research Associate at the University of Massachusetts, Amherst in 2020–2022 and was Visiting Faculty at IIM Rohtak, India in 2022. Prof. İnce-Yenilmez has been a Visiting Professor at the University of Tohoku, Japan since 2021. Prof. İnce-Yenilmez is an economist focused on labour economics, discrimination, sustainability, social policy, behavioural economics, and care work. Prof. İnce-Yenilmez has eight books published by Routledge, Palgrave, Rowman, and Peter Lang while the next book projects are Cyberfeminism, Migration Economy, and Economy, ecology, and Environment will be published by 2024.

Hakan YILDIRIM

is an Associate Professor at Istanbul Gelisim University, specializing in finance. His academic career focuses on financial markets, risk management, portfolio management, energy, and environmental economics. With expertise in finance and economics, Dr. Yıldırım has conducted extensive research on the functioning of the global financial system and its interaction with environmental factors. His studies primarily concentrate on risk analysis in financial markets, developing investment strategies, and portfolio optimization. Dr. Yıldırım has published numerous academic papers in these fields and regularly conducts training sessions for professionals. His work on energy and environmental economics explores sustainable finance practices and how environmental factors influence financial risks. Understanding the economic impact of fluctuations in energy markets and innovative strategies in portfolio management are key themes in his research. Having participated in various national and international conferences, Dr. Yıldırım provides valuable insights into the latest developments in the field, applying an academic perspective to contemporary issues. At Istanbul Gelisim University, he continues to educate students not only with theoretical knowledge but also by offering practical applications and real-world examples.

CHAPTER 1

Multidisciplinary Perspectives on the Definition of Happiness: a Global Endeavour

Burcu Türkcan and Merve Özcan Altan

Happiness has always had remarkable attention in social sciences research, but it has become a famous concept since the 1990s. Although defining the concept is quite hard owing to its complex structure, different opinions about its definition have also emerged. Psychologists have constructed happiness functions based on people's self-reports about the satisfaction of their lives. However, economists have tried to build more concrete indexes based on objective observable values such as income level and income inequality. Nowadays, happiness is also an agenda for sociologists. Sociologists examine the well-being of the whole society in terms of happiness and hence try to use both psychological and economic scaling factors. A true definition of happiness is in direct linkage with politics and other disciplines. Due to the philosophical background of happiness, the fundamental question here is what is the complete definition of happiness? In the context of this question, this study aims to enlighten the worldwide definition of happiness in terms of different scientific perspectives. Following this aim, after a brief introduction, the first section gives the definitions of happiness in different disciplines. The second section gives a synthesis of the worldwide definition of the concept. Lastly, the conclusion develops a discussion about the definition of happiness and future research. This chapter aims to contribute to the literature by exploring a commonly held definition constructed from different perspectives.

1   Introduction

We are all probably sure that no one in the world wants to be happy or not to have a blessed life filled with lots of pleasant emotions and memories. From a practical point of view, unless there is a tendency towards an exaggerated depression or a psychological disorder, all people are inclined to search for happiness at the end of everything they do. It stems from the shared idea that happiness is a good thing which triggers enjoyable feelings and makes people feel good.

The desire to be happy is not only related to today's world although its ongoing discussions are still on the table. Contrary to what is believed, happiness has been one of the most questioned things in the world since the birth of philosophical thought in ancient Greece (Veenhoven, 1995). Some outstanding philosophers attempted to define happiness by linking it with ethics. At this point, Aristotle came to the forefront as the first person to define happiness in his Nicomachean Ethics (Annas, 1993).

Since the times of ancient Greece, the concept of happiness has always had remarkable attention in social sciences research, but it has become a famous concept since the 1990s due to significant breakthroughs in technological advancements and empirical methods. Although defining the concept is quite hard owing to its complex structure, different opinions about its definition have also emerged. While psychologists define happiness as subjective well-being, economists define it as economic well-being in terms of income and wealth (Powdthavee, 2007). Psychologists have constructed happiness functions based on people's self-reports about the satisfaction of their lives. However, economists have tried to construct more concrete indexes based on objective observable values such as income level and income inequality. It's sure that both views have some deficiencies due to the complexity and inclusivity of the concept but at the same time, they provide good insights for the understanding of the issue. Nowadays, happiness is also on the agenda for sociologists. Although happiness from a sociological perspective dates back to Herbert Spencer and Auguste Comte, it has become popular in the last three decades (Veenhoven, 2018). Sociologists examine the well-being of the whole society in terms of happiness and hence try to use both psychological and economic scaling factors. Moreover, happiness level is also a concern of politics. Happiness level is an important indicator for politicians to evaluate their actions and forecast voting behaviours. Hence, it's seen that happiness has become one of the main research areas of various social science disciplines. What is more, is that some other disciplines like migration studies and sports sciences also deal with happiness issues from different perspectives.

Due to the philosophical background of happiness and the wide interest in this topic in ongoing research efforts from different disciplines, the fundamental question here is what is the complete and de facto definition of happiness? In the context of this question, this study aims to enlighten the worldwide definition of happiness in terms of different social science perspectives. Following this aim, this chapter tries to give different definitions of happiness with a comprehensive analysis of various disciplines. In this context, after a brief introduction, the first section gives happiness definitions from different sciences' perspectives. The second section gives a synthesis of the worldwide definition of the concept. Lastly, the conclusion develops a discussion about the definition of happiness and future research. The main purpose of this chapter is to contribute to the literature by exploring a commonly held definition constructed from different perspectives.

2   Definition of Happiness in Different Social Disciplines

Happiness as a qualitative notion, has various definitions in different social disciplines ranging from philosophy to psychology, sociology and economics. In this section, a general overview of the definition of this concept is given by examining different social science disciplines.

2.1   *Happiness in Philosophy*

In his Nicomachean Ethics, the Greek philosopher Aristotle presented his famous concept of "Eudaimonia" which was believed to pave the way for happiness in the end. In-depth, "eudaimonia" refers to the highest and the best version of humankind, such that it is not a stable state but an aim that should be achieved throughout one's lifetime (Huta and Waterman, 2014). In Aristotle's definition of happiness, a person's character and his will to behave in a good and respectful manner in all aspects of life are important for society to be happy all together. Hence, behaving by virtue and aiming for the greatest benefit of all human beings are seen as the concrete ways towards happiness. Within this scope, the importance of institutions as the "rules of the game" both for individuals and entities was highlighted for the solid application of virtuous attitudes. For instance, Aristotle emphasised that politics, as one of the most important institutions, should aim to reach "eudaimonia" in pursuit of happiness (Helliwell et al., 2023).

The first attempts to shed light on happiness in ancient Greek philosophy were not solely limited to Aristotle even though his definition has been the most famous one up to date. Among other outstanding philosophers of those times, Plato and Socrates come to the forefront as other attempts to explain happiness. Plato paid special attention to the happiness of the society as a whole rather than the happiness of its single members and evaluated these two kinds of happiness as equal if the society is happy (Morrison, 2001). Likewise, Socrates was interested in the happiness of the city as a whole even if some of its members like guardians were unhappy. Following the eudaimonia philosophy, Epicurus was also another philosopher who emphasized the importance of the existence of pleasure and the absence of pain (Annas, 1987). He stated that all living things search for pleasure and this pursuit completely relies on feelings. He also classified the pleasure as kinetic and static. "Ataraxia" is a term used by Epicurus to define the situation in which an individual has no pain or any upsetting condition. So, suffering nothing is a type of pleasure which is also quite hard to have. However, kinetic pleasure is the search for pleasure and having an act for it. As an example, the pleasure of drinking is purely kinetic (Annas, 1987: 8). Epicurus underlines that searching for pleasure is a natural incentive and hence individuals are selfish. For the pleasure of the whole society, states should intervene in the individuals' actions. As seen, the philosophers of ancient times focused generally on the goodness of the system and its stability rather than the happiness of every single individual. They thought that behaving under virtuous and moral values would bring happiness and excellence to the cities and societies (Cooper, 1987).

During ancient times, it was seen that happiness was mostly evaluated on an intangible ground and generally based on subjective perceptions of the philosophers. The philosophers searching for the definition and meaning of happiness have—in general—been called 'hedonists'. This situation continued until the beginning of the usage of some quantitative techniques such as surveys and questionnaires to measure happiness. The timing of these measurement techniques does not go a long way back in the past. They became popular, especially in the second half of the 20th century. During the time between the birth of ancient thought and the application of quantitative measurement techniques, works about happiness remained also limited to intangible discussions. Therein, for instance, English philosopher Jeremy Bentham defined happiness again from an intangible perspective as "the sum of pleasures and pains" and similarly focused on the happiness of more people rather than individuals due to his "greater happiness for the greater number of people" principle (Veenhoven, 2010:606). Immanuel Kant was another famous philosopher work on morals and happiness. Although Kant describes happiness in several ways such as pleasure, well-being, and welfare, all the definitions are directly linked with complete and stable satisfaction (Wike, 1994: 1–2).

2.2   Happiness in Psychology

After being handled for a long time within the scope of philosophy, the direction of happiness was changed with the rise of other social disciplines such as psychology and sociology. With the rise of psychology in the 19th century, happiness began to be defined differently. Psychologists started to focus on some other aspects of happiness ranging from the state of emotions and well-being to the fulfilment of personal urges. For instance, the founder of psychoanalysis, Sigmund Freud (1930) defined happiness as "the satisfaction of needs" which are especially primitive urges. He asserted that modern man's constant search for physical satisfaction turns to a vicious circle of pleasure and pain cycle and thus the result would be chronic unhappiness instead of happiness (Akhtar, 2010). All in all, psychology's focus on happiness has been broadly on narrowing and describing it as a personal phenomenon not only from an emotional but also physical and biological point of view (Jacobsen, 2007).

Psychology's approach towards happiness has deepened and prospered with the usage of quantitative methods. These quantitative methods were milestones for those who want to investigate happiness in detail because the methods could prevent the works on happiness from being solely intangible and unquantifiable. With the help of quantitative methods, happiness could be measured and therefore evaluated on a common ground (Powdthavee, 2007). Moreover, they give the subject of happiness the chance to be compared between individuals, groups and even countries so that making some inferences might be possible. Some of the very first attempts at the usage of quantitative methods in happiness were Gallup-poll-type surveys and the Cantril approach that became especially popular in the 1950s and 1960s (Easterlin, 1974).

Within the context of these techniques, respondents are asked directly to express how happy they are in the former and to scale their happiness between the range of the lowest and the highest ends in the latter. Following these initial and most influential techniques, there have been other initiatives like the Experience Sampling Method and Day Reconstruction Method to measure happiness. Today, there are lots of surveys, questionnaires and reports based on these techniques like the World Values Survey, Eurobarometer Survey, World Happiness Report and Gallup Global Emotions Report. With the development of these quantitative techniques, scholars and especially psychologists have begun to express happiness in different words such as subjective well-being, life satisfaction and quality of life.

Kahneman and Dolan (2015), listed several factors at play. They proposed that the physiological processes of the body could hold the key to explaining happiness and that greater study in the fields of general health and neuroscience will clarify the relationship between these processes and life pleasure. Deaton and Stone (2012) studied two aspects of subjective well-being: everyday feelings and participants' overall assessment of their lives. Inquiries like: How far from perfect is your life? were posed to the participants. Also, to assess feelings, consider asking yourself: How did you feel yesterday? Happiness, sadness, rage, worry, and tension were among the responses.

2.3   Happiness in Sociology

The rise of quantitative measurement techniques has also been beneficial for the incorporation of sociology in happiness studies during approximately the same years as psychology. As distinct from philosophy and psychology, sociologists have been interested in understanding the dynamics of happiness in societies and the reasons for differences in happiness levels among countries (Jacobsen, 2007). Surveys and reports on the scale of countries are effective tools for sociologists to search for changing motivations behind happiness from one country to another. It is almost impossible to offer a "one-size-fits-all" prescription for happiness that could be applied to all countries. It stems from the fact that happiness is a very subjective phenomenon and as Veenhoven (2010:614) underlined that "conditions for happiness differ across cultures".

The roots of the search for happiness definition in sociology date back to the 19th century. Happiness has attracted the attention of the founders of sociology like Auguste Comte and Herbert Spencer (Plé, 2000). In the following years, the rise of the quantitative measurement techniques was a turning point for the incorporation of sociology in happiness studies coinciding with a similar time with psychology. As distinct from philosophy and psychology, sociologists have been interested in understanding the divergent dynamics of happiness in societies and the reasons for differences in happiness levels among countries (Jacobsen, 2007).

With the developments in large-scale evaluation techniques from the mid-20th century—especially in western countries—sociologists were able to measure the life satisfaction of mass populations more accurately (Veenhoven, 2016). Today, there are large databases such as the World Database of Happiness which aims to figure out not only the determinants of happiness but also the way these determinants make people happy in many different countries. Measuring happiness from a sociological perspective has also been important to ensure healthy mental ageing and to compare social policies affecting people's well-being in different countries.

Some mutual conclusions are drawn attention in the surveys, reports and questionnaires published about happiness around the globe. These conclusions are as follows: (i) the average level of happiness is increasing, (ii) inequality in happiness levels is reducing and (iii) characteristics of society such as importance given to the rule of law, democracy and climate crisis in addition to high living standards affect happiness (Veenhoven, 2016). These conclusions come to the forefront as important common features of happiness in different countries thanks to the rising income levels, higher living standards and considerable technological developments since the end of the world wars.

Although some general characteristics of happiness find common ground in different societies, it is nearly impossible to offer a "one-size-fits-all" prescription that could be applied to all countries. It stems from the fact that happiness is a very subjective phenomenon, and every country has differences in terms of history, institutions, rules, values, sensibilities, economic conditions and even personal characteristics. This situation is emphasised by Veenhoven (2010:614) who asserted that "conditions for happiness differ across cultures". The challenge of offering a single prescription of happiness applicable to the whole world can be easily illustrated by cultural differences in countries and continents. At this point, it is known that while people in Asian countries tend to be happier when they belong to a group, European societies are inclined to be individualistic, so they give more importance to their boundaries (Yong, 2019). Likewise, Hofstede (1984) showed that other important traits like gender roles namely masculinity and femininity in addition to time orientation such as short and long-run perspectives might largely vary among different societies so that one precise definition of happiness with its exact determinants is far from reality.

2.4   *Happiness in Political Science*

Political science is another important social discipline that has direct linkages with happiness. Like philosophy, politics and governance of mass populations have been deep-rooted parts of life since the birth of ancient thought. Some of the significant ancient Greek philosophers, Aristotle and Plato, who were discussed in detail under the "happiness in philosophy" section, had important works touching upon society's happiness from the viewpoint of politics and philosophy. The insistence of the ancient Greek thought on virtuous behaviour was also seen in explaining the linkages between politics and happiness. In his famous work, *Politics*, Aristotle asserted that the best type of government is the one where the society reaches its happiest version.

Until the rise of the nation-states in the 18th century, happiness had not been handled from the perspective of society but from that of the rulers and kings. To provide stability and strengthen the power, writers, philosophers and statesmen of those times had sometimes advised restrictive ways of governance which ignored the community's happiness (Ryan, 2010). Here, one of the most extreme supporters of this view was a Florentine diplomat, author and philosopher, Niccolò Machiavelli who is seen as the founder of modern political thought (Del Lucchese, 2017). In his famous work, *Prince*, Machiavelli recommended that a prince must be cruel, tyrannic and ruthless unless he wants to lose his sovereignty (Hösle, 1989). In The *Prince*, the significant power of fear rather than love to rule a community is repeatedly emphasised because according to Machiavelli people tend to obey the leaders from whom they are afraid. Therefore, cruelty and power were the driving forces of Machiavelli's understanding of necessary conditions for state governance, and the well-being of society was not paid attention.

The 16th century established a ground for the rise of critical and scientific thinking due to the diminishing power of the Catholic Church and the rise of an interest in art after the Reform and Renaissance movements in Europe (Cieslik, 2017). The Independence of America in 1776 and the French Revolution afterwards were historical turning points for the arousing of new political phenomena such as freedom, human rights, democracy and equity. Despite its failure, the French Revolution was very important in the sense that people started to ask for better and honourable living conditions in addition to their basic rights. During the bloody days, the young revolutionist Saint-Just articulated that "happiness is a new idea in Europe" (Geuss, 2002:15). This shows that nothing would be the same anymore since people were insistent on getting rid of their chains and having equal rights as "citizens".

The formation of nation-states in the following century accelerated the modern man's search for happiness as he climbed the social ladder from the peasant class with almost no rights to equal citizens with newly manifested freedoms (Wimmer and Feinstein, 2010). At first glance, the acquisition of unprecedented rights and the opportunity to have a life with dignity after bloody struggles were victorious occasions for the millions. However, well-being of world citizens was repeatedly interrupted by the never-ending wars in especially the European continent and the following two major world wars (Kesternich et al., 2014).

In the new world order after World War II, states began to prioritise improving their internal conditions from an economic and social perspective. During the following years, the establishment of some international and supranational organisations such as the United Nations (UN) and the European Union (EU) paved the way for the emergence of welfare states. With the rise of these states, public policy has started to be used for enhancing citizens' living conditions and well-being (Ryan, 2010). Thanks to the highly increasing number of countries governed by democracy, elections have become important enforcement mechanisms for the public to make the governments aware of their demands. Recent tensions and conflicts between Russia-Ukraine and Israel-Palestine have damaged the well-being of people in the affected regions but it can be still asserted that the rise of fundamental rights and freedoms in the political sphere has been beneficial for the prioritisation of people's happiness.

2.5   *Happiness in Economics*

In parallel with the research efforts in psychology, sociology and politics, efforts in economics have also been raised in the 20th century. Vilfredo Pareto (1909) has developed the cardinal utility term to define choice behaviours as to price and budget constraints. This was the first attempt to identify individual choices to attain the best position across different possible options. In economics, utility is based on revealed preferences and agents try to maximise it as a result of their choices among a set of goods and services. However, economic agents are restricted by their budget constraints so that they cannot have all the material things they wish to have. As seen, although happiness is more related to emotions and a state of well-being, utility is largely interested in people's choices among different bundles of goods and services, so these two terms do not indicate the same meaning exactly. Jeremy Bentham (1952) has enhanced the understanding of individual optimal utility choice with the proposition that society's welfare can be represented as the sum of utilities of different individuals. In following years, Hirschman (1973) suggested that others' income also a determinant of an individual's happiness level. Existence of richer people may create comparison effect on poorer people and may give hope and belief about their future welfare. This may increase the expectations about subjective well-being. Consequently, it can be said that utilitarian approach has started with Pareto, enlarged by Bentham and evolved through egalitarian approach by Hirshcman.

The first attempts of analysing the effect of utility on economic growth were the attempts of Barro (1990) and, Barro and Sala-I Martin (1992). They have tried to shape economic growth models with the addition of utility for the first time. From that time on several other studies examined the impacts of numerous micro and macro factors such as income, consumption, employment and inflation on people's well-being. At this point, it was long believed that rises in income would enhance people's well-being since more money could buy an enlarged set of goods and services (Hirschauer et al., 2014). However, Easterlin (1974) was the first economist who falsified the deep-rooted assumption of income's power to enhance happiness forever after having presented his well-known "Easterlin Paradox".[1] He asserted that after passing a certain income level, people's well-being does not continue to go upward. This trend has been especially prevalent in many developed countries in the last decades where happiness levels are said to be stable (Kimball and Willis, 2023).

---

1   Easterlin, R.A. (2010). Happiness, Growth, and the Life Cycle. New York: Oxford University Press.

For decades, scholars have been fascinated by—and, with the recent invasion of economists, have become obsessed with—whether money makes people happy. We've all heard that poverty makes people unhappy. Some academics contend, however, that having more money than is needed for basic security provides no additional enjoyment and may even cause misery. Making more money may also be fruitless since people adapt mentally to their levels of wealth and, like addicts and narcotics, require ever more money to induce a similar amount of pleasure. Or maybe it's not so much about money as it is about status. People seek money to feel superior to the parents next door. Of course, this creates a vicious and futile circle. Alternative academics, like Veenhoven, agree that the more money one makes, the more money it takes to move the happiness meter, but they also claim that more money does bring more happiness, albeit at a slower rate among the wealthy. The facts appear to back up such an assertion. All these discussions have brought about an emerging research field: "happiness economics".

Happiness economics is an emerging and quickly expanding branch of economics focusing on the measurement of well-being to evaluate the effectiveness of policies. It is rooted in the term of subjective well-being. Hence, happiness and well-being are generally used interchangeably in literature (MacKerron, 2012: 705–706). Happiness economics tries to attach welfare to subjective well-being and hence relies on surveys and reports that are heavily based on self-reports and subjective evaluations harmonized with objective indicators like gross domestic product (GDP), inflation, income inequality etc. Consequently, happiness economics uses interdependent utility functions, procedural utility and the interaction of rational and non-rational influences in determining economic behaviour (Graham, 2005: 41–42). Frey and Stutzer (2000) have listed the factors determining the level of happiness as (1) personality and demographic factors (2) microeconomic and macroeconomic factors, and (3) institutional conditions in an economy and society. Thus, apart from material well-being, there are several other intangible factors determining a person's happiness level. In this context, as underlined before, one of the fundamental efforts of happiness economics is measuring the level of happiness.

Happiness measurement efforts have started in psychology with the Gallup Poll Survey, Experience Sampling Method and Day Reconstruction Method (Easterlin, 1974). Then these methods have been enhanced by the inclusion of objective indicators. Measuring efforts have become firstly national and then global. In this sense, the U.S. Gallup-Sharecare Well-Being Index is an example of national affords. It has 6 dimensions to construct happiness levels: present and anticipated life conditions, daily feelings and mental well-being, job satisfaction and working conditions, physical well-being, healthy behaviour for physical conditions, and feeling safe and satisfied (GALLUP, 2024). This national measurement attempt has been enlarged through the global context with the emergence of the Gallup Global Emotions Report. However, since this survey excludes economic indicators and only focuses on emotions and experiences, some other measurement methods have been developed (GALLUP; 2023). As one of them, OECD Well-Being Report tries to measure happiness levels by including income and wealth, work and job quality, housing, health, knowledge and skills, environmental quality, subjective well-being, safety, work-life balance, social connections, and civic engagement (OECD, 2024). Another measurement method has been developed with a different perspective as the Happy Planet Index. It includes the parameters of environmental sustainability and tries to intersect these parameters with personal well-being (happyplanetindex.org). Lastly, as a commonly held report, the World Happiness Report tries to shed light on the happiness levels of countries across the World. It is based on six dimensions: income, health, social support, having a sense of freedom to make key life decisions, generosity, and the absence of corruption (Helliwell et al., 2023: 6).

2.6   *Happiness in Other Disciplines*

Apart from philosophy, psychology, sociology, economics and politics, some other research fields and sciences have also been examining the happiness concept. Migration studies is one of these fields. Studies searching for the nexus between happiness and migration focus on the factors pushing people to migrate and the consequences of migration in terms of happiness. They mainly examine the relationship between happiness and migration decisions, and the factors affecting the happiness of migrants (Hendriks and Bartram, 2018). Hence, pre-migration happiness and post-migration happiness are the key research areas for migration studies (Hendriks, 2015). Since migration decision is highly correlated with utility, income and poverty, it's related to happiness economics. Since this decision is also correlated with security, equity and future expectations, it's also related to politics, sociology and psychology (Polgreen and Simpson, 2011: 820–821). So, it's sure that happiness in migration can be identified with an interdisciplinary perspective. Especially, migration issue has been on the scene with the acceleration of the Global Climate Crisis, recently. Today climate migration is an emerging discussion topic that underlines the critical importance of near-future migration trends due to climatic changes across the World by 2050 (Rigaud et al., 2018). So, it seems that climate will also take apart across happiness factors of people soon.

Another research field for happiness is gender studies. Gender studies mainly focus on gender discrimination and its effects on happiness. However, there is also a strand of studies examining happiness factors for different sexes. It seems from the empirical studies that there is a positive correlation between lower gender discrimination and higher happiness levels of women (Mookerjee and Beron, 2005). Especially, gender roles in the family are highly impressive on women's happiness. Empirical studies prove that a high share of housework and childcare responsibilities decreases the happiness level of women (Mencarini and Sironi, 2010: 216). What is more is that emerging gender studies focus on the happiness of LGBTIQ persons also (Greene and Britton, 2015). Empirical results underline that acceptance of support in society for LGBTIQ individuals increases their happiness level (de Vries et al, 2020).

Recently, happiness studies also took part in health studies. Since being healthy is an important dimension of personal happiness, this indicator has been included in happiness measurement methods. Hence, the health and happiness relationship has come to be examined recently in health studies. Clinical health, perceived health status and wellness are positively correlated with personal happiness level (Mahon et al., 2005). Health—as a general definition—is a state of physical, mental and social well-being (Cloninger and Zohar, 2011). Hence, mental health status—which is also the research field of psychology—is also important for happiness since it affects the perceived subjective well-being.

Lastly, happiness is an emergent discussion topic in sports sciences. As Csikszentmihalyi (1992) stated in his Flow Theory, people's overall well-being is directly determined by their experiences in flow. Sports, dance, and yoga help people to connect their body and mind. Recent studies on the relationship between physical activity and happiness proved that engaging in physical exercise and maintaining an active lifestyle provides a good psychological state. Today, there is still an ongoing effort to obtain optimal physical activity levels to provide maximum happiness level for individuals (Zhang and Chen, 2019).

3   A Path toward a Common Definition of Happiness

Historically, from Ancient Greek to the Modern Age, humanity has been on the search for a valid and commonly held definition of happiness. Sometimes they have attached virtue and ethics and sometimes religion and belief to the concept. In this manner, it has been one of the main concerns of different research fields in philosophy, religion and science. From individual to society, being happy has always been in the spotlight. But, at the same time, the fundamental question has always been: "What is happiness?".

TABLE 1.1   Happiness definitions as to various scientific fields

Scientific field	Definition of happiness
Philosophy	Behaving under virtue while searching for sustained pleasure.
Psychology	Satisfaction of needs to provide subjective well-being.
Sociology	Society's subjective well-being which changes according to culture, historical background, economic conditions, institutions and laws.
Politics	Well-being of citizens by the courtesy of equity and fairness.
Economics	Individual and societal welfare attainment by a higher level of income and income equality, lower inflation and provision of sustainable development elements.
Migration Studies	Well-being of migrants and host country citizens in the post-migration period.
Gender Studies	Subjective well-being of different sexes by attainment of less gender discrimination and higher acceptance of society for different sexual choices.
Health Sciences	Physical and mental well-being of individuals.
Sport Sciences	Well-being of individuals' body and mind that connected by physical activity.

SOURCE: THE TABLE HAS BEEN CONSTRUCTED BY THE AUTHORS

As we have mentioned in the previous section, different scientific fields have different approaches to define happiness. From philosophy to sports sciences, each field has its own perspective. By obtaining these diversified perspectives, several happiness measurement methods have been constructed recently. OECD Well Being Report, Happy Planet Index, Gallup Global Emotions Report and World Happiness Report are the most famous attempts to measure happiness levels across countries and societies, to classify them according to their happiness levels. However, it's observed that different methods use different indicators to get happiness levels and hence it proves that there is still no common definition of happiness. Table 1.1 summarizes happiness definitions in various scientific fields.

All definitions seem right in their contexts. However, it seems that there is an ongoing need to merge them into a common definition. In this sense, happiness can be defined as:

Happiness is subjective well-being that is attained by behaving under virtue, a satisfaction of basic needs and wants, having physical and mental
health, being physically active, providing high welfare level, accepting
diversities and increasing equity across different groups of society.

4   Conclusion

The concept of happiness has always had remarkable attention in social sciences research, but it has become a famous concept since the 1990s. Although
defining the concept is quite hard owing to its complex structure, different
opinions about its definition have also emerged. From philosophy to economics, each scientific field has produced its own happiness definition. As
we have examined different approaches in this chapter, all definitions seem
quite right from their perspectives. But at the same time, each of them has its
limitations. In this context, we have tried to make a synthesis about the definition of happiness by merging different approaches. Although there are some
global attempts to measure happiness by taking together various indicators
covering diversified fields such as physical well-being, life satisfaction, income,
welfare, expectations and health; there is still a significant need to develop a
comprehensive definition of happiness. This chapter tries to contribute to the
literature by enhancing happiness definition from the lens of different scientific disciplines.

Defining happiness is important since it helps us understand what brings
fulfilment and contentment in life. It allows us to set meaningful goals for
both our individual lives and socioeconomic development. It also allows us to
make informed decisions and prioritize activities contributing to well-being.
Consequently, true and complete definition is critical both for individual and
societal decisions. In this chapter, we have melted different definitions in the
same pot by an inductive approach. In this manner our happiness definition
is as follows:

Happiness is subjective well-being that is attained by behaving following
virtue, satisfaction of basic needs and wants, having physical and mental
health, being physically active, providing high welfare level, accepting
diversities and increasing equity across different groups of society.

References

Akhtar, S. (2010). Happiness: origins, forms and technical relevance. The American Journal of Psychoanalysis 70: 219–244.

Annas, J. (1993). The morality of happiness. Oxford University Press.

Annas, J. (1987). Epicurus on Pleasure and Happiness. Ancient Greek Philosophy. 15(2): 5–21.

Aristotle. (1988). The Politics. Trans. Benjamin Jowett; ed. Stephen Everson. Cambridge: Cambridge University Press.

Bentham, J. (1952). The Philosophy of Economic Science. In Werner Stark, (ed.), Jeremy Bentham's Economic Writings, Vol. I. London: Published for the Royal Economic Society by George Allen and Unwin, pp. 81–119.

Cieslik, M. (2017). The Happiness Riddle and the Quest for a Good Life. Palgrave Macmillan. London, United Kingdom.

Cloninger, C. R. and Zohar, A. H. (2011). Personality and the perception of health and happiness. Journal of Affective Disorders. 128 (1–2): 24–32.

Cooper, J. M. (1987). Contemplation and happiness: a reconsideration. Synthese 72(2): 187–216.

Csikszentmihalyi, M. (1992). Flow—The classic work on how to achieve happiness. Harper & Row. The USA.

Del Lucchese, F. (2017). Machiavelli and constituent power: The revolutionary foundation of modern political thought. European Journal of Political Theory. 16(1): 3–23.

De Vries, J. M. A., Downes, C., Sharek, D., Doyle, L., Murphy, R., Begley, T., McCann, E., Sheerin, F., Smyth, S. and Higgins, A. (2020). An exploration of happiness within the Irish LGBTI community. Journal of Gay & Lesbian Mental Health. 24(1): 40–76.

Easterlin, R. A. (1974). Does economic growth improve the human lot? Some Empirical Evidence. In (P. A. David and M. W. Reder eds) Nations and Households in Economic Growth: Essays in Honour of Moses Abramowitz. New York and London: Academic Press, pp. 89–125.

Freud, S. (1930). Civilization and its discontents. Standard edition 21:64–145.

Frey, B. S. and Stutzer, A. (2000). Happiness, economy and institutions. The Economic Journal 110: 918–938.

GALLUP. (2024). How does the U.S. Gallup-share care well-being index work? https://news.gallup.com/poll/128186/gallup-healthways-index-work.aspx.

GALLUP. (2023). Gallup Global Emotions 2023. https://www.gallup.com/.

Geuss, R. (2002). Happiness and Politics. A Journal of Humanities and the Classics. 10(1): 15–33.

Graham, C. (2005). The economics of happiness: insights on globalization from a novel approach. World Economics. 6: 41–53.

Greene, D. C. and Britton, P. J. (2015). Predicting adult LGBTQ happiness: impact of childhood affirmation, self-compassion, and personal mastery. Journal of LGBT Issues in Counseling. 9 (3): 158–179.

Happy Planet Index. https://happyplanetindex.org/.

Helliwell, J. F., Layard, R., Sachs, J. D., De Neve, J-E., Aknin, L. B. and Wang, S. (2023). World happiness report 2023. https://worldhappiness.report/ed/2023/.

Hendriks, M. and Bartram, D. (2018). Bringing happiness into the study of migration and its consequences: what, why and how? Journal of Immigrant & Refugee Studies. 17 (3): 279–298.

Hendriks, M. (2015). The happiness of international migrants: a review of research findings. Migration Studies. 3(3): 343–369.

Hirschauer, N., Lehberger, M. and Musshoff, O. (2015). Happiness and utility in economic thought—Or: what can we learn from happiness research for public policy analysis and public policy making? Social Indicators Research 121: 647–674.

Hirschman, A. O. (1973). The changing tolerance for income inequality during economic development. Quarterly Journal of Economics 87: 544–566.

Hofstede, G. (1984). Culture's Consequences: International Differences in Work-Related Values. Sage, Beverly Hills, California.

Hösle, V. (1989). Morality and Politics: Reflections on Machiavelli's "Prince". International Journal of Politics, Culture, and Society. 3(1): 51–69.

Huta, V. and Waterman, A. S. (2014). Eudaimonia and Its Distinction from Hedonia: Developing a Classification and Terminology for Understanding Conceptual and Operational Definitions. Journal of Happiness Studies, 15: 1425–1456.

Jacobsen, B. (2007). What is Happiness? The Concept of Happiness in Existential Psychology and Therapy. Existential Analysis. 18(1): 39–50.

Kesternich, I., Siflinger, B., Smith, J. P. and Winter J. K. (2014). The Effects of World War II on Economic and Health Outcomes across Europe. The Review of Economics and Statistics 96(1): 103–118.

Kimball, M. S. and Willis, R. J. (2023). Utility and happiness NBER Working Paper Series. National Bureau of Economic Research. Cambridge, USA.

MacKerron, G. (2012). Happiness economics from 35 000 feet. Journal of Economic Surveys. 26(4): 705–735.

Mahon NE, Yarcheski A, Yarcheski TJ. (2005). Happiness as Related to Gender and Health in Early Adolescents. Clinical Nursing Research. 14(2): 175–190.

Mencarini, L. and Sironi, M. (2010). Happiness, housework and gender inequality in Europe. European Sociological Review. 28 (2): 203–219.

Mookerjee, R. and Beron, K. (2005). Gender, religion and happiness. The Journal of Socioeconomics. 34 (5): 674–685.

Morrison, D. (2001). The Happiness of the City and the Happiness of the Individual in Plato's Republic. Ancient Philosophy 21.

Pareto, V. (1909). Manuel d'économie politique. Paris: Giard and E. Brière.

Plé, B. (2000). Auguste Comte on Positivism and Happiness Journal of Happiness Studies, 1, 423–445.

Polgreen, L. A. and Simpson, N. B. (2010). Happiness and international migration. Journal of Happiness Studies. 12: 819–840.

Powdthavee, N. (2007). Economics of happiness: a review of literature and applications. Chulalongkorn Journal of Economics 19(1): 51–73.

Rigaud, K. K. de Sherbinin, A., Jones, B., Bergmann, J., Clement, V., Ober, K., Schewe, J., Adamo, S., McCusker, B., Heuser, S., Midgley, A. (2018). Groundswell: Preparing for internal climate migration. World Bank, Washington, DC. http://hdl.handle.net/10986/29461.

Ryan, A. (2010). Happiness and Political Theory. Social Research: An International Quarterly. 77(2): 421–440.

Veenhoven, R. (1995). World database of happiness. Social Indicators Research 34: 299–313.

Veenhoven, R. (2010). Greater Happiness for a Greater Number—Is that Possible and Desirable? 11:605–629.

Veenhoven, R. (2016). The sociology of happiness: Topic in social indicators research. Proceedings of Common Sessions of the ISA Forum 2016 1–13.

Wike, V. S. (1994). Kant on happiness in ethics. SUNY Press. New York. The USA.

Wimmer, A. and Feinstein, Y. (2010). The rise of the nation-state across the world, 1816 to 2001. American Sociological Review 75(5): 764–790.

Yong, E. L. (2019). Understanding divergence of living standards between Asia and Europe: a proposition of regionally dominant cultural effects. Asian Journal of German and European Studies 4(1):1–21.

Zhang, Z. and Zhen, W. (2019). A systematic review of the relationship between physical activity and happiness. Journal of Happiness Studies. 20: 1305–1322.

CHAPTER 2

Financial Frameworks and Contentment: the Financial Aspects of Well-Being

Begüm Yurteri Kösedağlı

Financial matters constitute an important part of people's daily lives. Hence the uncertainty around finances, worry about the future and the lack of financial security can be leading causes of stress in an individual's life and may give rise to important physical, psychological and social problems. At this point, regarded as one of the essential elements of overall well-being, the concept of "financial well-being" has emerged as a new research area in the last decades. Nowadays, it continues to be an important pillar of happiness economics with the growing interest of policymakers, regulators, and organizations as well as private companies. In this context, this chapter aims to provide a comprehensive definition of financial well-being, examine the financial well-being levels at the global level and evaluate the efforts to promote financial well-being in developed and developing countries. Our analysis shows that it's globally accepted that material resources are not enough to sustain individual financial well-being as perceived financial satisfaction is of great importance. The determinants of financial well-being vary among countries, but the fact that high-income countries with lower income inequality and higher financial literacy seem to be performing better in terms of financial well-being justifies the need for fixing the income disparities and effective financial education programs designed for different sociodemographic groups.

1   Introduction

The General Assembly of the United Nations proclaimed 20 March "the International Day of Happiness" in 2012, stating that happiness is an essential goal for humans and calling for "*a more inclusive, equitable and balanced approach to economic growth that promotes the happiness and well-being of all peoples*". The proclamation originates from Bhutan, a landlocked country in South Asia, where the "Gross National Happiness (GNH)"[1] was valued over

---

1   More information can be found at https://www.gnhcentrebhutan.org/gnh-happiness-index/.

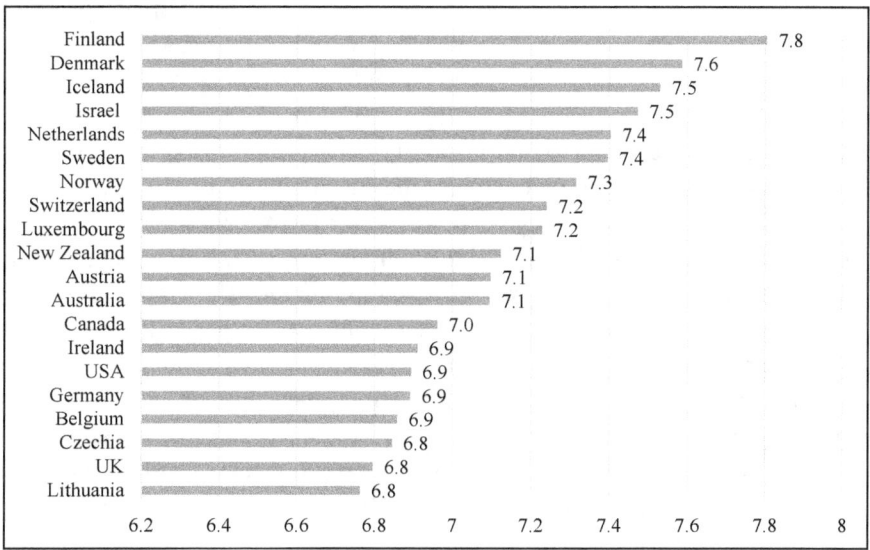

FIGURE 2.1 Happiness score of the top 20 happiest countries, average of 2020–2022
SOURCE: WORLD HAPPINESS REPORT, 2023

national income back in the late 1970s. Under this initiative, a World Happiness Report (WHR) is published annually since April 2012. Based on survey data for more than 150 countries; the report provides rankings of the countries according to their happiness scores where Afghanistan has the lowest (1.859) and Finland has the highest (7.804) score, as can be seen in Figure 2.1 (Helliwell et al., 2023). It's the sixth consecutive year that Finland placed at the top rank with a happiness score significantly higher than its followers.[2]

The WHR highlights that GDP per capita, having someone to rely on at hard times, physical and mental health, satisfaction of the freedom about own life, and community interaction (in terms of donation) positively affect happiness scores while the perceived corruption in a country or business environment has a negative effect.[3]

The studies focusing on the relationship between life satisfaction (happiness) and income have been conducted primarily in the fields of psychology and philosophy. It was after the 20th century that economists started to

---

2 One can argue why the country where the "Gross National Happiness" model is developed, Bhutan, is not ranked among the happiest countries. The reason for that is no survey data has been available for Bhutan in recent years. Instead, The Royal Government of Bhutan's Centre for Bhutan & GNH Studies releases the GNH Index scores annually (https://ophi.org .uk/policy/bhutan-gnh-index/).

3 For more information, please see https://worldhappiness.report/.

investigate the association between happiness and income, both at the country level and international level. Especially, the pioneering study of Easterlin (1974) focuses on the question: "Does money buy happiness?". Subsequently labelled as "*the Easterlin paradox*"; he states that although happiness and income are positively related up to a point, this positive impact does not exist in the long run. This outcome led researchers to shed light on the relationship between happiness and various (socio-economic factors. Nowadays, the literature on "happiness" is still growing with different aspects. Although the terms "happiness" and "well-being" are often used interchangeably in the literature; they are two different concepts, the latter being a multidimensional concept combining feeling good and functioning effectively. The concept of "feeling good" is accepted to be mostly about overall happiness, but it also incorporates various emotions such as interest, engagement, confidence, passion and affection. On the other hand, the concept of "functioning effectively" is about one's potential, control over his/her life, ambition on the goals and positive relationships (Huppert, 2009).

The five essential elements of holistic well-being can be vastly summarized as in Figure 2.2. The most important feature of these five elements is that an individual can control and further that he/she can improve each of them. Although the relative importance of each pillar may change during a person's life course, keeping them in balance is of great importance. Easier said than done, this could unfortunately be challenging considering the modern life problems.

Considering that financial matters constitute an important part of the daily lives of people, there's no doubt that financial well-being is one of the essential pillars of an individual's overall well-being. Hence the uncertainty around finances, worry about the future and the lack of financial security can be leading causes of stress in an individual's life and may give rise to important physical, psychological and social problems. In the meantime, the financial and economic turmoil in recent years as well as the COVID-19 pandemic gave rise to considerable financial distress among households and individuals. Household savings started to decrease dramatically in OECD countries after the outbreak of the COVID-19 pandemic (Figure 2.3).

The countries that have the highest saving ratio are no exception. Reaching its peak in 2020, the household saving ratio as a proportion of net disposable household income continued to fall until 2022 even for top-savers (Figure 2.4).

On the other hand, the growing indebtedness of households both in developed (USA) and in developing countries (Brazil[4]) gives rise to concerns about

---

4   https://en.mercopress.com/2023/07/12/number-of-brazilians-in-debt-on-the-rise.

FIGURE 2.2 The five elements of wellbeing
SOURCE: RATH AND HARTER (2010)

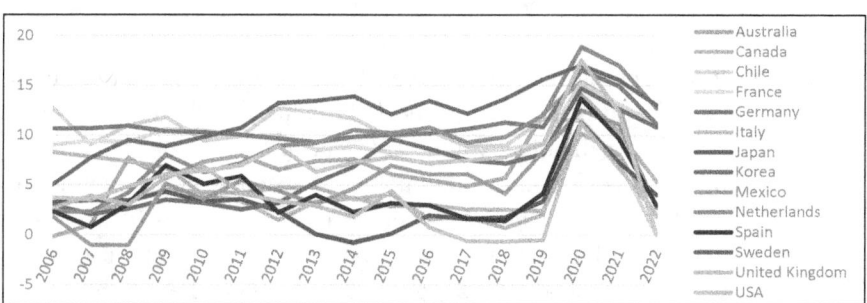

FIGURE 2.3 Household savings of selected OECD countries, % of net disposable household income, 2006–2022
SOURCE: OECD.STAT

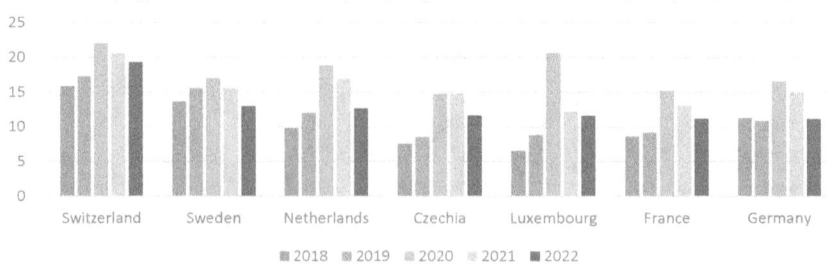

FIGURE 2.4 Household savings of the top savers, % of net disposable household income, 2018–2022
SOURCE: OECD.STAT

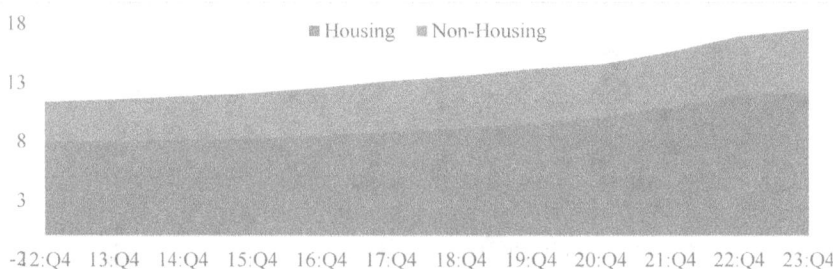

FIGURE 2.5 Total household debt balance, USA, 2012:Q4–2023Q4, trillion dollars
SOURCE: HOUSEHOLD DEBT AND CREDIT REPORT, FED NEW YORK

a lack of healthy spending-savings balance which can affect the current financial situation and the future achievements of individuals of all ages (Figure 2.5).

Regarding employee financial wellness, financial distress hurts employee well-being and work performance like increased absenteeism, presenteeism (being present at work but underperforming), or health issues (CIPD, 2021). As the global cost of living increases, its impact on mental health also arises. The report by Champion Health (2023) on employee mental health shows that financial pressure is the most important cause of stress (40%) outside work; among relationships, parenting, health, caring responsibilities, bereavement and COVID-19. It's also stated that 19% of employees experiencing thoughts of suicide or self-harm experience financial stress while 10% do not experience any financial stress. CIPD (2021) states that nearly half of UK employees are having financial problems, while 16% are experiencing difficulties in paying their bills. Moreover, one of every three employees in the UK has stated a worse financial security and 63% of US workers said that their level of financial stress has escalated since the onset of the pandemic showing that COVID-19 exacerbated the situation in both countries.

At this point, the concept of "financial well-being" which has emerged as a new research area in the last decades, is an important pillar of happiness economics with growing interest of policymakers, regulators, and organizations as well as private companies. In this context, the main purpose of this chapter is to provide a comprehensive view of financial well-being, to examine the financial well-being scores of countries at a global level and to evaluate the efforts to promote financial well-being in developed and developing countries. For this aim, the distinct definitions and elements of financial well-being will be reviewed in the first part. The efforts on the measurement of the concept will be analyzed in the second part while the last part will be devoted to the policies promoting or raising awareness about the financial well-being in developed and developing countries.

1.1   *Comprehension of Financial Well-Being and Its Determinants*

Despite drawing social, academic and political attention, there is still no universally accepted definition of financial well-being while the concepts *"financial wellness, financial satisfaction, financial health, financial resilience"* are also used interchangeably in the literature.[5] The Consumer Financial Protection Bureau (CFPB) of the USA states that *"financial well-being can be defined as a state of being wherein a person can fully meet current and ongoing financial obligations, can feel secure in their financial future, and can make choices that allow enjoyment of life"* (CFPB, 2015).

The growing literature insists that financial well-being is a concept beyond an individual's income or wealth. It is accepted to be a highly personal state regardless of income level. This is why, although having material resources like bank assets, a savings account, health insurance, and job benefits are all financial blessings; these objective (or observable) measures are not enough to define the financial well-being of individuals. For this reason, taking into consideration the subjective elements (personal characteristics such as self-control, optimism, or the personal perception of financial problems) is of great importance although they complicate the conceptualization of financial well-being (Sorgente and Lanz, 2017). On the other hand, one should not fail to notice that despite capturing different dimensions of the concept, the observed and perceived financial well-being are accepted to be interrelated (Comerton-Forde et al., 2018).

Although decent income and a strong political and economic environment may seem adequate to secure financial well-being, there are other several factors affecting the perception of financial well-being. First, competing with

---

5   The term "financial well-being" will be used for consistency throughout this chapter.

others can make someone view his/her financial situation as worse than it is (the so-called "keep up with the Joneses syndrome"), despite having a high income. Second, a negative correlation is found between the Gini coefficient and financial well-being, showing that higher income inequality is associated with lower financial well-being. Third, it is observed that the perception of financial security may vary within a short time depending on the timing of the assessment. The individuals feel more stressed about their financial situation before paydays, or they may feel more optimistic after paydays or receiving tax refunds. Moreover, life events, news, political incidents, and future outlooks can also have a positive or negative impact on the perception of financial well-being depending on the nature of the information contained (Riitsalu et al., 2023).

The comprehension of financial well-being may also differ among people with different age groups, underlining the importance of age-specific components of the concept. There are qualitative studies investigating the evaluation of the meaning and components of financial well-being among age groups. Riitsalu et al. (2023) demonstrate that different age groups attribute several different dimensions of financial well-being. For example, while young people evaluate financial freedom as earning passive income and not having to work (FIRE—Financial Independence Retire Early) such an assessment is not mentioned by working-age or older people in Estonia. Salignac et al. (2020) report that young, working and retired people in Australia have different assessments of financial well-being and recommend an *"ecological life course approach"* considering both where the people are in their life course as well as the interaction with their environment should be adopted. On the other hand, there is mixed empirical evidence about the relationship between age and financial well-being. Besides a positive or negative relation, a U-shaped relation showing that middle-aged people have lower FWB than younger and older people is reported in Ritsalu and Murakas (2019).

Individual differences in the self-control of behavioural heterogeneity play an important role in the perception of anxiety about the consequences of financial decisions. Strömback et al. (2017) find that non-cognitive processes such as self-control, optimism and deliberative thinking are found to be important determinants of financial well-being for Swedish people affecting both aspects of financial anxiety (negatively) and financial security (positively). This finding is consistent with Castro-Gonzalez et al. (2020) who find that the attitude towards money (measured by the careful handling of the budget) which is a subjective characteristic, plays an important role in the financial well-being of Spanish people by positively affecting financial planning horizon (savings) and actual financial behaviour (closely watching individual financial transactions and settings goal for the future) while negatively effecting financial risk tolerance.

Using an online survey for the United Kingdom and Sweden, Barrafrem et al. (2020) investigated people's anticipations about the future economic situation at personal, national and global levels. Despite having pessimistic perceptions of the future economic situation, the households in both countries reported that their situation will be better off respected to the countries or world's situation, a phenomenon to be called "financially better-than-average". They also find that financial ignorance, measured by Financial Homo Ignorans Scale, has a negative impact on the financial well-being of both countries. On the other hand, financial literacy has a positive impact on Swedish people's financial well-being, but no relation is found for the UK sample. Besides, the role of demographic characteristics such as income, gender, and education level are also found to be important, especially for Swedish people's financial well-being.

In their study of Norway, a high-income country with one of the lowest Gini coefficients among the OECD countries, Kempson and Rompe (2017) state that, individuals from different age groups, income levels, and family and work status have different assessments of financial well-being. It is noted that financial well-being is found to be higher for people older than 50, and especially for the retired ones, who are living as a couple, either childless or with non-dependent children. The key determinants of financial well-being are found to be money-use behaviours such as *spending restraint, active saving, not borrowing for daily expenses* and *restrained consumer borrowing* with different effects on the three components of financial well-being, two of which are about the current financial situation (meeting current financial commitments, being comfortable financially) and one is about the expectation for future (having financial resilience for the future).

Conformingly, it can be emphasized that besides depending on demographic variables, financial well-being is often linked to demographic financial attitude, financial behaviour, financial literacy (knowledge), financial security in the present (feeling in control) and in the future (capacity to absorb a financial shock), financial freedom in the present (flexibility to make choices) and in the future (setting goals and being on track to meet them) showing that it depends both the current situation and the future achievements of an individual.

1.2   *Global Comparison of Financial Well-Being*

As mentioned before, the measuring of financial well-being is quite complex. Because it consists of both objective and subjective elements. This is why, the construction of a financial wellbeing index or just measuring the financial wellbeing within a country needs reliable survey data. However, various studies are measuring financial well-being within a country and for different socioeconomic groups (Vieira et al., 2022; Norvilitis et al., 2003; Comerton-Forde et al., 2018, CFPB, 2015).

Using an "*Observed Financial well-being scale*" and "*Reported Financial well-being scale*", Comerton-Forde et al. (2018) found that the observed and perceived financial well-being are interrelated as the reported and observed financial well-being of the customers of a Major Australian bank has a positive correlation of 40%. They state that each scale is positively linked with income, home ownership, metropolitan residence, financial windfalls, financial knowledge, thrifty attitudes, and good financial habits and negatively related to poor health and financial setbacks.

"*The Financial Wellbeing Scale*" developed by Norvilitis et al. (2003) for university students is widely used in literature as a dependent variable to investigate the determinants of financial wellbeing. It considers both the current financial situation and future expectations.

"The CFPB Financial Well-Being Scale" is developed for U.S. adults under the national strategy of empowering individuals to manage their financial situation. The average financial well-being for U.S. adults in 2017 is reported to be 54 out of 100; and financial well-being is reported to be positively associated with age, level of education, and physical health while an identical score emerged for men and women.

Consumer and Community Research Section of the Federal Reserve Board's Division of Consumer and Community Affairs (DCCA, 2023) also releases a report based on the Survey of Household Economics and Decision Making (SHED) annually to measure the economic well-being of U.S. households. According to the latest data in 2022 the financial wellbeing of U.S. households, falling sharply concerning the previous year, is among the lowest observed since 2016, with 73% reporting "*doing okay financially*". Adults with at least a bachelor's degree are more likely to be doing okay financially. Meanwhile, adults with less than a high school degree report the lowest financial well-being among others. Despite diminishing since 2020, the education gap in terms of self-reported financial well-being remains important for U.S. households.

Nevertheless, while doing a cross-country analysis, one should avoid comparing the financial well-being scores of different countries based on different methodologies. In this chapter, firstly the financial well-being of European countries measured by D'Agostino et al. (2020) will be analyzed and then the financial well-being across different countries all over the world will be evaluated in an international context as published by OECD (2023).

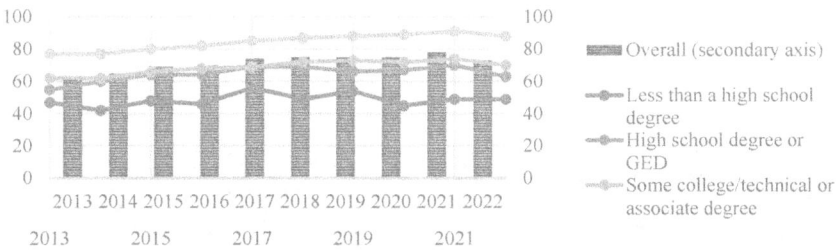

FIGURE 2.6   U.S. households reporting at least doing okay financially (overall and by
education)
SOURCE: DCCA (2023)

D'Agostino et al. (2020) measured the financial well-being of 27 European
Union, and 7 non-EU countries. Although the related survey[6] dates to 2012,
the financial well-being scores of the countries are noteworthy. With a value
of 0 (1) showing the lowest (highest) financial well-being score, it is reported
that the scores lie between the values 0.56 and 0.69. The Northern (Iceland,
Sweden, Denmark and Finland) and Southern countries (Cyprus and Greece)
show remarkable differences in terms of financial well-being. Another important point is that Germany has relatively higher financial well-being than
France and the UK despite having similar wealth indicators. This is stated as
proof that the degree of financial well-being and wealth are not directly related
as in Easterlin (1974).

Analyzing the financial well-being scores of different countries all over the
world, it is first seen that the scores vary significantly across the countries. The
average across participating OECD countries is 47 out of 100, which is higher
than the overall average (42 out of 100). Among all the countries, Germany
has the highest score of financial well-being (73 out of 100) remarkably higher
than any other country listed. The other countries with the highest financial
well-being score are Hong Kong, Ireland, Sweden and the Netherlands. On the
other hand, Yemen, Paraguay and the Philippines have the lowest financial
well-being scores.

The financial well-being scores listed in Figure 2.8 consider the two aspects
of the concept, which are the observable and the subjective measures that
are rebelled as "financial resilience" and subjective financial well-being".
Financial resilience is measured by considering the respondents' answers on
their observable financial situation (the ability to pay a major expense without

6   Third European Quality of Life Survey of the European Foundation for the Improvement of
    Living and Working Conditions.

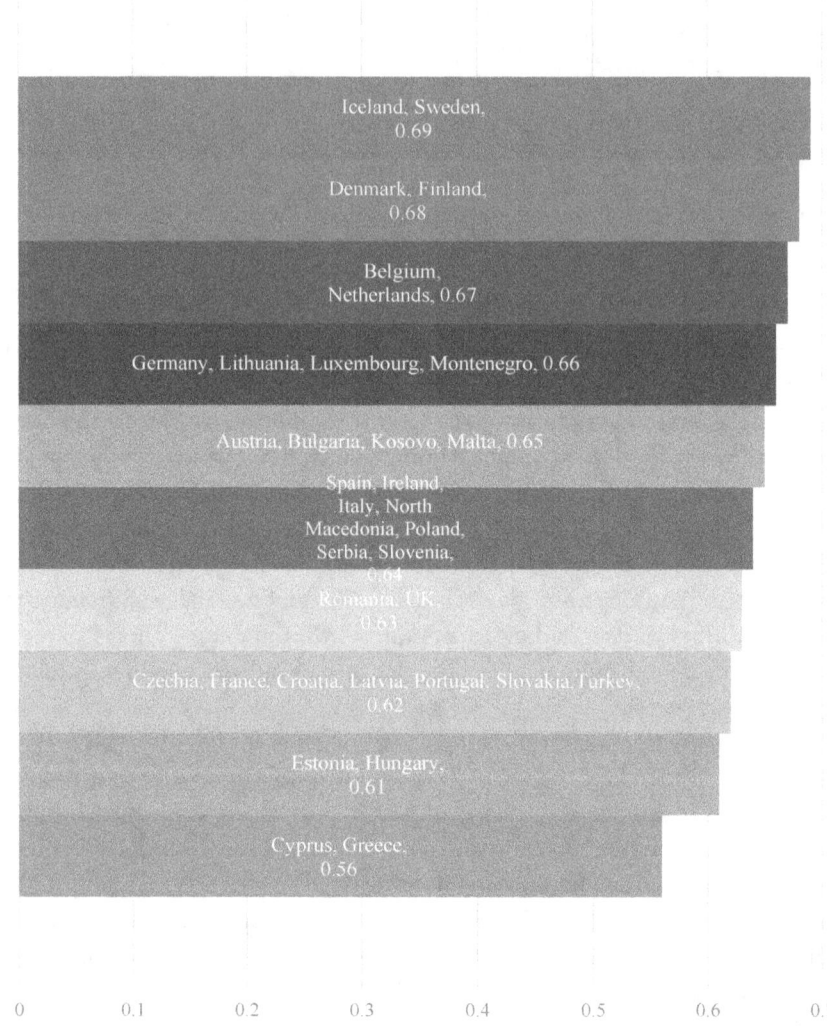

FIGURE 2.7 Financial wellbeing in European countries
SOURCE: D'AGOSTINO ET AL. (2020)

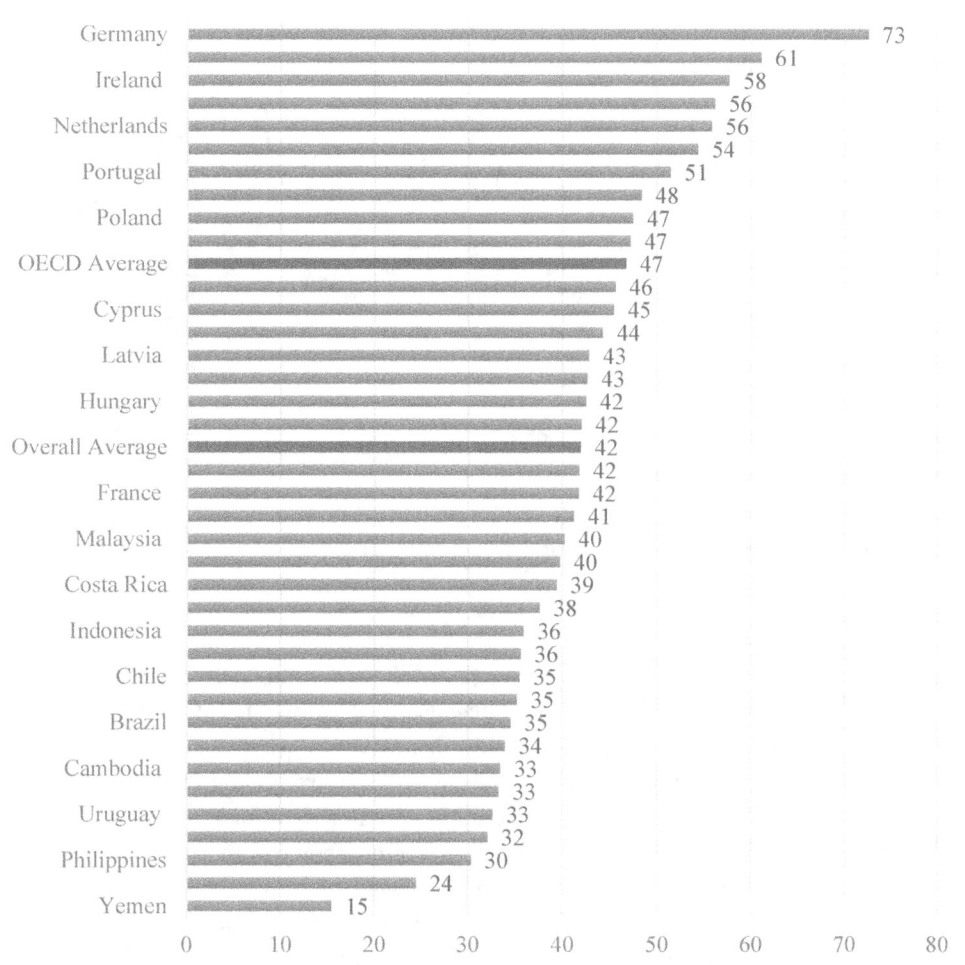

FIGURE 2.8 Financial wellbeing around the world (out of 100)
SOURCE: OECD (2023)

borrowing or asking family or friends for help, the ability to survive financially for at least three months without a main source of income, having enough income to cover the expenses, having some money leftover at the end of the month) as well as the subjective aspects (overall satisfaction of finances, anxiety about the future and the sense of control over finances). It can be noted that the financial resilience component gives a higher positive contribution to the financial well-being in countries with the highest financial well-being score, while the contribution of the two components is mixed for the countries with the lowest score.

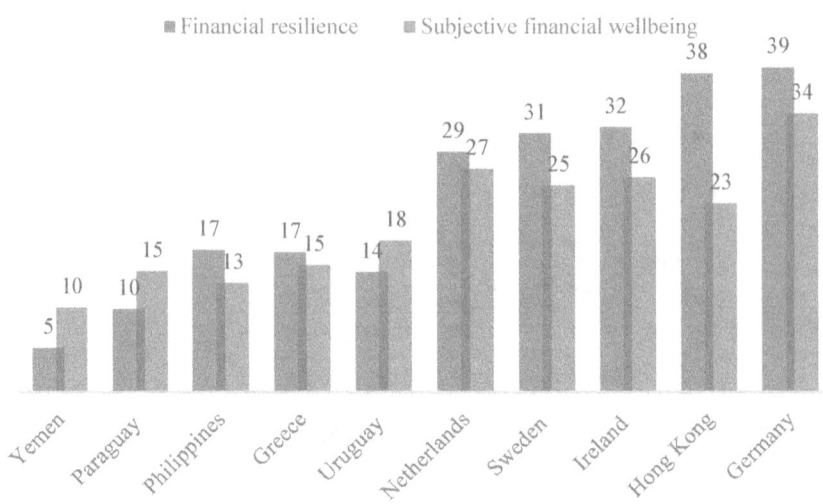

FIGURE 2.9 The composition of financial wellbeing (each out of 50)
SOURCE: OECD (2023)

As mentioned before, comparing the individual financial well-being scores across countries may be deceptive because of the possible differences in survey questions. However, the Global Findex Database provides comprehensive data on financial measures related to the financial well-being of individuals in an international context. As the database contains data for 100+ countries for several years, we believe that examining countries according to their income groups (low, lower-middle, middle, upper-middle and high income) will reveal some important points about financial well-being. The indicators we'll consider are the distress of not being able to pay for medical costs in case of a serious illness/ accident, the distress of not being able to pay school fees or fees for education, anxiety about not having enough money for old age as well as for the ability to pay monthly expenses and bills. Besides, the financial distress caused by COVID-19 will also be analyzed. The individuals are grouped in three according to their worry levels very worried, somewhat worried, and not worried at all.

Starting with the distress on emergency payments, it is seen that a greater proportion of the population (73%) in low-income countries is very worried about not being able to pay for medical costs in case of a serious illness or accident as well as the lower-middle and middle-income countries. The countries with the highest proportion to worry about any serious emergency payments are Malawi, South Sudan and Mali, all located in sub-Saharan Africa. It can

FIGURE 2.10   Worried about not being able to pay for medical costs in case of a serious
illness or accident, % of age 15+
SOURCE: THE GLOBAL FINDEX DATABASE, 2021

be well noticed that the proportion of the worried population decreases for
higher-income country groups. 45% of the population living in high-income
countries does not worry at all about emergency finances. The countries where
a high proportion of the population does not worry at all about any emergency
finances are the United Kingdom, Denmark and Sweden.

Similar results can be reported for the anxiety about not being able to pay
school fees or fees for education. A greater proportion of the population (62%)
in low-income countries is very worried about not being able to finance education. The countries with the highest proportion of worry about education fees
are Malawi, Liberia and South Sudan again all located in sub-Saharan Africa.
The gap between low and high-income countries is striking as 60% of the population living in high-income countries does not worry at all about education
fees. The top 3 countries where a high proportion of the population does not
worry at all about education finances are all Scandinavian countries: namely
Denmark, Norway and Sweden.

The perception of having enough money for old age is an important indicator of financial security for the future. The proportion of the population
worrying about not having enough money for old age decreases as the income
level increases. A greater proportion of the population (63%) in low-income
countries is very worried about not being able to have enough money in the
future with Sub-Saharan African countries having the most anxious population about their financial situation in the future. The proportion of the population that is not worried at all and somewhat worried is identical (39%) for
high-income countries. The top countries where a high proportion of the population does not worry at all about having enough money for the future are
Denmark, Sweden and the United Arab Emirates.

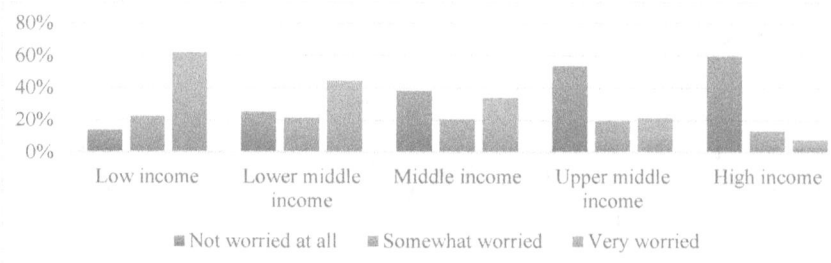

FIGURE 2.11   Worried about not being able to pay school fees or fees for education,
               % age 15+
               SOURCE: THE GLOBAL FINDEX DATABASE, 2021

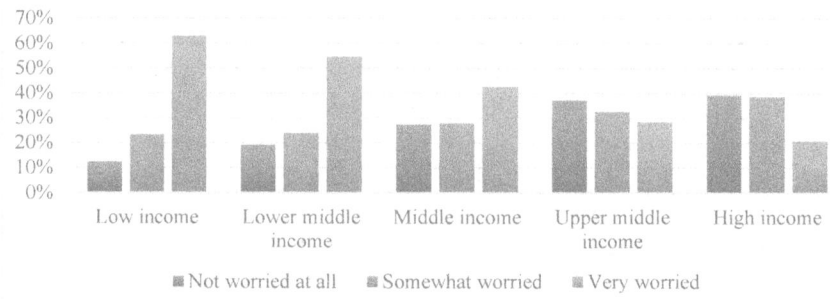

FIGURE 2.12   Worried about not having enough money for old age, % age 15+
               SOURCE: THE GLOBAL FINDEX DATABASE, 2021

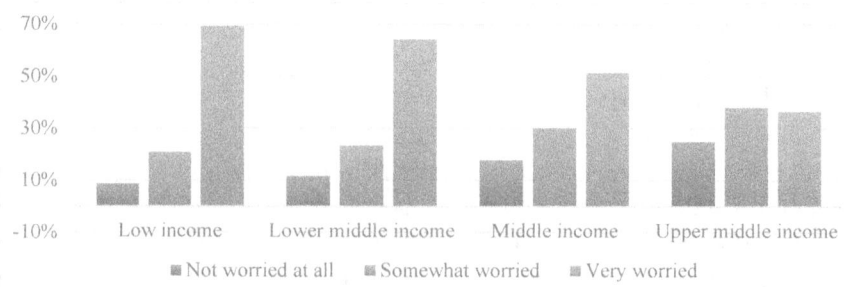

FIGURE 2.13   Worried about not having enough money for monthly expenses or bills,
               % age 15+
               *No data for high-income countries is provided.
               SOURCE: THE GLOBAL FINDEX DATABASE, 2021

The results for the assessment of the current financial situation through the ability to pay monthly expenses and bills look quite like the previous indicators. A greater proportion of the population in low, lower-middle and middle-income countries are worried about being able to pay their monthly expenses or bills. On the other hand, the proportion of the population that is not worried at all is higher for upper-middle- and high-income countries. The countries with the highest proportion of worry about monthly expenses are Malawi, Liberia and Mali; while the countries with the highest proportion of feeling secure about monthly finances are Sweden, Denmark and Norway.

The financial challenges caused by the COVID-19 pandemic look more severe in lower-income countries than expected. The proportion of individuals experiencing severe financial hardship because of COVID-19 is strikingly higher in low and lower-middle-income countries. The countries where most of the population is experiencing hardships due to COVID-19 are Malawi, Liberia and Zambia, the latter being a lower-middle-income country. The fact that no data is provided for high-income countries on this measure limits the interpretation, but it is noteworthy that, the proportion of people who do not worry at all about the financial hardships caused by COVID-19 is the lowest (25%) among all indicators for upper-middle-income countries. This means that nearly a quarter of the population in upper-middle-income countries are at least a little bit worried about the challenges faced after the COVID-19 pandemic showing the magnitude of the impact the pandemic caused globally.

To summarize this part, it is obvious that the majority of the people living in low-income countries, especially the Sub-Saharan countries, report high levels of worry about all indicators showing their lack of financial security for both the present and the future while nearly half of the people living in higher income countries such as Scandinavian region do not worry at all for any emergency payments, education finances or their future financial situation.

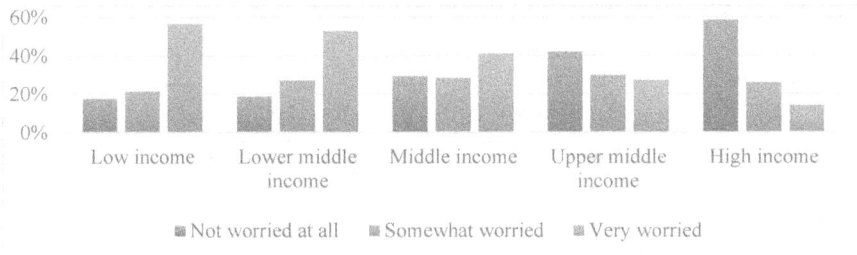

FIGURE 2.14   Experience or continue to experience severe financial hardship as a result of the disruption caused by COVID-19, % age 15+
SOURCE: THE GLOBAL FINDEX DATABASE, 2021

1.3   *Financial Literacy as a Means of Promoting Financial Well-Being*

The impact of financial literacy on financial well-being is a widely popular subject with a growing literature. Considering different countries and demographic groups, studies are showing that there is a positive association between financial literacy and financial well-being (Taft et al., 2013; Lone and Baht, 2022; Bai, 2023; Lusardi and Streeter, 2023; Sticha and Setika, 2023) Individuals with higher financial literacy are reported to spend less than their income, to have emergency funds and to save future retirement plans, to be more cautious on credit card spending and borrowing behaviours (Lin et al., 2022). This fact shows that individuals with higher financial literacy are associated with both current and future financial security which is an essential element of financial well-being.

In this context, financial literacy has been one of the most popular elements of financial education during the last decade. The USA adopted a national strategy to promote financial literacy in 2010. The Consumer Financial Protection Bureau (CFPB) of the USA describes that promoting financial literacy and capability through financial education and thus empowering individuals to manage their financial situations is one of its essential missions. On the other hand, OECD (2023:6) states that *"Financial literacy has been recognized at a global level as a core life skill in the 21st century, one that is essential for the empowerment of individuals and for supporting individual and societies' financial well-being"*.

At this point, analyzing financial literacy at a global level will give us important insights into the need for financial education. As of 2023, Germany has the highest financial literacy score (76 out of 100), followed by Thailand and Hong Kong. On the other hand, Yemen, Cambodia and Paraguay have the lowest financial literacy scores. The overall average for the 39 countries listed is 60 out of 100, while the OECD average is slightly higher with a score of 63. It should be noted that Germany and Hong Kong are the two countries with the highest financial well-being and financial literacy scores.

Going into detail, financial knowledge, financial behaviour and financial attitude are regarded as the essential components of financial literacy. Considering financial knowledge, Hong Kong has the highest score (91 out of 100), followed by Germany and Estonia scoring well above the overall average which is 63 out of 100. The countries with the lowest scores for financial knowledge are the Philippines, Cambodia and Indonesia. The countries with the highest financial behaviour scores are Malta with a score of 77 out of 100, followed by Saudi Arabia and Germany, while the overall average is 61 out of 100. The countries with the lowest scores for financial behaviour are Cyprus,

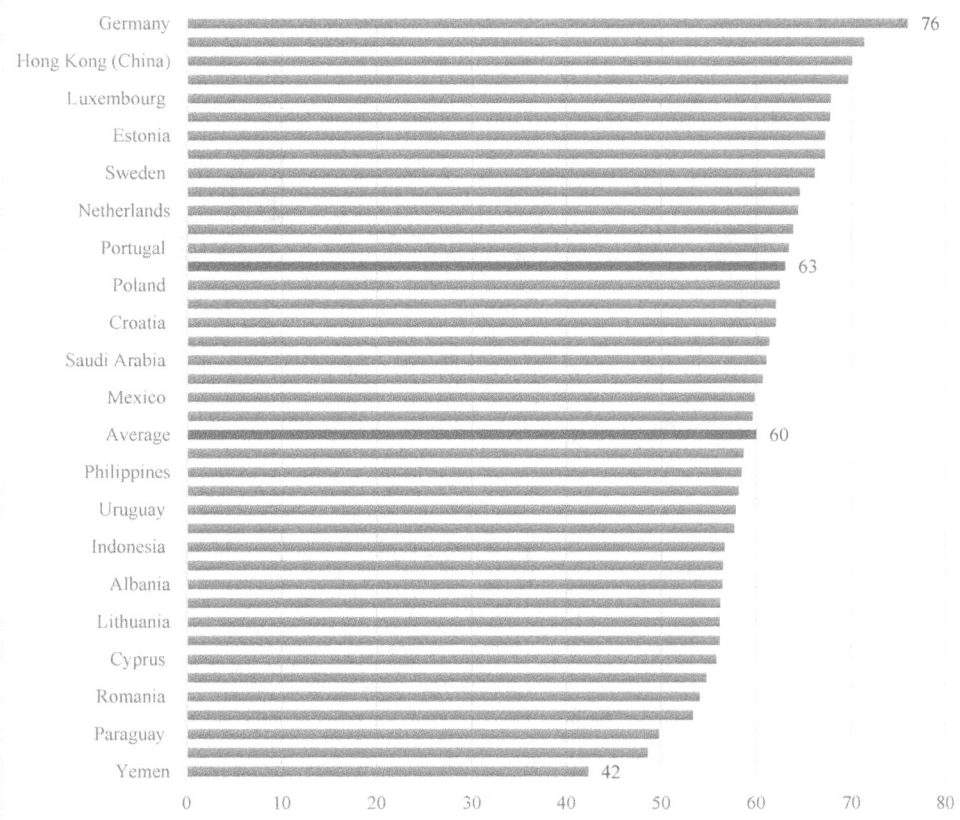

FIGURE 2.15   Financial literacy scores (out of 100)
SOURCE: OECD (2023)

Hungary and Yemen. For the third component, financial attitudes, Thailand
has the highest score (77 out of 100) and places just above Spain and Sweden.
The countries with the lowest scores for financial behaviour are Lithuania,
Saudi Arabia and Yemen. It's striking that Saudi Arabia has the second-highest
score for financial behaviour while having the second-worst score for financial
attitudes.

Considering the rapid growth of digital products and services in finance,
digital financial literacy among adults with internet access also comes out as
an important indicator measuring individuals' awareness and capability to
safely use these technologies (OECD, 2022). Hong Kong has the highest digital
financial literacy score (69 out of 100), followed by Ireland and Germany, while
Albania Indonesia and Cambodia have the lowest scores.

Financial Knowledge
Financial Behaviour
Financial Attitudes
91
85
78
77
75
74
77
70
67
Hong Kong (China)
Germany
Estonia
Malta
Saudi Arabia
Germany
Thailand
Spain
Sweden

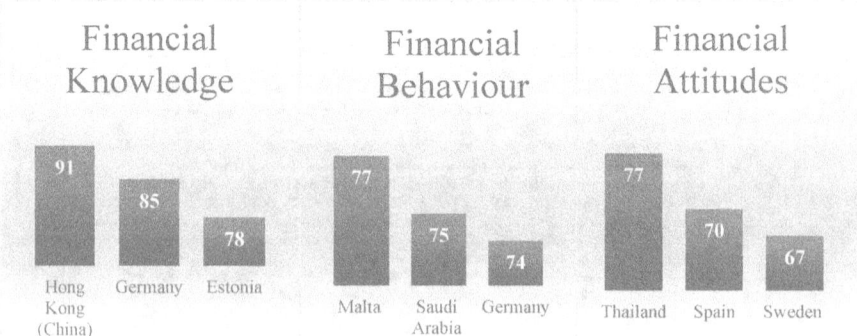

FIGURE 2.16 Countries scoring highest for the components of financial literacy (out of 100)
SOURCE: OECD (2023)

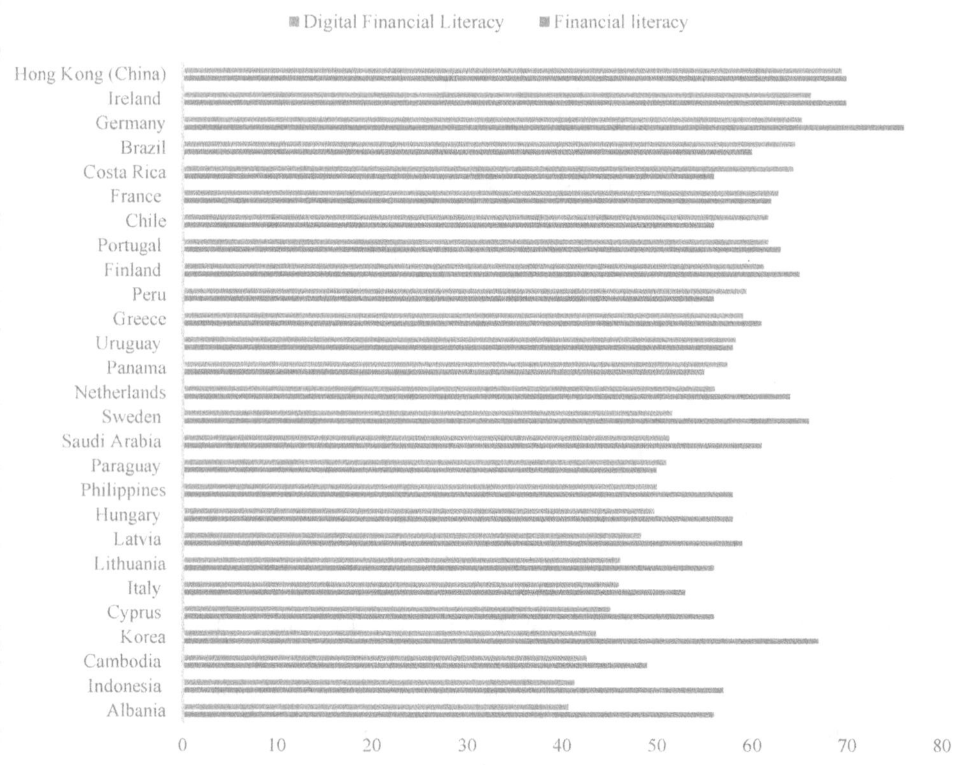

Digital Financial Literacy
Financial literacy
Hong Kong (China)
Ireland
Germany
Brazil
Costa Rica
France
Chile
Portugal
Finland
Peru
Greece
Uruguay
Panama
Netherlands
Sweden
Saudi Arabia
Paraguay
Philippines
Hungary
Latvia
Lithuania
Italy
Cyprus
Korea
Cambodia
Indonesia
Albania
0
10
20
30
40
50
60
70
80

FIGURE 2.17 Financial literacy and digital financial literacy scores among those with internet access
SOURCE: OECD (2023)

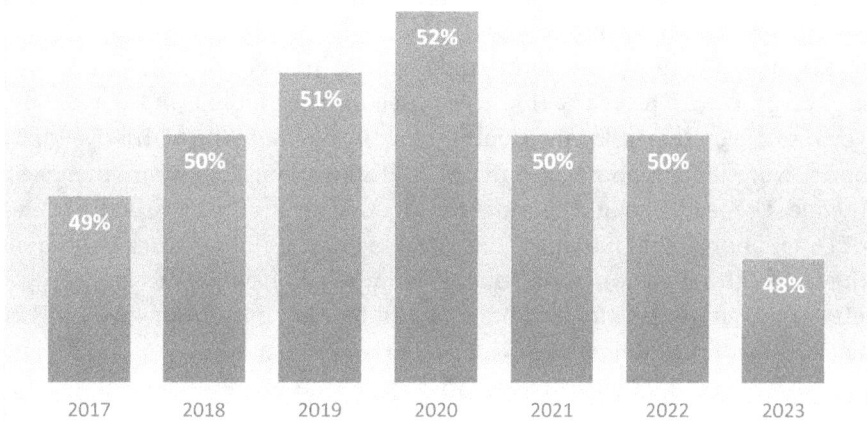

FIGURE 2.18   Financial literacy among U.S. adults, 2017 to 2023, as % of questions answered
correctly
SOURCE: YAKOBOSKI ET AL. (2023)

Despite being a member of the OECD, no data on financial literacy for the USA, a well-developed and Turkey, a developing country is available in OECD publications. However, numerous studies are focusing on financial literacy in the USA. Among all, the pioneering study of Lusardi and Mitchell (2011) where they developed "the big three" approach consisting of three basic questions on interest, inflation and risk, leads the field in measuring financial literacy. Using the 2021 National Financial Capability Study, Lusardi and Streeter (2023) report that 69.4% of the respondents answered the question on interest rate correctly, while this number decreases to 53.1% and 41.5% for inflation and risk questions, respectively. While it is stated that the overall financial literacy is alarmingly low in the USA, the financial literacy of young, less educated, female and not employed people is especially low. Based on another comprehensive survey, Yakoboski et al. (2023) report that the percentage of questions answered correctly is 48% in 2023, which is labelled as a poor level of financial literacy for the USA. Moreover, it is seen that there haven't been any significant changes in the Personal Finance Index (P-Fin Index) over the years.

Established in 2003, the Financial Literacy and Education Commission (FLEC) of the USA is committed "*to improve the financial literacy and education of persons in the United States through the development of a national strategy to promote financial literacy and education.*" To realize this aim, the commission holds three meetings per year to coordinate the 24 federal agencies, publishes a report to update the Congress on its process, implements and updates the National Strategy to Promote Financial Literacy and Education and manages a resource webpage (MyMoney.gov).

Klapper et al. (2015) reveal that the financial literacy of adults in Turkey is also very low with just 24%. However, based on The Methods of Payment survey results conducted for the Central Bank of the Republic of Türkiye; Bilici and Çevik (2023) report that only 7% of Turkish households are financially literate. The reader should consider the fact that each survey method adopts a different approach to measuring financial literacy, and this causes a variation in results. Although academics, non-governmental organizations and companies carry out projects to promote financial literacy, it is obvious that Turkey needs to implement effective financial literacy programs at the governmental level as a major emerging country with a rapidly developing financial sector.

2   Conclusion

Financial matters constitute an important part of the daily lives of people and the financial situation of an individual affects his/her life in numerous aspects (quality of life, success, mental health, relationship quality). Hence the uncertainty around finances, worry about the future and the lack of financial security can be leading causes of stress in an individual's life and may give rise to important physical, psychological and social problems. For this reason, this chapter focuses on the financial aspects of happiness, for which various concepts (such as financial wellness, financial satisfaction, financial health, financial resilience, and financial well-being) are used in the growing literature with an increasing interest of policymakers, regulators and organizations. We concentrate on financial well-being, which is respected as an essential element of overall well-being. Considering that financial well-being is more susceptible to times of economic uncertainty, the financial and economic turmoil in recent years as well as the COVID-19 pandemic gave rise to considerable financial distress among individuals and households, which increases the importance of financial well-being.

Numerous studies are measuring the financial well-being within a country showing that the assessment of financial well-being varies among different socioeconomic groups (depending on age, gender, education level, and work status). On the other hand, the cross-country analysis shows that Nordic countries and Germany have higher financial well-being scores than other countries. Being an important indicator of perceived financial well-being, the sentiment of financial security for both the present (the anxiety level for not being able to pay emergency payments, education fees, monthly bills or expenses) and the future (the anxiety level for not being able to have enough money for old age) in low-income countries, especially for the Sub-Saharan countries, is very low. Additionally, the hardships caused by the COVID-19 pandemic hit all countries regardless of income level.

Besides having its reflections on the individual level, it's well-accepted that financial well-being is also important at organizational and societal levels. Recognizing its importance at the organizational level, an increasing number of companies offer their employees financial wellness programs such as financial coaching or online financial management tools, mainly to help their employees who are struggling financially and to boost employee performance by helping them to have a financially sound future.

Given the fact that higher financial skills and knowledge are associated with higher financial well-being, as shown in the case of Germany and Hong Kong and vice versa as in the case of Yemen and Paraguay; the governments and intergovernmental organizations mainly focus on financial education on macro-level, especially through promoting financial literacy. Unfortunately, financial literacy around the world levels remains low, even in well-developed markets such as the USA. This reflects the fact that many people do not have the knowledge and capability to make sound financial decisions. However, while well-developed markets like the USA put more effort into promoting the financial well-being of their households for a long time, there are minor solid actions in developing countries. In addition to effective financial education programs designed specifically for each gender of all ages but especially for younger people; financial counselling, financial advice or generating awareness will help individuals to improve their financial well-being.

References

Bai, R. (2023) Impact of financial literacy, mental budgeting and self-control on financial wellbeing: Mediating impact of investment decision making. PLoS ONE 18(11): e0294466. https://doi.org/10.1371/journal.pone.0294466.

Barrafrem, K., Västfjäll, D., and Tinghög, G. (2020). Financial well-being, COVID-19, and the financial better-than-average effect. Journal of Behavioral and Experimental Finance, 28, 100410.https://doi.org/10.1016/j.jbef.2020.100410.

Bilici, M. R. & Çevik, S. (2023). Financial literacy and cash holdings in Türkiye, Central Bank Review 23 (4): 1–7.

Castro-González, S., Fernández-López, S., Rey-Ares, S., Rodeiro, L. and Pazos, D. (2020). The Influence of Attitude to Money on Individuals' Financial Well-Being, Social Indicators Research, 148: 747–764.

CFPB (2015). Measuring financial well-being: A guide to using the CFPB Financial Well-Being Scale. Consumer Financial Protection Bureau.

CFPB (2017). Financial well-being in America, Consumer Financial Protection Bureau

Champion Health (2023). The Employee Mental Health Handbook, https://champion health.co.uk/insights/guides/employee-mental-health-handbook/.

CIPD (2021). Financial well-being: An evidence review, https://www.cipd.org/globa lassets/media/knowledge/knowledge-hub/evidence-reviews/financial-wellbeing -evidence-review-scientific-summary-1_tcm18-102718.pdf.

Comerton-Forde, C., Ip, E., River, D. C., Ross, J., Salamanca, N., Tsiaplias, S. (2018). Using Survey and Banking Data to Measure Financial Wellbeing, Commonwealth Bank of Australia and Melbourne Institute Financial Wellbeing Scales Technical Report No. 1, Chapters 1–6, March.

D'Agostino, A., Rosciano, M., and Grazia Starita, M. (2020). Measuring financial well-being in Europe using a fuzzy set approach, International Journal of Bank Marketing, (39):1 48–68.

DCCA (2023). Economic Well-Being of U.S. Households in 2022, Consumer and Community Research Section of the Federal Reserve Board's Division of Consumer and Community Affairs, https://www.federalreserve.gov/publications/files/2022 -report-economic-well-being-us-households-202305.pdf.

Easterlin, R. A. (1974). Does Economic Growth Improve the Human Lot? Some Empirical Evidence. In Paul A. David; Melvin W. Reder (eds.). Nations and Households in Economic Growth: Essays in Honor of Moses Abramovitz. New York: Academic Press, Inc.

Helliwell, J. F., Layard, R., Sachs, J. D., De Neve, J.-E., Aknin, L. B., and Wang, S. (Eds.). (2023) World Happiness Report 2023. New York: Sustainable Development Solutions Network.

Huppert, F. (2009). Psychological Well-being: Evidence Regarding its Causes and Consequences, applied Psychology: Health and Well Being, 1 (2), p. 137–164, doi:10.1 111/j.1758-0854.2009.01008.x.

Kempson, E. and Poppe, C. (2017). Understanding Financial Well-Being and Capability—A Revised Model and Comprehensive Analysis, Consumption Research Norway—SIFO. (Professional Report No. 3).

Klapper, L., Lusardi, A., and Van Oudheusden, P. (2015). Financial Literacy around the World. Washington DC: Standard & Poor's Ratings Services Global Financial Literacy Survey.

Lin, J. T., Bumcrot, C., Mottola, G., Valdes, O., Ganem, R., Kieffer, C., Lusardi, A., and Walsh, G. (2022). Financial Capability in the United States: Highlights from the

FINRA Foundation National Financial Capability Study (5th Edition). FINRA Investor Education Foundation. www.FINRAFoundation.org/NFCSReport2021.

Lone, U. M. and Bhat, S. A. (2022). Impact of financial literacy on financial well-being: a mediational role of financial self-efficacy. Journal of Financial Services Marketing, 3:1–16. doi: 10.1057/s41264-022-00183-8.

Lusardi, A. and Streeter, J. L. (2023). Financial literacy and financial well-being: Evidence from the US, Journal of Financial Literacy and Wellbeing (2023), 1, 169–198 doi:10.1017/flw.2023.13.

Lusardi, A., and Mitchell, O. S. (2011). Financial literacy and retirement planning in the United States, Journal of Pension Economics and Finance; 10(4):509–525. doi:10.1017/S147474721100045X.

Norvilitis, J. M., Szablicki, P. B., and Wilson, S. D. (2003). Factors Influencing Levels of Credit-Card Debt in College Students. Journal of Applied Social Psychology, 33(5), 935–947.

OECD (2023). OECD/INFE 2023 International Survey of Adult Financial Literacy, OECD Business and Finance Policy Papers, No. 39, OECD Publishing, Paris, https://doi.org/10.1787/56003a32-en.

Rath, T. and Harter, J. (2010). The Five Essential Elements of Well-Being, Gallup at Work newsletter, May 4, https://www.gallup.com/workplace/237020/five-essential-elements.aspx, accessed 04 March 2024.

Riitsalu, L., and Murakas, R. (2019) Subjective financial knowledge, prudent behaviour and income: the predictors of financial wellbeing in Estonia. International Journal of Bank Marketing, 37(4), 934–950. https://doi.org/10.1108/IJBM-03-2018-0071.

Riitsalu, L., Sulg, R., Linden, H., Remmik, M. and Vain, K. (2023). From Security to Freedom—The Meaning of Financial Well-being Changes with Age, Journal of Family and Economic Issues, https://doi.org/10.1007/s10834-023-09886-z.

Salignac, F., Hamilton, M., Noone, J., Marjolin, A., and Muir, K. (2020). Conceptualizing Financial Wellbeing: An Ecological Life-Course Approach. Journal of Happiness Studies, 21(5), 1581–1602. https://doi.org/10.1007/s10902-019-00145-3.

Sorgente, A. and Lanz, M. (2017). Emerging Adults' Financial Well-being: A Scoping Review, Adolescent Research Review, 2:255–292, DOI 10.1007/s40894-016-0052-x.

Sticha, A. and Sekita, S. (2023). The importance of financial literacy: Evidence from Japan, Journal of Financial Literacy and Wellbeing (2023), 1, 244–262, doi:10.1017/flw.2023.9.

Strömbäck, C., Lind, T., Skagerlund, K., Västfjäll, D., and Tinghög, G. (2017). Does self-control predict financial behavior and financial well-being?, Journal of Behavioral and Experimental Finance, 14, 30–38.

Taft, M. K., Hosein, Z. Z., Mehrizi, S. M. T., and Roshan, A. (2013). The Relation between Financial Literacy, Financial Wellbeing and Financial Concerns, International Journal of Business and Management; Vol. 8, No. 11, 63–75.

Vieira, K. M., Matheis, T. K., Bressan, A. A., Potrich, A. C. G., Klein, L. L. and Rosenblum, T. O. A. (2023). Construction and validation of a perceived financial well-being scale (PFWBS), International Journal of Bank Marketing, Vol. 41 No. 1, pp. 179–209. https://doi.org/10.1108/IJBM-04-2022-0148.

Yakoboski, P., Lusardi, A., and Hasler, A. (2018). Financial well-being and literacy in a high-inflation environment: The 2023 TIAA Institute-GFLEC Personal Finance Index, TIAA Institute; Global Financial Literacy Excellence Center, https://gflec .org/wp-content/uploads/2023/04/2023-P-Fin-Index-report-TIAA-Inst-and-GFLEC -Apr-2023.pdf.

Online Data Sources

The Global Findex Database (2021), https://www.worldbank.org/en/publication /globalfindex.

OECD Stat, https://stats.oecd.org/.

FED Nex York, https://www.newyorkfed.org/microeconomics/hhdc.

CHAPTER 3

Consumption and Happiness

Gül Huyugüzel Kışla

The subject of happiness has been widely analyzed by different disciplines. While there is much empirical research in social sciences, various research focusing on happiness related to mental health and health-related issues have been examined in the context of psychological and medical studies. The term happiness can be sometimes thought of as an inclusive term for "the good life". The concept of happiness is generally related to economic terms like utility, income, unemployment, human needs and consumption. Different disciplines also try to discuss the relationship between consumption and happiness from different perspectives. For example, the negative properties of consumerism have been underlined in psychology literature. However, it is assumed that the level of satisfaction or happiness that we gain will increase when we consume more. The neoclassical economic theory also asserted that individuals are labelled as the "insatiable consumer" and hence more consumption will bring more satisfaction. In general, consumer choices are a little more complex than we might think. Consumer behaviour relies on preferences, expectations, income level, wealth or other individuals' preferences. Even the concept of happiness in economics has been discussed in the 2000s with some studies (e.g. Frey and Stutzer, 2002; VanPraag and Ferrer-i Carbonell, 2010), this issue was examined firstly in the study of Richard Easterlin (1974) who brought the association of income and happiness called Easterlin paradox. With the rising importance of changing the behaviour of consumers, this study aims to discuss the relationship between consumption and happiness from a theoretical and empirical perspective. The concept of happiness and consumption is discussed at first sight, the views of the earlier economists on happiness are mentioned and then the statement that "spending on material goods can or can't buy you happiness" is examined with the help of a literature review. Afterwards, some concluding remarks will be proposed at the end of the chapter.

1   Introduction

There is an ongoing debate on happiness which has been going on for years. Is it coming out of experiential purchasing or material purchasing? Which consumption do we need to be happy? Those questions remain in the heart of happiness from different disciplines. Many researchers tried to explain the concept of consumption and happiness from their perspectives. For example, Aristotle once said that *"true happiness flows from the possession of wisdom and virtue and not from the possession of external goods"*. On the other hand, a well-known economist Adam Smith, said that *"Consumption is the sole end and purpose of all production; and the interest of the producer ought to be attended to, only so far as it may be necessary for promoting that of the consumer"* which was mentioned in his book of "Wealth of Nations". Smith believed that people consume to satisfy their needs and wants. He acknowledged that people would gain utility or satisfaction by consuming goods and services which contribute to their overall well-being (Guillen-Royo, 2011). Well, the concept of happiness and consumption is at the core of investigating individuals' behaviour in the field of economics and psychology. While studies continue to focus on consumption, happiness is also being discussed by many philosophers and social scientists. Some studies use large-scale welfare surveys to understand levels of happiness, while research on mental and medical health is linked to happiness. In particular, the empirical studies gained momentum with the Easterlin paradox (Stanca and Veenhoven, 2015). More specifically, it is believed that higher income can lead to a higher level of happiness. In the period of rising capitalism, countries mainly focus on raising their income or Gross Domestic Product (GDP) levels. With higher income levels, it is expected that higher income levels will bring more happiness to human beings. Because of this importance, studies generally focus on the impact of income on happiness. However, the relationship between consumption and happiness deserves to be analyzed in more detail. From this point of view, the concept of happiness and consumption will be examined in the next section.

2   Take a Quick Lens at the Concepts of "Happiness" and "Consumption"

2.1   *The Concept of Happiness*

Happiness itself has a broad meaning. It is sometimes used interchangeably with the term 'subjective well-being (SWB)'. According to Layard (2005), happiness is an experience of positive affect and life satisfaction and can be thought of as good feelings that people want to maintain. However, there is no clear consensus among philosophers and psychologists about the concept of happiness and well-being. Also, the economists did not like the obvious question "What is happiness?". Rather, they used other terms like pleasure, satisfaction, welfare, subjective well-being (SWB) or utility interchangeably (Bruni, 2006). From the psychological side of happiness, it is a state of well-being that includes a meaningful and satisfying life. Most people want to live a better life, and their expectation is usually to be a happy person. In our society, we demand so many things and we focus on our quality of life. One of the leading psychologists, Ed Diener and his colleagues noted that happiness can mean, among other things, pleasure, life satisfaction, positive emotions, a meaningful life, or a sense of contentment (Diener et al. 2003).

Oishi et al. (2012) mentioned happiness by looking at ancient Greece and America. According to many philosophers, while luck and fortune are essential factors, Americans generally see happiness as the goal of life. Daniel Haybron (2013) mentioned the three dimensions of happiness in his book. Concerning Haybron (2013), the feeling of joy and sadness make up the "endorsement dimension", "engagement with our life" is the second dimension of happiness. The third dimension is called 'attunement', which includes peace of mind, confidence and expansion of mood or spirit. In the case of the source of happiness, it is believed that people's intrinsic motivations are also essential. Feeling secure, being positive and accepted, and caring for others can bring happiness. On the other hand, Weiss et al. (2008) proposed that happiness has a strong genetic side, but external factors may also affect people's happiness. In addition to different approaches to understanding the concept of happiness, earlier economists such as Adam Smith and Thomas Malthus were concerned with people's happiness as well as their material wealth. Other economists, such as Jevon, Walras and Menger, supported the idea that well-being was an ultimate goal and a central motivation for people (Rojas, 2019). Nowadays, with the rise of capitalism, expectations about life and consumer behaviour have changed. The economic theories emphasize the materialist approaches more often. Indeed, neoclassical economic theory supports the importance of consumption that will bring happiness. Until the pioneering work of Richard Easterlin (1974) which turned over a new leaf in literature, the main focus of economics was to expand consumption and production. Countries mainly aim to have higher economic growth rates in successive years. Easterlin (1974) presented the idea that "high-income people tend to report a high level of happiness compared to low-income people". However, this situation may not last forever. Indeed, as the income grew over time, there were no significant changes in people's happiness. This finding was unexpected for the economists who gave importance to economic growth (and hence named as Easterlin paradox). With the help of Easterlin's studies on happiness and income, it would take some time to include the discussions of happiness in the economic era. With the rising interest in happiness, many studies are being conducted to discuss the relationship between income and happiness. The main focus is generally on the relationship between income and happiness while the studies focusing on the relationship between consumption and happiness is a little bit scarce. Before presenting the empirical studies which focus on consumption and happiness, let's discuss consumption itself at first.

2.2   The Concept of Consumption

So, what is consumption? Well, we can give the basic definition of consumption as the act of buying and using goods and services. It can also relate to the utilization of resources. According to Ackerman (1997), the study of consumption is a dynamic field and researchers from sociology, anthropology, philosophy and economics have made noteworthy contributions to this field. Hereby, the three important assumptions of the neoclassical theory of consumption can be listed as "asocial individualism", "insatiability" and "commodity orientation". Asocial individualism refers to an individual point of view that is characterized by a lack of concern for social interaction or engagement with the community. Insatiability means not being able to stop wanting more and commodity orientation emphasizes the importance of goods and services to be bought and sold as commodities. The economic value of goods and services is much more important than their intrinsic or social worth. Veblen[1] criticized asocial individualism which saw consumers' desires and preferences as exogenous. According to Veblen, people consume goods and services to display social status rather than satisfy their actual needs and this is called "conspicuous consumption". In addition, people buy goods not for their utility, but they want to signal their economic achievement. Veblen criticized this type of consumption as wasteful and argued that it could be replaced with more socially beneficial production. Nevertheless, consumption behaviour is also discussed by many economists. One of the important contributions to this issue has been made by John Maynard Keynes. According to Keynes, consumption is determined by current income and as income rises so does consumption with a diminishing rate. Nobel prize-winning economists Franco Modigliani and Richard Brumberg emphasized not only current income but also considered future income and wealth in the determination of consumption decisions (called the "life-cycle hypothesis"). Milton Friedman introduced the "permanent income hypothesis" in 1957 and emphasized the idea that consumers prefer smooth consumption flows over time, considering their lifetime resources rather than just current income. With the help of studies on behavioural

---

1   Veblen (1899) introduced the concept of "conspicuous consumption" in his seminal work *"The Theory of the Leisure Class"*.

economies, Richard Lucas and Daniel Kahneman have changed the economic perspective by introducing psychological factors into consumption analysis. Beyond rational decisions, individuals may be influenced by cognitive biases and heuristics. Rational expectation theory, which is associated with the work of Robert Lucas and Thomas Sargent, supports decisions based on the individuals' expectations of future income and economic conditions.

Apart from the different approaches of the economists, the consumption decisions of individuals may change from time to time. Given these changing behaviours, the consumption of different goods and services may arise. While the basic distinction of consumption can be thought of as durable goods and non-durable goods, an alternative analysis has been made for hedonic goods and utilitarian goods (Dhar and Wertenbroch, 2000). Hedonic goods bring experiential consumption, the fun, pleasure and excitement that comes from luxury goods, clothes and sports cars, while utilitarian goods are more functional (like durables goods). According to Zhang and Xiong (2015), consumption is a multifaceted concept in which different types of consumption (such as education, housing, cars, leisure, daily shopping and so on) should be considered.

3   Do We Need to Consume to Be Happy, or Not?

Most of the empirical studies focusing on happiness are related to the income effect. In particular, the role of income in understanding individual life satisfaction or happiness is well documented. Many studies concluded that people with higher incomes are happier than people with lower incomes, and on average, people living in rich countries are happier than those living in poor countries. However, the effect of income on happiness may vary across societies (see, Easterlin 1995,[2] Frey and Stutzer, 2000; Blanchflower and Oswald, 2004; Shields and Wheatley Price, 2005; Clark et al., 2005; Caporale et al. 2009; Di Tella et al., 2010; Becchetti et al. 2011; Lim et al. 2019). According to the World Happiness Report (2023) and World Bank (2023), income and happiness seem to go together within countries. Figure 3.1 presents the relationship between life satisfaction and GDP per capita.

We now turn our attention from the effect of relative or permanent income levels on happiness to the importance of consumption, whether it leads to

---

2 Easterlin (1995) stated an important point in which within a given time those with higher incomes are on average, happier. However, raising the incomes of all does not increase the happiness of all.

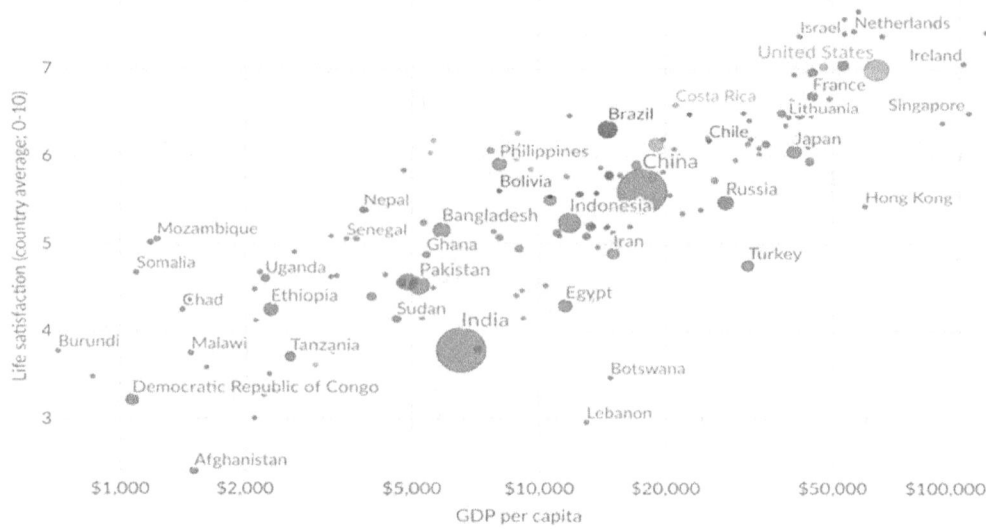

FIGURE 3.1   Self-reported life satisfaction vs. GDP per capita, 2022
            SOURCE: OUR WORLD IN DATA

higher or lower levels of happiness. The expectations about consuming more will bring higher happiness. Is it true? The alternative answer can be given as "yes" because consumption increases happiness or well-being by making life easier. In the case of consumption behaviours, absolute consumption and relative consumption may lead to a higher level of happiness or a lower level of happiness. While absolute consumption refers to the consumption of goods and services without comparison with others, relative consumption refers to the comparison of one's level of consumption or possessions with those of others. Regarding relative consumption, people may make choices taking into account social comparisons (comparing themselves with other individuals), their status, hedonic adaptations (maintaining the same level of satisfaction or happiness by consuming more) and their cultural norms. As Veblen (1899) mentioned, some "conspicuous goods" may increase the level of happiness, particularly because the status of the individuals is increasing. According to Duesenberry (1949), everyone's preferences are interdependent on behaviour of other individuals and those consumption habits are required to maintain social status. As social status increases so does happiness. The other consumption types may also affect the happiness levels depending on what kind of life you are expecting (Deleire and Kalil, 2010).

According to Venhooven (2012), when it comes to making comparisons between people with savings and people with debts, the former case is valid for greater happiness. Some consumption behaviours like owning a car, a house and a garden will bring more happiness than those who don't have. Likewise, possessing luxury goods and electronic devices may also bring more happiness. Spending more on clothing, cosmetics, expensive vacations, hobbies, medical treatment and fitness may contribute to higher happiness of individuals (Dutt, 2006; Wang et al. 2019).

In contrast to earlier statements which present the positive side of consumption, it is not always as true as we might expect. As Stutzer and Frey (2010) mentioned in their study, additional material goods and services initially provide additional pleasure, but this situation is temporary. There would be a phase where the increased happiness with material things would diminish. Satisfaction will disappear with continued consumption. Therefore, the effect of consumption can be changeable due to consumption types or expectations of the individuals.

Whereby the major concern in literature is about the effect of relative income or permanent income on happiness, there are a limited number of studies which consider the effect of consumption on happiness. In particular, most studies focused on developed countries to analyze the relationship between consumption and happiness (see, Headey et al. 2008; Deleire and Kalil, 2010; Zhang and Xiong, 2015; Noll and Weick, 2015; Brown and Gathergood, 2017).

Heady et al. (2008) used panel data (including Australia, Britain, Germany, Hungary and the Netherlands) to show the effect of economic well-being on happiness. The results show that wealth affects life satisfaction more than income and nondurable consumption is important for happiness. *Deleire and Kalil (2010)* examined the relationship between various components of consumption and happiness for older Americans. They found that only leisure consumption is positively related to happiness. The results support the importance of social connectedness. *Zhang and Xiong (2015)* collected data from 2178 respondents who are living in various cities in Japan. According to different approaches (Chi-Squared automatic interaction detector and Bayesian belief network) used in the study, 41 out of the 77 consumption variables were found to influence happiness. The study by *Noll and Weick (2015)* is based on the data from the German Socio-Economic Panel Study. They found that life satisfaction increases with increasing consumption expenditures and low levels of expenditure because of voluntary choices do not reduce life satisfaction. Lastly, expenditures on clothing and leisure are found to be important factors for subjective well-being (SWB) but expenditures on food and housing do not affect life satisfaction at all. In the study of *Brown and Gathergood (2017)*, US micro-level panel data is used to analyze the effect of consumption on life satisfaction. The estimation results indicate that consumption has a much larger effect on life satisfaction than income. Also, the effect of conspicuous consumption on life satisfaction is much more than the of non-conspicuous consumption.

The interest in the relationship between consumption and happiness is also examined for developing or underdeveloped countries (see, Fafchamps and Shilpi, 2008; Guillen-Royo, 2011; Dumludağ, 2015; Linnsen et al. 2011; Gökdemir, 2015; Wang et al., 2019; Jaunky et al., 2020; Dumludağ et al. 2021).

The study of *Fafchamps and Shilpi (2008)* discussed the relative consumption of Nepal. The empirical results show that Nepalese households do not differ from their counterparts in wealthier economies. Their subjective assessment of the adequacy of their consumption rises with their consumption and falls with the average consumption of their neighbours. In addition, the authors stated that relative assessment has an impact on subjective welfare even among poor households that are isolated from the market. *Guillen-Royo (2011)* examined the relationship between reference group consumption and subjective well-being (SWB) among Peruvians. The main emphasis is on the importance of relative consumption for people's sense of adequacy in different consumption areas (food, housing, education, clothing and health care). The results indicate that relative consumption has a negative effect on participants' assessment of household clothing, housing and children's education. *Dumludağ (2015)* investigated the impact of consumption categories on life satisfaction for transition and developed European countries. According to the estimation results, the relationship between life satisfaction and consumption differentiated at different levels of development, especially some consumption categories have a negative effect on life satisfaction. This situation is explained by the fact that increased spending on utilities may reduce the resources available for luxury spending and therefore have a negative effect on life satisfaction. *Linssen et al. (2011)* examined the effect of relative income and conspicuous consumption on subjective well-being (SWB) for low-income households in India. The multi-level regression analyses show that individuals who spent more on conspicuous consumption ensured lower levels of SWB.

In the study of *Gökdemir (2015)*, the impact of the seven different components of consumption expenditures and saving patterns on subjective well-being is examined for Türkiye. The regression analysis has been made for different gender groups and the results are somehow different. The estimation results indicate that for every sample, durable goods have a significant effect on life satisfaction. Wang et al. (2019) indicate a positive relationship between consumption and happiness using Chinese panel data. According to the analysis, in the case of the same age, education and gender, consumption has a positive effect on happiness (i.e. signalling effect) but an increase in consumption by the highest spenders among people of the same age, education and gender lowers happiness (i.e. jealousy effect). *Jaunky et al.* (2020) tried to explore the nexus between socioeconomic dimensions, basic needs, luxury personality traits and happiness in Mauritius. The results show that material consumption and happiness are positively related. The study by *Dumludağ et al.* (2021) discussed the role of consumption on life satisfaction. By adopting a survey method, they gathered 3008 data from individuals. They run a regression analysis considering different consumption types. According to the results, there is a negative relationship between life satisfaction and most consumption categories. On the other hand, they found a positive correlation between expenditure in the case of eating out and vacations.

According to the related literature, there is a tendency for happiness to increase with consumption. However, this statement can be subject to change depending on the country group. Individuals' consumption patterns and expectations of life are quite different. While some people expect to be happy when they consume more, others need to be more social or go on a holiday. According to TurkStat, Life Satisfaction Survey, the source of happiness can be identified as "health", "love", "success", "money", and "job". Health is the most important source of happiness for Turkish people with a figure of over 68%. The second most important source of happiness is love. To compare consumption and happiness, let's consider the average rate of satisfaction and household consumption for the European Union countries as of 2022.

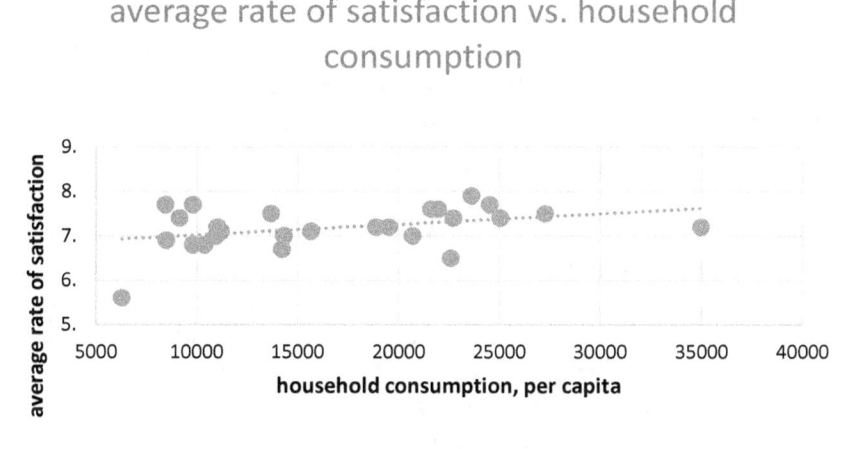

FIGURE 3.2 Average rate of satisfaction vs. household consumption expenditure per capita, 2022
SOURCE: EUROSTAT AND WORLD BANK WORLD DEVELOPMENT INDICATORS—WDI

Figure 3.2 shows that there is a positive relationship between consumption and the average rate of satisfaction, but the correlation coefficient is 0.37 which is slightly low. This finding is somewhat consistent with the other studies that emphasize the other factors that might influence happiness or life satisfaction. For example, Dutt (2006) mentioned that "happiness does not depend on consumption and income alone, but on many other things." However, it needs to take time to consider all consumption types in one study and deserves further investigation.

4   Conclusion

The concept of happiness has been widely discussed from many different perspectives. Of course, we want to be happy and what makes us happy is still a question mark. The debate about understanding the concept of happiness has been going on for a long time. Sometimes we think that happiness comes from our family through genetic factors, sometimes it comes from our wealth or higher income, or it comes from consuming more and more. According to Dutt (2006), consumption may give people incentives to work, trade and innovate which leads to a higher level of production and hence economic growth. Increased economic activity can strengthen societies. There are many types of consumption and yet there is still no consensus about which one is more important. Do we need to consume more and more durable goods, nondurable goods or should we change our consumption behavior? The answer is still unclear. Spending patterns can make a difference in individuals' happiness. Spending on experiences such as holidays, social activities (theatre, cinema, going out with friends, etc.), and sports activities can change the level of happiness (Venhooven, 2012). Many arguments support the idea that experiential consumption brings more happiness than material consumption. While the emphasis is on the source of happiness, it is worth noting that human behaviours can also support happiness from within and without. In this study, the concept of happiness and consumption is discussed in detail and the relationship between happiness and consumption is examined with the help of the related empirical studies. The issue of happiness is still a newsworthy issue that requires more attention from researchers. As Socrates once said, *"The secret of happiness, you see, is not found in seeking more, but in developing the capacity to enjoy less"*, perhaps it is also true for our time.

References

Ackerman, F. (1997). Consumed in theory: alternative perspectives on the economics of consumption. Journal of Economic Issues 31(3), 651–664.

Becchetti, L., Trovato, G., and Londono Bedoya, D. A. (2011). Income, relational goods and happiness. Applied Economics 43(3), 273–290.

Blanchflower, D. G. and Oswald, A. J. (2004). Well-being over time in Britain and the USA. Journal of Public Economics (88), 1359–1386.

Brown, G. D. A. and Gathergood, J. (2017). Consumption and Life Satisfaction: A Micro Panel Data Study (May 3, 2017). Available at SSRN: https://ssrn.com/abstract=2962837 or http://dx.doi.org/10.2139/ssrn.2962837.

Bruni, L. (2006). Civil happiness: economics and human flourishing in historical perspective. Routledge, London.

Caporale, G. M., Georgellis, Y., Tsitsianis, N., and Yin, Y. P. (2009). Income and happiness across Europe: Do reference values matter? Journal of Economic Psychology 30(1), 42–51.

DeLeire, T., and Kalil, A. (2010). Does consumption buy happiness? Evidence from the United States. International Review of Economics 57(2), 163–176.

Dhar, R., & Wertenbroch, K. (2000). Consumer choice between hedonic and utilitarian goods. Journal of Marketing Research 37(1), 60–71.

Diener, E. and Seligman, M. E. P. (2003). Beyond money: toward an economy of well-being, Psychological Science in the Public Interest 5, 1–31.

Di Tella, R., Haisken-De New, J., and MacCulloch, R. (2010). Happiness adaptation to income and status in an individual panel. Journal of Economic Behavior & Organization 76(3), 834–852.

Duesenberry, J. S. (1949). Income, saving, and the theory of consumer behaviour. Cambridge, MA: Harvard University Press.

Dumludag, D., Gokdemir, O. and Veenhoven, R. (2021). Does Spending Make Us Happy? The Role of Consumption on Life Satisfaction, International Journal of Business and Applied Social Science 7(10), 37–48.

Dutt, A. K. (2006). Consumption and happiness: Alternative approaches. New Directions in the Study of Happiness 1–58.

Easterlin, R. (1974). Does economic growth improve the human lot? In: P. A. David, M. W. Reder (eds.) Nations and households in economic growth: essays in honour of Moses Abramovitz. Academic Press, New York.

Easterlin, R. A. (1995). Will raising the incomes of all increase the happiness of all? Journal of Economic Behavior and Organization (27), 35–47.

Fafchamps, M., and Shilpi, F. (2008). Subjective welfare, isolation, and relative consumption. Journal of Development Economics 86(1), 43–60.

Frey, B. S., and Stutzer, A. (2000). Happiness, economy and institutions. The Economic Journal 110(466), 918–938.

Frey B. S., and Stutz, A. (2002). Happiness and economics. Princeton University Press, Princeton.

Gokdemir, O. (2015). Consumption, savings and life satisfaction: The Turkish case. International Review of Economics 62(2), 183–196.

Guillen-Royo, M. (2011). Reference group consumption and the subjective well-being of the poor in Peru. Journal of Economic Psychology 32(2), 259–272.

Haybron, D. M. (2013). Happiness: A very short introduction, Vol. 360, Oxford University Press, USA.

Headey, B., Muffels, R., and Wooden, M. (2008). Money does not buy happiness: Or does it? A reassessment based on the combined effects of wealth, income and consumption. Social Indicators Research 87(1), 65–82.

https://ourworldindata.org/happiness-and-life-satisfaction. (accessed 28 February 2024).

https://ec.europa.eu/eurostat/databrowser/view/ilc_pw01_custom_10524929/default/table?lang=en&page=time:2023. (accessed 28 February 2024).

https://data.tuik.gov.tr/Bulten/Index?p=Life-Satisfaction-Survey-2021-45832&dil=2. (accessed 27 February 2024).

https://www.azquotes.com/quotes/topics/happiness.html?p=3. (accessed 26 February 2024).

https://www.azquotes.com/quotes/topics/overconsumption.html. (accessed 20 February 2024).

Jaunky, V. C., Jeetoo, J., and Rampersad, S. (2020). Happiness and consumption in Mauritius: An exploratory study of socio-economic dimensions, basic needs, luxuries and personality traits. Journal of Happiness Studies 21, 2377–2403.

Layard, R. (2005). Happiness. London: Penguin Books.

Lim, H. E., Shaw, D., Liao, P. S. and Duan, H. (2020). The Effects of Income on Happiness in East and South Asia: Societal Values Matter? J Happiness Stud. 21, 391–415. https://doi.org/10.1007/s10902-019-00088-9.

Linssen, R., van Kempen, L. and Kraaykamp, G. (2011). Subjective Well-being in Rural India: The Curse of Conspicuous Consumption. Soc Indic Res. 101, 57–72. https://doi.org/10.1007/s11205-010-9635-2.

Noll, H.-H., and Weick, S. (2015). Consumption expenditures and subjective well-being: Empirical evidence from Germany. International Review of Economics 62(2), 101–119.

Oishi, S., Graham, J., Kesebir, S., and Galinha, I. C. (2013). Concepts of happiness across time and cultures. Personality and Social Psychology Bulletin 39(5), 559–577.

Rojas, M. (2019). The relevance of Richard A. Easterlin's groundbreaking work. A historical perspective. In: M. Rojas (eds.) The Economics of Happiness: How the Easterlin Paradox Transformed Our Understanding of Well-Being and Progress, 3–24.

Shields, M. A. and Wheatley Price, S. (2005). Exploring the economic and social determinants of psychological well-being and perceived social support in England. Journal of the Royal Statistical Society Series A, (168), 513–538.

Stanca, L. and Veenhoven, R. (2015). Consumption and happiness: An introduction. International Review of Economics 62, 91–99.

Stutzer, A., and Frey, B. S. (2010). Recent Advances in the Economics of Individual Subjective Well-Being. Social Research 77(2), 679–714. http://www.jstor.org/stable/40972234.

VanPraag, B., and Ferrer-i-Carbonell, A. (2010). Happiness economics: a new road to measuring and comparing happiness. Found Trends Microecon. 6, 1–97.

Veblen, T. (1899). The theory of the leisure class. New York, NY: Macmillan.

Veenhoven, R. (2012). Evidence-based pursuit of happiness: What should we know, do we know and can we get to know? https://mpra.ub.uni-muenchen.de/41924/ (accessed 26 February 2024).

Wang, H., Cheng, Z., and Smyth, R. (2019). Consumption and happiness. The Journal of Development Studies 55(1), 120–136.

Weiss, A., Bates, T. C., and Luciano, M. (2008). Happiness is a personal (ity) thing: The genetics of personality and well-being in a representative sample. Psychological Science 19(3), 205–210.

Zhang, J., and Xiong, Y. (2015). Effects of multifaceted consumption on happiness in life: a case study in Japan based on an integrated approach. International Review of Economics 62, 143–162.

CHAPTER 4

Happiness and Income: Understanding the Complex Relationship

Meltem İnce Yenilmez

The lord of a state or a family concerns himself not with scarcity
but rather with uneven distribution ... For where there,
is even distribution there is no poverty.—Confucius

•••

This study examines the complex relationship between wealth and happiness, taking its cues from Confucius's thesis that the well-being of a state or family is more significantly impacted by unequal distribution than by scarcity. It expands on Easterlin's work by examining the "Easterlin Paradox," which casts doubt on the notion that having more money equates to a higher level of subjective well-being. The investigation addresses psychological, social, and economic aspects and casts doubt on the idea that a consistent rise in money leads to a lifetime of happiness. It also recognizes the shifting dynamics of income and job happiness, particularly in light of expanding work trends such as remote work and the gig economy. The idea that more economic inequality is linked to lower happiness is supported by regression analysis, which links variables including GDP, household income, unemployment, income inequality, and life expectancy to happiness. The unexpected discovery that there is no statistically significant correlation between changes in household income and happiness, however, emphasizes the necessity of more investigation into these intricate relationships. In conclusion, this study adds to the current body of knowledge regarding the relationship between wealth and happiness. It examines psychological, social, and economic aspects and makes recommendations for particular laws and practices to improve social welfare as a whole. The multidisciplinary approach and empirical results provide insightful information about the complex relationship between wealth and happiness.

1 Introduction

Following the groundbreaking research of Easterlin (1974), one of the first economists to examine the connection between real GDP per capita and subjective well-being, there has been a surge in interest in the study of subjective well-being. He noticed that although income levels increased in the decades after World War II, average levels of satisfaction hardly changed when examining the historical evolution of these two variables in developed countries such as the United States. This problem, sometimes known as the "Easterlin Paradox," has also been verified for China (Easterlin et al. 2012), European transition countries (Frey and Stutzer 2002a; Clark et al. 2008), and other industrialised nations.

Academics from a wide range of fields have long been fascinated by the intricate relationship between wealth and happiness. To fully understand the complex links between material wealth and subjective well-being, a multidisciplinary investigation is necessary. The central focus of this study is the analysis of how income levels affect happiness from a psychological, social, and economic perspective. Early studies have historically frequently shown a clear-cut positive association between happiness and income. Nevertheless, more complex insights have emerged from later research, casting doubt on this oversimplified perspective and highlighting the necessity of a careful examination of moderating factors.

Psychological variables are crucial in determining how money and happiness interact. According to the hedonic treadmill theory, when people's wealth varies, they gradually lose the benefits of their transient improvements in happiness. This casts doubt on the widely held notion that a consistent rise in income corresponds to a lifetime of contentment. Furthermore, the subjective sense of happiness is highly influenced by individual differences in personality, values, and psychological qualities, which further complicates the relationship between well-being and wealth.

Societal and cultural factors further complicate the relationship between money and happiness. According to the relative income theory, people frequently gauge their degree of satisfaction by comparing it to others in their social circle and giving relative riches a higher weight than absolute money. The relationship between wealth and happiness varies depending on the cultural context and is impacted by social comparisons, financial inequality, and societal expectations.

A significant role for economic issues also plays in this complex interaction. The idea of marginal utility captures the saturation barrier, beyond which increased money produces diminishing rewards in terms of enjoyment. This barrier must be understood by economists and policymakers to develop policies that enhance societal well-being. The distribution of income and the availability of job possibilities also have a major role in determining the general level of happiness in communities.

The relationship between money and happiness is taking on new dimensions as a result of the changing nature of work and trends like remote work and the gig economy. To comprehend the current state of the economy, it is necessary to investigate how conventional ideas of income and job satisfaction are changing. Taking into account social, cultural, and economic aspects is crucial for overall well-being, as this literature review concludes by highlighting the necessity for a thorough understanding of the complex interactions between wealth and happiness. The results highlight the need for customized treatments and policies that take into account the various contextual factors affecting the happiness-income link and recognize the shortcomings of a one-size-fits-all strategy.

2   Literature Review

The "Easterlin Paradox" has been the subject of lengthy discussion. According to the "Easterlin Paradox" (Easterlin, 1974), there is no positive correlation between happiness and inequality. This study is at the confluence of two distinct research strands. Research on the boundaries of economic growth is one. Evidence from the literature suggests that nonmaterial factors, such as air pollution (Zhang et al., 2017), traffic congestion (Smyth et al., 2008), crime (Powdthavee, 2005), etc., are what endangers the subjective well-being of the average citizen and counteract the positive effects of material factors on subjective well-being. Specifically, economic expansion is invariably accompanied by economic disparity, which may undermine communal unity and residential segregation (Bjorvatn and Cappelen, 2003; Engler and Weisstanner, 2021).

According to Festinger's (1954) social comparison theory, an individual's happiness is significantly influenced by their relative economic status. If they live in a reasonably wealthy environment, those who are poorer may be happier than those who are richer. Furthermore, those with lower economic standing tend to sense relative deprivation, and economic disparity serves as a catalyst for people to become conscious of their economic status. One gets less happy the more deprived they feel (D'Ambrosio and Frick, 2007). The reason happiness does not keep pace with economic growth can be explained by both the vertical and horizontal social comparisons, which compare an individual's riches to their surroundings. It might be the outcome of vertical social comparison-based hedonic adaptation. People recover from abrupt shocks to their income, according to research (Di Tella and MacCulloch, 2010; Di Tella et al., 2010). Happiness thus returns to normal following the economic shock.

Individuals are always assessing who they are, particularly in terms of financial aspects like money, income, and consumption. As a result, people are worried about both their relative wealth and their absolute wealth when compared to those who are better and worse off. The distinction between an individual's distance from better-off people and their distance from worse-off people is made by Fehr and Schmidt (1999), who also define these terms as upward and downward inequality, respectively. In addition, they propose four conditional expressions of people's love for them. The "tunnel effect," which refers to the perception of having the chance to keep up with the rich, is at play if someone is glad with the strong upward inequality. But, if someone feels cheated by it, they are jealous. Meanwhile, researchers empirically validate those feelings of pride and altruism in response to substantial downward inequality (Hopkins, 2008; Espín et al., 2018). Alternatively, an individual may feel joyful about the inequality. In the relationship between inequality and pleasure, Yu and Wang (2017) analyze two opposing effects: the envy effect and the signal effect.

A broad assessment of one's life is the definition of subjective well-being (Diener and Seligman, 2002). According to Frey and Stutzer (2002b), it is about the respondents' assessment and judgment of several facets of an individual's life. According to studies, people typically equate happiness with life satisfaction, which is a component of the subjective well-being construct (Easterlin, 2001; Brockmann and Delhey, 2010; Leung et al., 2011).

As per Frey and Stutzer (2002a), some argue that happiness and life satisfaction might be defined differently due to their influence from diverse aspects of people's lives. Happiness is a transient, instantaneous, transient, and retroactive mental state, while life satisfaction is a reasonably long-term assessment of an individual's well-being (Gamble and Gärling, 2012; Chui and Wong, 2016).

Indeed, studies have indicated that greater income inequality can lead to social and economic issues that would ultimately harm SWB. Less egalitarian societies, for example, would have negative consequences for investment, economic growth, and political stability (Alesina and Perotti, 1996; Oishi et al., 2011; Baten and Mumme, 2013). Furthermore, Delhey and Dragolov (2014) who demonstrate that inequality causes status anxiety and distrust in Europe and hence lowers Europeans' SWB, support Wilkinson and Pickett (2010) claim that higher inequality increases status competition and status anxiety.

According to Oishi et al. (2011), inequality in the USA has a detrimental impact on lower-class people's satisfaction because it heightens feelings of unfairness and a lack of truth in society.

According to Schneider (2019), people's perceptions of their social standing can help to explain why people in European cultures with higher levels of inequality are less content with their lives.

Due to the tunnel effect argument put forth by Hirschman and Rothschild (1973), a crucial component in determining how income disparity affects people's SWB is the "hope factor." If people perceive income inequality as a chance to advance in society, they might be able to put up with it. But that tolerance wanes and their SWB decreases if their expectations are not fulfilled. According to Grosfeld and Senik (2010), Poland's situation closely matches the tunnel theory's forecast. Growing income disparity did not translate into decreased personal satisfaction during the first phase of the transition period since it represented a chance for people to climb the socioeconomic ladder.

Individuals' expectations were not fulfilled throughout the last phase of the transition process, and they saw the income distribution mechanism as unjust and corrupted, which reduced their level of happiness overall. In China, Wang et al. (2015) discovered more evidence in favour of the tunnel theory. In both rural and urban China, their empirical results highlight the inverse U-shaped relationship between an individual's self-reported happiness and economic disparity. According to Kelley and Evans (2017), the beneficial impact of inequality is limited to developing nations because of the swift institutional and social transformations that occur there, leading people there to perceive inequality as a sign of progress. However, because of "the relatively stable opportunity structures and existential security," people in industrialized nations do not care about economic inequality.

The people in Turkey are diverse. It is unclear if society as a whole is doing better overall, even though many are pursuing material prosperity. Specifically among those in the higher income levels, Easterlin (2001), Frey, and Stutzer (2002a) claimed that an increase in income only slightly increases happiness. Veenhoven and Vergunst (2014), however, argued that income increases are correlated with increases in happiness, especially in countries where average happiness increases along with economic expansion. In industrialized countries, relative income—defined as the difference between an individual's income and the state income per capita—was found to have a more significant impact on human well-being than absolute income (Blanchflower and Oswald, 2004; Blanchflower and Oswald, 2016). Yu and Chen (2016) discovered that in China, the impact of income on well-being varied depending on the individual. Household income was found to be positively correlated with happiness and life satisfaction on an individual basis. In contrast, only relative wealth was linked to pleasure and life satisfaction at the national level.

Some research has expanded the influence of predicted income on happiness (Caner, 2015; Tsui, 2014), while other studies have looked at the relationship between absolute and relative income and happiness (Blanchflower and Oswald, 2004; Oshio et al., 2011; Yu and Chen 2016). Other sociodemographic characteristics (Tambyah and Tan, 2011; Howell et al., 2012; Yiengprugsawan et al., 2012), social capital (Leung et al., 2011), the senior population (Eshkoor et al., 2015), and gender (Chui and Wong, 2016) have all been mentioned in literature on happiness. Concerning the relationship between various forms of income (absolute, relative, and expected) and subjective well-being in Türkiye, this study aims to offer more thorough coverage.

3   Data and Methodology

3.1   *Data*

The research makes use of yearly data collected between 2005 and 2012. The Organization for Economic Co-operation and Development's (OECD) iLibrary website provided the data points. Twenty of the thirty-four nations covered by publicly available OECD data were chosen at random for this study. An overview of the information gathered and used in an empirical model to examine the implications of measured happiness may be found in Table 4.1. The World Bank website and the World Database of Happiness archive both include more information:

TABLE 4.1   Data and statistics

Variable	Obs.	Mean	Std. Dev.	Min	Max
Life Expectancy (OECD, ILO)	160	81.13	3.17	74.19	11.13
Unemployment (ILO, WB)	170	3.48	3.19	0.14	15.90
Household Income (OECD, ILO)	184	38917.40	9017.25	12573.25	48139.47
GDP (WB, OECD)	184	39152.80	9473.08	8735.03	48042.67
GINI Index (WB, OECD)	160	38.14	8.17	27.30	40.95

TABLE 4.1   Data and statistics (*cont.*)

Variable	Obs.	Mean	Std. Dev.	Min	Max
Happy Years Index (World Database of Happiness)	184	5.30	0.96	5.40	12.15

3.2   *Empirical Model*

This work adheres closely to the model and research of Verme (2011). This study looks at the problem from a new angle by altering the variables and data sources in the model. To obtain a perspective on income and inequality that is more in line with what an individual perceives and realizes, the model that is employed combines a pre-tax Gini and the post-tax Household Income (HI). To account for the demotivation of the underemployed, the model additionally includes a metric of work security. The model is expressed as follows:

$$HY_{it} = \beta_0 + \beta_{it}GN_{it} + \beta_{it}HI_{it} + \beta_{it}UE_{it} + \beta_{it}LE_{it} + \beta_{it}GDP_{it} \qquad (4.1)$$

The Happy Years (HY_{it}) of a country i at a given year t is its annual average. The dependent variable in question is HY_{it}. This metric assesses happiness by considering both the duration and the level of satisfaction. It provides a broader perspective on a nation's level of well-being. Applying this measure also fosters common sense. It makes sense that someone would rather live a long and happy life than a short and unhappy one. Last but not least, it compares and measures with current public and economic policies. According to a review of the academic literature, HY_{it} is the best technique for measuring the many forms of life satisfaction and quality indicators (Hagerty et al., 2001).

The five measurements that make up the study's independent variables were gathered from different databanks and archives. First, the GN_{it}, an online measure of inequality for the nation I at year t, from the World Bank DataBank. The wealth disparity in a given country (i) at a given year (t) is represented by the GN_{it} coefficient. The OECD iLibrary is the source of HI_{it}, an alternative to the income metric. To examine a household's income available for spending before progressive tax brackets affecting the amounts of yearly income, this includes a post-tax measure of household income.

The unemployment rate in the country i at year t is measured by UE_{it} or long-term unemployment. The World Bank DataBank website is where the information was gathered. Life Expectancy, or LE_{it}, is the fifth variable. To guarantee that we have a measure of both the duration of HYS and the projected time of life for an individual, a quantity that has a significant impact on how society uses the limited resource of time, the data was taken from the OECD iLibrary databank. GDP_{it}, or GDP per capita after accounting for purchasing power parity, is the study's sixth independent variable. Measuring not just an individual's wealth but also the wealth of their community is crucial. GDPit, which accounts for currency exchange rate fluctuations, measures GDP growth per person in the economy. With the use of this metric, the financial gains that every person experiences are taken into account equally. The research anticipates a strong negative association between the GN_{it} and HY_{it} using these variables in an empirical model.

4   Empirical Results

Regarding the equation and data, Tables 4.2, 4.3, and 4.4 display the findings of the empirical estimation. The results of the regression analysis demonstrate the anticipated negative association between the Happy Years index and the degree of income inequality as indicated by a Gini index.

TABLE 4.2   1st regression results

Variable	Coefficient	Std. Error
GN**	−0.047192	0.034729
LE**	0.094781	0.045915
UE***	−0.31885	0.067103
GDP*	0.18672	1.170842
HI	3.79E-05	9.08E-05
C	0.78105	5.134795
R-squared	0.59704	
F-statistic	15.0834	
Number of Obs.	160	

Note: ***, **, and * denotes significance at the 1%, 5%, and 10% respectively.

TABLE 4.3   2nd regression results

Variable	Coefficient	Std. Error
GN*	−0.03471	0.00854
HI	−7.49E-05	9,06E-05
LE	0.074581	0,049856
UE***	−0.35902	0,047821
C	4.078127	3.15972
R-squared	0.597453	
F-statistic	28.01975	
Number of Obs.	150	

Note: ***, **, and * denotes significance at the 1%, 5%, and 10% respectively

TABLE 4.4   3rd regression results

Variable	Coefficient	Std. Error
GN*	−0.07246	0.02136
HI	−0.00009	0.00008
GDP***	0.00078	1.49E-05
UE***	−0.28102	0.061547
C	18.34972	3.47982
R-squared	0.81457	
F-statistic	41.36080	
Number of Obs.	150	

Note: ***, **, and * denotes significance at the 1%, 5%, and 10% respectively

Relativity to changes in the independent variables can be used to explain the findings of the empirical model with all the variables, as shown in Table 2, as well as with a few modifications, such as the removal of GDPit in Table 3 and LEit in Table 4. A nation's satisfaction levels are being impacted by the tendency of the rich-poor divide to grow wider. As anticipated, there is a considerable expected correlation between HY and LE, UE. Interestingly, though, HI is found to be statistically insignificant for HY even when it increases. This means that a person's degree of happiness won't rise or fall in response to rising incomes and salaries or falling taxes. This is an unexpected result. Even with a higher HI not influencing HY, there is still a negative correlation with the Gini coefficient. These findings support the theory that income disparity increases unhappiness and harms happiness and life satisfaction, but they also indicate something unexpected.

5   Conclusion

A multidisciplinary inquiry is required to fully understand the complicated relationships between tangible riches and subjective well-being since scholars from a variety of fields have long studied the nuanced relationship between wealth and happiness. This research primarily examines the psychological, social, and economic effects of income levels on happiness. While mitigating factors have been taken into account in subsequent studies, the initial findings of a clear positive correlation between happiness and income have been refuted.

The understanding of the relationship between happiness and money depends heavily on psychological factors. Contrary to the notion that a steady increase in income results in lifetime contentment, the hedonic treadmill theory contends that people gradually lose the advantages of fleeting increases in happiness as their wealth fluctuates. Further complicating the relationship between money and well-being are individual variances in personality, values, and psychological traits. Further complicating aspects are societal and cultural circumstances and social comparisons, which are highlighted by the relative income theory. Social expectations, socioeconomic disparity, and cultural factors all affect how wealth and happiness are related. The distribution of income and other economic factors, such as marginal utility, are also important in this complex relationship.

New perspectives on the relationship between money and happiness are brought about by the evolving nature of employment, including remote work and the gig economy. To be well overall, one must comprehend these changes and take into account social, cultural, and economic factors. The necessity for a full knowledge of the intricate relationships between wealth and happiness is emphasized in the literature review's conclusion, which also promotes the need for tailored interventions and laws that take context into account.

The examination of the literature starts with Easterlin's pioneering work, which revealed the "Easterlin Paradox," which states that higher income levels did not correspondingly result in higher subjective well-being. Understanding the complex relationships between wealth and happiness has made subjective well-being—which includes life satisfaction and happiness—a central concern. The review delves into how cultural and sociological elements contribute to the happiness-income relationship, as well as the effects of income disparity on social and economic issues.

The empirical part of the study uses a model to look at how happiness relates to several variables, such as GDP, household income, unemployment, life expectancy, and income inequality. Regression analysis supports the hypothesis that more economic inequality is associated with lower happiness by confirming the expected negative relationship between the Happy Years index and income inequality. The study's surprising conclusion—that changes in household income had no statistically significant effect on happiness—highlights the necessity for more research into these intricate relationships.

In conclusion, by exploring psychological, social, and economic aspects, the study adds to the continuing conversation on the connection between wealth and happiness. To improve general social well-being, more specialized policies and interventions will be possible thanks to the multidisciplinary approach and empirical findings, which offer insightful information on the complex nature of this interaction.

References

Alesina, A. and Perotti, R. (1996). Income distribution, political instability, and investment. *European Economic Review* 40(6): 1203–1228.

Blanchflower, D. G. and A. J. Oswald (2004), 'Well-being over time in Britain and the USA,' Journal of Public Economics, 88, Issues 7–8: 1359–1386.

Blanchflower, D. G. and A. J. Oswald (2016). Antidepressants and age: a new form of evidence for U-shaped well-being through life, *Journal of Economic Behavior & Organization* 127: 46–58.

Brockmann, H. and Delhey, J. (2010). Introduction: The dynamics of happiness and the dynamics of happiness research. *Social Indicators Research* 97(1): 1–5. https://oi.org10.1007/s11205-009-9561-3.

Bjorvatn, K., and Cappelen, A. W. (2003). Inequality, segregation, and redistribution. J. Public Econ. 87, 1657–1679. https://10.1016/S0047-2727(01)00202-X.

Caner, A. (2015). Happiness, comparison effects, and expectations in Turkey. *Journal of Happiness Studies* 16(5): 1323–1345. https://doi.org/10.1007/s10902-014-9562-z.

Chui, W. H., and Wong, M. Y. H. (2016). Gender differences in happiness and life satisfaction among adolescents in Hong Kong: Relationships and self-concept. *Social Indicators Research* 125(3): 1035–1051. https://doi.org/10.1007/s11205-015-0867-z.

Clark, Andrew E., Paul Frijters, and Michael A. Shields. 2008. Relative Income, Happiness, and Utility: An Explanation for the Easterlin Paradox and Other Puzzles. Journal of Economic Literature, 46 (1): 95–144.

Delhey, J. and Dragolov, G. (2014). Why Inequality Makes Europeans Less Happy: The Role of Distrust, Status Anxiety, and Perceived Conflict, *European Sociological Review*, Volume 30, Issue 2, April 2014, Pages 151–165, https://doi.org/10.1093/esr/jct033.

Diener, E and Seligman, M. E. P. (2002). Very happy people. *Psychological Science, 13*(1), 81–84. https://doi.org/10.1111/1467-9280.00415.

Easterlin, R. (2001). Income and Happiness: Towards a Unified Theory. *Economic Journal,* 111, 465–484. http://dx.doi.org/10.1111/1468-0297.00646.

Eshkoor, S. A., Hamid, T. A., Chan, Y. M. and Shahar, S. (2015). An investigation on predictors of life satisfaction among the elderly. *International E-Journal of Advances in Social Sciences* 1(2): 207–212. https://doi.org/10.18769/ijasos.86859.

Easterlin, R. A. (1974). Does economic growth improve the human lot? Some empirical evidence. In *Nations and Households in Economic Growth*, David and M. W. Reder (New York, NY: Academic Press), 89–125. https://10.1016/B978-0-12-205050-3.50008-7.

Easterlin, R. A., Morgan, R., Switek, M., and Wang, F. China's life satisfaction, 1990–2010. Proc Natl Acad Sci USA. 2012 Jun 19;109(25):9775–80. https://10.1073/pnas.1205672109.

Espín, A. M., Moreno-Herrero, D., Sánchez-Campillo, J., and Rodríguez Martín, J. A. (2018). Do envy and compassion pave the way to unhappiness? Social preferences and life satisfaction in a Spanish city. J. Happiness Stud. 19, 443–469. https://10.1007/s10902-016-9828-8.

Engler, S., and Weisstanner, D. (2021). The threat of social decline: income inequality and radical right support. J. Eur. Public Policy 28, 153–173. https://10.1080/13501763.2020.1733636.

Easterlin, R. (2001) Income and Happiness: Towards a Unified Theory. *Economic Journal,* 111, 465–484. http://dx.doi.org/10.1111/1468-0297.00646.

Eshkoor, S. A., Hamid, T. A., Chan, Y. M. and Shahar, S. (2015). An investigation on predictors of life satisfaction among the elderly. *International E-Journal of Advances in Social Sciences* 1(2): 207–212. https://doi.org/10.18769/ijasos.86859.

Espín, A. M., Moreno-Herrero, D., Sánchez-Campillo, J., and Rodríguez Martín, J. A. (2018). Do envy and compassion pave the way to unhappiness? Social preferences and life satisfaction in a Spanish city. J. Happiness Stud. 19, 443–469. https://10.1007/s10902-016-9828-8.

Fehr, E., and Schmidt, K. M. (1999). A theory of fairness, competition, and cooperation*. Q. J. Econ. 114, 817–868. https://10.1162/003355399556151.

Festinger, L. (1954). A theory of social comparison processes. Hum. Relat. 7, 117–140. https://10.1177/001872675400700202.

Frey, B. S. and Stutzer, A. (2002b). What can economists learn from happiness research? Journal of Economic Literature 40(2): 402–435.

Hagerty, M. R., Cummins, R. A., Ferriss, A. L. *et al.* Quality of Life Indexes for National Policy: Review and Agenda for Research. *Social Indicators Research* 55, 1–96 (2001). https://doi.org/10.1023/A:1010811312332.

Hirschman, A. O., and Rothschild, M. (1973). The changing tolerance for income inequality in the course of economic development. Quarterly Journal of Economics, 87(4), 544–566.

Hopkins, E. (2008). Inequality, happiness and relative concerns: what is their relationship? J. Econ. Inequal. 6, 351–372. https://10.1007/s10888-008-9081-4.

Howell, R. T., Chong, W. T., Howell, C. J. and Schwabe, K. (2012). Happiness and life satisfaction in Malaysia. In *Happiness across culture: View of happiness and quality of life in non-Western cultures*, eds. H. Selin and G. Davey, 43–55. New York: Springer.

Gamble, A. and Gärling, T. (2012). The relationships between life satisfaction, happiness, and current mood. *Journal of Happiness Studies* 13(1): 31–45. https://doi .org/10.1007/s10902-11-9248-8.

Grosfeld, I. and Senik, C. (2010). The emerging aversion to inequality—Evidence from subjective data, CEPREMAP Working Papers (Docweb) 1006, CEPREMAP.

Leung, A., Kier, C., Fung, T., Fung, L. and Sproule, R. (2011). Searching for happiness: The importance of social capital. *Journal of Happiness Studies* 12(3): 443–462. https:// doi.org/10.1007/s10902-010-9208-8.

Oishi, S., Kesebir, S. and Diener, E. (2011). Income Inequality and Happiness. *Psychological Science*, 22(9), 1095–1100. https://doi.org/10.1177/0956797611417262.

Schneider, S. M. (2019). Why Income Inequality Is Dissatisfying—Perceptions of Social Status and the Inequality-Satisfaction Link in Europe, *European Sociological Review*, Volume 35, Issue 3, June 2019, Pages 409–430, https://doi.org/10.1093/esr/jcz003.

Tambyah, S. K. and Tan, S. J. (2011). Subjective well-being in ASEAN: A cross-country study. *Japanese Journal of Political Science*, 12(3): 359–373. https://doi.org/10.1017 /S1468109911000168.

Tsui, H. C. (2014). What affects happiness: Absolute income, relative income or expected income? *Journal of Policy Modeling* 36(6): 994–1007. https://doi.org/10.1016/j.jpol mod.2014.09.005.

Veenhoven, R. and Vergunst, F. (2013). *The Easterlin illusion: economic growth does go with greater happiness*, MPRA Paper 43983, University Library of Munich, Germany.

Verme, P. (2011). Life Satisfaction and Income Inequality, *Review of Income and Wealth*, 57(1): 111–127.

Wang, P., Pan, W., and Luo, Z. (2015). The impact of income inequality on individual happiness: evidence from China, *Social Indicators Research*, 121, 413–435.

Wilkinson, R. and Pickett, K. (2010). The Spirit Level: Why Equality is Better for Everyone. London: Penguin.

Yiengprugsawan, V., Somboonsook, B., Seubsman, S. and Sleigh, A. C. (2012). Happiness, mental health, and socio-demographic associations among a national cohort of Thai adults. *Journal of Happiness Studies*, 13(6): 1019–1029. https://doi.org/10.1007 /s10902-011-9304-4.

Yu, Z. and Chen, L. (2016). Income and well-being: relative income and absolute income weaken negative emotions, but only relative income improves positive emotion. *Frontiers in Psychology*, 7, 2012.

Zhang, X., Zhang, X., and Chen, X. (2017). Happiness in the air: how does a dirty sky affect mental health and subjective well-being? J. Environ. Manage. 85, 81–94. https://10.1016/j.jeem.2017.04.001.

CHAPTER 5

Life Satisfaction, Happiness, and Contemporary Development Economics: Insights from Data and the Discussions on Circular Economy Policy

Özge Kozal

This chapter has two aims: First, it seeks to investigate the factors influencing individual-level life satisfaction in the 21st century, using the most recent data from the World Values Survey, Wave 7. It encompasses demographics, material well-being, social capital, and macro-level variables. Secondly, the chapter discusses the limits of the capitalist world economy and its mainstream economic paradigm in ensuring life satisfaction. Results, obtained through logistic regression analysis with 80,189 individuals from 56 countries, reveal correlations between life satisfaction and age, religion, education level, employment status, number of children, and personal income. Higher material well-being levels notably correspond to elevated life satisfaction. Individuals with greater interpersonal trust, institutional trust, and active membership in volunteer organizations tend to experience higher life satisfaction. All macro-level indicators—GDP per capita, unemployment rate, and women's representation in parliament—show a positive association with higher life satisfaction. Country-level income per capita emerges as the most influential factor, even with country-level variations indicated by further quantitative analysis. The study concludes with discussions on how a circular economy can foster a more redistributive and socially inclusive environment, aligning with the vision of a 21st-century economist as articulated by doughnut economics.

1   Introduction

The concepts of happiness and life satisfaction are closely related but not entirely synonymous. However, both happiness and life satisfaction are integral elements in contemporary development economics and are acknowledged as core components of subjective well-being (SWB) (Diener et al., 2002). Essentially, SWB involves individuals' evaluations of their lives, encompassing general assessments or various dimensions. Gamble and Gärling (2012) note that there are two aspects to consider SWB: the cognitive aspect involves individuals forming assessments of their life satisfaction, while the affective aspect pertains to the moods and emotions they experience.

Even though understanding the dynamics of life satisfaction and establishing connections between happiness are essential for comprehending human life holistically, particularly from an interdisciplinary perspective, in the social sciences, debates on how to measure SWB are even controversial. Yet, the general tendency is to focus on self-reporting methods to understand moods, emotions, or the overall evaluation of life. And what about economics? It is not incorrect to say that economics is intertwined with everything. In the field of contemporary development economics, comprehending the factors affecting life satisfaction or happiness involves considering two key concepts: material well-being and non-material, or subjective, well-being. As Todaro and Smith (2014) assert, there are three core values of development: sustenance, self-esteem, and freedom. Sustenance refers to meeting basic material needs to survive, but self-esteem and freedom are more complex and non-material aspects of human life that can be related to life satisfaction and happiness. Economics attempts to understand the basic mechanisms contributing to the life satisfaction and happiness of individuals to create a more resilient and inclusive society.

As mentioned earlier, measuring happiness and life satisfaction can be challenging, and assigning scores to life satisfaction introduces a numeric aspect. Despite the inherent limitations, economic analyses often rely on quantitative measures. While recognizing the pervasive nature of the capitalist world economy's emphasis on measuring performance through numerical metrics, it is acknowledged that thinking in numbers is beneficial and more manageable for reductive human brains, particularly for some social scientists, especially economists. In the literature, questionnaires typically employ the following queries for evaluation: 'Taking all together, how would you say things are these days? Would you say you are very happy, rather happy, or not happy at all?' For a more comprehensive assessment, the question 'How satisfied are you with your life these days?' is asked, commonly using Cantrill's ladder scale to order the responses. Although the questions remain consistent in academic research, the factors explaining variations in life satisfaction or happiness levels vary significantly. In mainstream development economics, the accepted wisdom once held that income, happiness, and life satisfaction were closely intertwined. On one side, research suggested a positive trend in the average happiness and life satisfaction levels of citizens as the income of countries increased. On the other side, some studies found little to no impact of income on life satisfaction. Ultimately, the literature on this topic is controversial, and results are mixed (Blanchflower and Bryson, 2024; Boyce et al., 2010; Boes and Winkelmann, 2010; Easterlin, 1973; 1974; Cheung and Lucas, 2015; Masuda et al., 2021; Veenhoven, 1989; Veenhoven and Vergunst, 2014; Verme, 2011, and so forth).

Understanding income and life satisfaction levels across individuals, communities, and countries is essential. However, focusing solely on the income or material well-being side of well-being can result in missing the big picture and overlooking other important factors. In the 21st century, there are numerous challenges and opportunities in the world economy. On one side, there are economic crises, health crises, or environmental crises; on the other side, there is an increasing number of social movements, changing norms, a rise in artificial intelligence, and a transformation in the organization of the state. If we see the bigger picture, we have to recognize other opportunities and boundaries that we must face and mitigate in society. In this respect, examining both individual-level and macro-level factors that affect life satisfaction or happiness from a multidimensional perspective is crucial to design policies more accurately. In this regard, this chapter aims to shed light on the factors correlated with life satisfaction by focusing on demographics, and material well-being, and attempting to go beyond demographic differences and income-related factors by controlling for social capital and macro-level variables. World Values Survey (wvs, Wave 7, Edition 5, 2017–2022) data from more than 80,000 individuals in 56 countries is used for quantitative analysis.

In the next section, we will briefly discuss breakpoints in the economic development approach regarding the concepts of life satisfaction and happiness. Then, utilizing individual and country-level data, we will provide an overview of worldwide life satisfaction, happiness, and income. Employing logistic regression, we will attempt to capture individual and macro-level differences related to the level of life satisfaction. Following this, we will pose the question: Does the capitalist world economy aim to ensure life satisfaction and happiness? The chapter will conclude by raising questions about a path-breaking approach: the "circular economy" and whether it can be a tool to address the life satisfaction side of well-being by exploring what kind of economic design genuinely cares about life satisfaction.

2   Stating the Obvious: Is the Life Satisfaction and Economics Related?

In this section, our focus will be on the roots of development economics, delving into the emergence of concepts like happiness and life satisfaction. Let's rewind the story and revisit the crucial moments in the post-World War II rise of development economics. Discussing the entire process comprehensively is challenging; attempting to tell the story would require a detailed exploration of the changes throughout the history of capitalism.

In this narrative, it becomes essential to specifically address the roots of the dependency approach and the narrative of "development of underdevelopment" or "dependent development." This transition didn't occur solely at the country level; global economic relations underwent significant changes. This would necessitate a detailed discussion involving numerous influential social scientists such as Prebisch, Singer, Frank, Sweezy, Arrighi, Amin, Mandel, and Wallerstein who emphasized the ideology of capital accumulation, exchange forms, and states. However, undertaking such an extensive task is beyond the scope of this study. Instead, we will touch upon certain waypoints, inevitably leaving out many aspects, including discussions on the ideology of development up to the present. In summary, this flow can be considered the "mainstream story of the breakpoints in the human and planet-centric development idea".

There is no doubt that World War II (WWII) was one of the most important breakpoints, bringing about economic, social, and cultural transformations worldwide. In the process of reconstructing the aftermath of the war, economic growth became the fundamental motivation for national policy pursuits. During this time, the singular focus on "quantitative increase" in production and the widespread adoption of the Fordist production and consumption style paved the way for a lack of emphasis on equality, redistribution policies, and human well-being. This transformation ushered in a golden age for capitalism (Lipietz, 1990; Perelman, 2007) until the beginning of the discussion on the dynamics of the 1973 economic crisis. The problems stemming from the rapid industrialization race and Fordism were initially deliberated in the 1960s. However, during this period, terms such as industrialization, growth, development, and modernization were almost synonymous. Consequently, there was limited space for discussions on resource use, human welfare and well-being, equality and justice, and environmental pollution. In the 1970s, the economic repercussions of the crisis, the emergence of energy supply problems due to escalating oil prices, and mounting concerns about the finite nature of non-renewable energy sources sparked new conversations. Furthermore, the consequences of environmental damage during this period and the deepening income inequality resulting from the liberalization policies of the 1980s emphasized the need for a more comprehensive approach. This underscored the importance of considering social equality, justice, individual well-being, and the environmental dimension in development approaches.

The term "sustainable development" was first used in the 1987 report known as the "Our Common Future" (Brundtland Report) by the United Nations

(UN). The concept was conceptualized as a development approach capable of meeting the basic needs of the current generation without compromising the opportunities to meet the needs of future generations (UN, 1987; Brundtland, 1985). In the 1990s, the understanding of "sustainability" and "sustainable development," systematized by the UN, led to a significant questioning of growth approaches in economics, ultimately resulting in a paradigm shift. This development perspective, contrary to the limitless pursuit of growth until that time, triggered a model search that acknowledges the limits of economic growth and development while considering the social, ecological, economic, spatial, and cultural dimensions, and of course intergenerational aspects of human well-being. From now on, different dimensions of human well-being are extensively studied by scholars from various disciplines, including economics, psychology, and sociology.

Even the roots of happiness economics can be traced back to early works by economists such as Richard Easterlin, who, in the early 1970s, conducted influential research on the relationship between economic growth and well-being, well-known as the Easterlin paradox. Easterlin's seminal research, particularly his paper "Does Economic Growth Improve the Human Lot? Some Empirical Evidence" published in 1974, explored that within a society, higher income levels did not necessarily correlate with higher levels of happiness. Even the contribution of Easterlin to development economics by emphasizing that happiness is important, the emergence of happiness economics as a sub-discipline of happiness economics gained momentum in the 1990s with scholars like Richard Layard, Daniel Kahneman, Amartya Sen and others contributing to the development of the subject and the important breakpoint in economic paradigm title with sustainable development or sustainable development.

Until the end of the 1960s, development had been accepted as a sustainable rate of growth of income to enable a nation to expand its output at a rate faster than the growth rate of its population, and this trend has been measured with gross domestic product per capita. Yet now, in development economics, we aim to broaden our perspective by going beyond GDP-type variables and considering two dimensions of well-being. The first pertains to the materialistic aspect, referred to as material well-being, which relies on income support. On the second axis lies the non-materialistic facet of well-being, covering happiness, life satisfaction, dynamics of community building, institutional trust, and psychological well-being as well. The contribution of Amartya Sen is especially important in comprehending factors affecting human well-being rather than focusing solely on subjective well-being, often measured through self-reported life satisfaction or happiness, as seen with pioneers of happiness economics such as Easterlin. Amartya Sen's capabilities approach takes a broader

perspective by emphasizing individuals' capabilities—their real opportunities to achieve valuable functioning (the various things a person may value
doing or being). Sen argues that true well-being is achieved when individuals
have the freedom and capabilities to pursue their chosen ways of living. This
represents an important paradigm shift by emphasizing objective and measurable capabilities, focusing on what individuals can do and be, rather than
solely relying on subjective feelings. At their core, both happiness economics
and Amartya Sen's capabilities approach share a common goal, which is the
enhancement of human well-being (Todaro and Smith, 2012; Sen, 1999).

Today, within the field of economics, happiness and life satisfaction stand
out as two crucial concepts that have been extensively discussed. Numerous
theoretical and empirical research studies on this subject have been conducted
using various methodologies, examining different country cases and periods
(Easterlin and Veenhoven, 1989; Veenhoven and Vergunst, 2014; Easterlin, 2003;
Easterlin, 1973, 1974; Abdallah et al., 2008; Pittau et al., 2010; Kapteyn et al., 2010;
Pavot and Diener, 2008; Graham, 2005). The inclusion of happiness and life
satisfaction aspects in economics has been described by some scholars as "revolutionary" (Frey, 2010). Emerging paradigms, such as the circular economy,
are aiming to address not only human well-being but also planetary boundaries, integrating both human-centric and planet-centric perspectives. These
holistic approaches acknowledge the interdependence of human prosperity
and environmental sustainability, emphasizing the imperative for a balanced
and sustainable coexistence.

3   What Do Data Say? Insights from a Basic Quantitative Analysis

According to Easterlin (1974), there exists a positive relationship between per
capita income and happiness within a country. However, he deemed it "uncer-
tain" whether such a positive relationship exists between the incomes and
happiness of countries at a specific point in time. Notably, he observed that
individual happiness did not necessarily increase, and the average happiness
of wealthy countries did not surpass that of poor countries. These findings are
commonly referred to in the literature as the Easterlin Paradox. The argument
does not explicitly state that income growth cannot influence happiness at all;
rather, any effect can only occur under the restrictive assumption of ceteris
paribus (Beja, 2014). Veenhoven, a leading figure in happiness economics, dis-
agreed with Easterlin's findings that more money doesn't lead to more happiness. Veenhoven argued the opposite, suggesting that as a country's income
per person increases, so does its overall happiness. Veenhoven believed that

the Easterlin Paradox, implying that higher income doesn't always equate to more happiness, was more of a illusion than a rule (Kamilcelebi, 2023).

As it seen there is no consensus on income and happiness relationship. Conducting an individual-level quantitative analysis of capabilities and functioning's, as suggested by Amartya Sen, proves challenging. In this section, we try to take a further step to analyze the individual level life satisfaction variations in the world. Life satisfaction is chosen the dependent variable for the analysis, while happiness and life satisfaction are interconnected in economics, they represent distinct facets of well-being that are influenced by various economic and social parameters (Ortiz-Ospina and Roser, 2017). The discussion of the determinants of life satisfaction, considered a more comprehensive indicator of overall well-being (Diener et al., 2002), in the 21st century is essential using questions based on Easterlin's conceptualization. The main research question of this chapter is that what drives higher level of life satisfaction and why it differs widely between people and countries.

In this section, we first evaluate the most recent individual-level data from the World Values Survey, providing a comprehensive understanding of both materialistic and non-materialistic well-being. This dataset covers various dimensions of everyday life and essential aspects of community building, including trust, religiosity, interpersonal and institutional trust. The questionnaire encompasses several dimensions of well-being. In the literature, the World Values Survey is recognized as a credible individual-level dataset and one of the most reputable cross-national surveys on value changes and well-being (Abdallah et al., 2008; Bjørnskov et al., 2008; Yin, 2023; Cheng et al., 2023). National-wide representative samples of the adult population have been surveyed in every country/territory in every wave, but there is no continuity between the samples across waves. This is the reason to focus on the last wave of the study. In the latest wave, individuals from 91 countries answered questions related to life satisfaction and happiness; however, we could cover responses from 57 countries. This exclusion was based on the criteria presented in Table 5.1, where individuals with missing answers were excluded.

Before delving into the econometric analysis, let's take a broader view by examining the distribution of happiness and life satisfaction across countries. Figure 5.1 depicts the distribution of happiness levels among 155,642 individuals from 91 countries, with individual responses ranging from 442 to 4.554 participants. Vietnam, Kyrgyzstan, Iceland, Andorra, Tajikistan, Norway, Indonesia, Sweden, Northern Ireland, and Switzerland exhibit the highest individual happiness levels, with over 90% of respondents stating they are "very happy" or "quite happy". On the other end of the happiness spectrum, Lithuania, Mongolia, Bolivia, Nigeria, Egypt, Greece, Iran, Iraq, Bulgaria, and

share of people (%, high life satisfaction)

9.3　　　　76.4

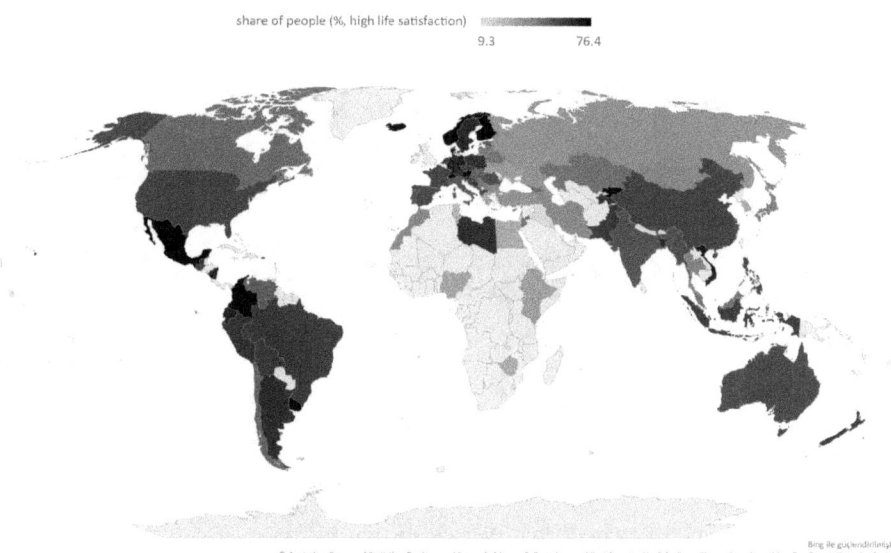

© Australian Bureau of Statistics, GeoNames, Microsoft, Microsoft Crowdsourced Enrichments, Navinfo, Open Places, OpenStreetMap, TomTom, Wikipedia, Zenrin

FIGURE 5.1　Share of very happy and quite happy people (% of country sample)
SOURCE: AUTHORS' CALCULATION BASED ON WVS, WAVE 7 DATA

Zimbabwe have over 30% of respondents defining themselves as "Not very happy" or "Not at all happy".

When considering life satisfaction within the total sample, the results differ from happiness, showing lower overall satisfaction levels. Only 16.2% of the total sample reports being completely satisfied with their lives. Countries such as Kyrgyzstan, Puerto Rico, Colombia, Libya, Nicaragua, Mexico, Azerbaijan, Malaysia, Turkey, Japan, Canada, Macau SAR, Greece, Iraq, Lebanon, South Korea seem to have a relatively low percentage of people who are completely satisfied with their lives. Recognizing that being completely satisfied is an extreme case, we calculated the share of people indicating life satisfaction levels 7, 8, 9, and 10 out of 10 as representing high life satisfaction. In this case, Puerto Rico, Iceland, Uruguay, Norway, Finland, Colombia, Mexico, Kyrgyzstan, Switzerland, and Denmark have the highest levels. On the other hand, Turkey, Ukraine, Ethiopia, Kenya, Macau SAR, Nigeria, South Korea, Greece, Zimbabwe, Lebanon, Egypt, Tunisia, Iraq have the lowest life satisfaction levels, ranging from 31% to 9%.

In addition to individual-level data, the last World Happiness Report (2023) also presents country rankings based on life evaluations from 2020 to 2022. Utilizing a three-year average, the global mean life satisfaction value is 5.5 out of 10 across 137 countries. At the summit of the life satisfaction hierarchy

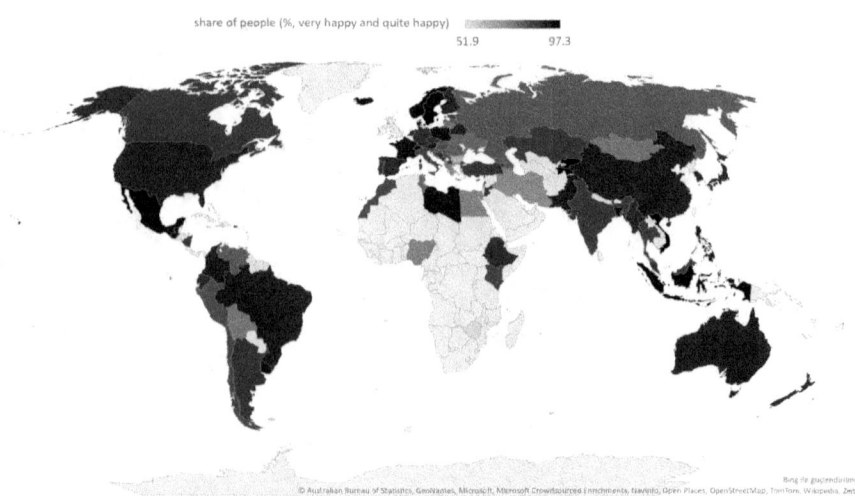

share of people (%, very happy and quite happy)

51.9   97.3

FIGURE 5.2   Share of people completely satisfied with their life (%)
SOURCE: AUTHORS' CALCULATION BASED ON WVS, WAVE 7 DATA

share of people (%, completely satisfied wih their life)

0.7   59.1

FIGURE 5.3   Share of people with high life satisfaction (%)
SOURCE: AUTHORS' CALCULATION BASED ON WVS, WAVE 7 DATA

FIGURE 5.4   The countries highest and lowest life evaluations based on three-years-average
SOURCE: WORLD HAPPINESS REPORT, 2023

are Finland, Denmark, Iceland, Israel, and the Netherlands, while Zimbabwe, Sierra Leone, Lebanon, and Afghanistan find themselves at the lower end of the spectrum.

Is the level of life satisfaction related to income? We selected countries by considering both the highest self-reported life satisfaction levels in the World Values Survey (WWS), Wave 7, and the World Happiness Report (2023). The countries presented in Table 5.1 exhibit a higher level of life satisfaction. When examining the personal income scale, we observed that in Colombia, where 14.6% of individuals with a high income level reported a life satisfaction level of 10 out of 10, and in the Netherlands, only 30% of those with the highest income reported the highest level of life satisfaction. In Mexico, only 14% of high-income individuals reported being completely satisfied with their lives. This basic quantitative analysis indicates that we need to look beyond income to comprehend the variations in life satisfaction levels within a country.

Notably, financial security is just one among several factors influencing life satisfaction or happiness. Layard (2005) identifies seven factors that surveys indicate affect the average national happiness: family relationships, financial situation, work, community and friends, health, personal freedom, and personal values. Besides avoiding poverty, research suggests that individuals are happier when they are employed, not divorced, or separated, and exhibit a high level of trust in others within society. Additionally, happiness is associated with experiencing high government quality with democratic freedoms and having religious faith. The significance of these factors may provide insights into the substantial variation in the reported percentages of people who are not happy or satisfied among developing countries with similar incomes. Drawing inspiration from Layard's (2005) work, our analysis aims to explore the individual

TABLE 5.1 Life satisfaction and individual level income relationship in selected countries

Income level	Completely satisfied = 10			Satisfaction level = 9			Satisfaction level = 8			Satisfaction level = 7		
	Low	Medium	High	Low	Medium	High	Low	Medium	High	Low	Medium	High
Colombia	40	45.4	14.6	30.8	53.3	15.9	29.5	60	10.5	34.2	61.6	4.1
Denmark	29.3	27.1	37.5	18.9	30.1	46.7	25.8	28.9	40.8	32.7	31.4	31.6
Finland	26.2	30	28.2	23.2	31.9	39.4	30.1	32.5	31.9	43.2	34.5	21.1
Iceland	20.1	41.5	30.4	16.5	30.6	45	24.4	38.4	29	32.3	33.9	25.9
Kyrgyzstan	16.8	67.7	14.1	20.7	63.2	13.9	12.3	77.5	9.2	13.7	81.1	3.8
Mexico	42.3	45.3	11.3	35.8	49	13.7	39.7	49.2	9.7	42.5	46.2	10.8
Netherlands	17.2	29.7	29.7	8.4	41.6	32.5	14	40.6	29.5	18.5	41.1	21.4
Norway	29.3	41.1	26.2	23.7	38.9	33.4	33.1	32	28.9	41.6	32.6	22.5
Puerto Rico	23.4	59.9	15.2	11.6	69	16.8	15.1	73.5	10.3	23.5	64.2	12.3
Sweden	23.7	30.7	43.8	15.1	36.2	46.3	18.4	30	46.9	21.8	39.2	33.9
Switzerland	28	32.3	27.9	23.3	33.4	35.1	27.6	33.8	30.5	30.3	34.7	25.5
Uruguay	27.5	54.4	14.9	15.2	67.7	15.6	15.1	71.8	12.2	18.8	74.2	3.3

Note: Other missing, Multiple answers, don't know, and no answer excluded, this is why the total is not 100 percent.

SOURCE: HAERPFER, C., INGLEHART, R., MORENO, A., WELZEL, C., KIZILOVA, K., DIEZ-MEDRANO, J., LAGOS, M., NORRIS, P., PONARIN, E. & PURANEN B. (2022): WORLD VALUES SURVEY WAVE 7 (2017–2022) CROSS-NATIONAL DATASET. VERSION: 4.0.0. WORLD VALUES SURVEY ASSOCIATION. DOI: DOI.ORG/10.14281/18241.18

and macro-level dynamics influencing life satisfaction globally. The dependent variable is constructed using the following question:

> Q49. All things considered, how satisfied are you with your life these days? (Scale from 1 to 10 (from "completely dissatisfied" to "completely satisfied")

Initially, we transformed the life satisfaction variable into three categories: Level 1–4 (low), 5–7 (moderate), and above 7 (high life satisfaction). We then conducted an ordinal logistic regression. Subsequently, we constructed a binary life satisfaction variable, where 0 represents not satisfied with life (0–5) and 1 indicates being satisfied with life (6–10). The results were highly consistent across categories in the ordinal logistic regression and remained robust when comparing them with the binary logistic regression. Therefore, for simplicity, we present the results from the binary logistic regression in our analysis.

Conducting a comprehensive econometric analysis is not the primary aim of this research but serves to understand the relationship between individual-level life satisfaction and relevant factors. In the literature, income is often considered a primary driver, with higher income positively correlated with life satisfaction. However, the figures mentioned earlier, and Table 5.1 indicate that while income is significant in understanding variations in life satisfaction levels, it alone is insufficient to capture the bigger picture. Therefore, we perform a binary logistic regression analysis to explore the hypothesis that other factors, such as material well-being, institutional trust, and social capital (measured by interpersonal trust and active membership in volunteer organizations), are also correlated with life satisfaction, and this correlation may be even stronger than observed with income.

We utilized World Values Survey Wave 7, the most recent wave of the survey. After excluding missing answers accompanying the questions in Table 5.1, the model included 80,189 individuals from 56 countries. The countries are Argentina, Armenia, Australia, Bangladesh, Bolivia, Brazil, Canada, Chile, China, Colombia, Cyprus, Czech Republic, Germany, Ecuador, Egypt, Ethiopia, United Kingdom, Greece, Guatemala, Indonesia, Iraq, Jordan, Japan, Kazakhstan, Kenya, Kyrgyzstan, South Korea, Lebanon, Libya, Morocco, Maldives, Mexico, Myanmar (Burma), Mongolia, Malaysia, Nigeria, Nicaragua, Netherlands, New Zealand, Pakistan, Peru, Philippines, Romania, Russia, Singapore, Serbia, Slovakia, Thailand, Tajikistan, Tunisia, Turkey, Ukraine, Uruguay, United States, Vietnam, Zimbabwe.

This survey encompasses a broad range of values and demographics, including sex, age, religiosity, education, and employment status, as well as core human values such as trust, memberships, views on migration, and ethnicity. We selected the main socio-demographic variables, including Religiosity, Sex, Age groups, Education level, Employment status, and an income-related indicator categorized as low-middle- and high-income groups. Additionally, different from income level, we defined material well-being as the situation of individuals in meeting basic needs, such as food, safety, access to medicine and medical treatment, cash income, and shelter—the bottom line of Maslow's hierarchy of needs. Inclusion of individual-level income level and material well-being can be problematic for the analysis, and hence in Model 1, we exclude material well-being. In Model 2, we add material well-being, and due to robust signs and magnitudes between models, we include material well-being in the final model, which is Model 2 in Table 5.2.

To explore the potential relationship between social capital and life satisfaction, we included three variables: interpersonal trust (measuring how much trust individuals have for others), institutional trust, and active membership in volunteer organizations. Lastly, we incorporated country-level indicators to capture the relationship between life satisfaction and macro indicators. This includes income per capita, the total unemployment rate, and the number of women represented in parliament as a proxy for gender equality in the country. The logistic regression was conducted in Stata 16, and the regression coefficients and marginal effects are presented in Table 5.3, while Table 5.2 provides the variables and their definitions.

TABLE 5.2   Variables and definitions

Individual-level variables

Question	Variable name	Scale
Q49. How satisfied are you with your life these days?	Life Satisfaction	Binary (0-1) low-high

Independent variables

In the last 12 months, how often have your or your family, Q51 Gone without enough food to eat. Q52 Felt unsafe from crime in your home. Q53 Gone without medicine or medical treatment that you needed. Q54 Gone without a cash income. Q55 Gone without a safe shelter over your head.	Material well-being	Binary (0-1) low- high
Q64–Q89 Churches, armed forces, the press, television, labour unions, police, courts, government, political parties, parliament, civil service, universities, elections, major companies, banks, environmental organizations, women's organizations, charitable or humanitarian organizations, the European Union, the United Nations, the International Monetary Fund, the International Criminal Court, the North Atlantic Treaty Organization, the World Bank, the World Health Organization, the World Trade Organization	Institutional Trust	1 low 2 moderate 3 high 4 very high

TABLE 5.2   Variables and definitions (*cont.*)

Q58 Your family Q59 Your neighbourhood Q60 People you know personally Q61 People you meet for the first time Q62 People of another religion Q63 People of another nationality	Interpersonal Trust	1 low 2 moderate 3 high 4 very high
Q94 Church or religious organization Q95 Sport or recreational organization, football/baseball/rugby team Q96 Art, music or educational organization Q97 Labor Union Q98 Political party Q99 Environmental organization Q100 Professional association Q101 Humanitarian or charitable organization Q102 Consumer organization Q103 Self-help group, mutual aid group Q104 Women's group Q105 Other organization	Active membership	0: no active membership 1: active member
Q.288. Income group	Income	1 low 2 middle 3 high
Q173. Are you religious or not?	Religiosity	Binary (1-0) Religious-Not religious
Q260. Respondent's sex	Sex	Binary (1-2) Male-female
Q261. How old are you?	Age groups	<=30, 31–45, 45–60, 60 =>
Q275. What is the highest educational level that you have attained?	Education level	(1–4) primary-high school-university-graduate
Q279. Are you employed now or not? How many hours a week?	Employment status	1 full-time, 2 part-time, 3, self-employed, 4 retired/pensioned, 5 housewives not otherwise employed, 6 student, 7 unemployed, 8 others

Macro-level variables

gdppc	Logarithm of gross domestic product per capita, PPP (constant 2017 international $)

TABLE 5.2   Variables and definitions (*cont.*)

unemployment	Logarithm of the unemployment rate (% of the labor force)
women representation	Logarithm of Proportion of seats held by women in national parliaments

SOURCE: COMPILED BY THE AUTHOR USING WVS, WAVE 7 DATA. THE AVERAGE 2019–2020 IS USED FOR THE MACRO VARIABLES

Table 5.3 presents the results, including both regression coefficients and marginal effects. Starting from the demographics, individuals aged between 41–64 and those aged 65 and older are less likely to report high life satisfaction and no statistically significant differences were observed between genders. Higher religiosity is associated with increased life satisfaction. Individuals with at least one child are more likely to report higher life satisfaction. Employment status shows variations, where part-time employees are more likely to report higher life satisfaction compared to full-time employees, while retired/pensioned and unemployed individuals are less likely to report higher life satisfaction. The personal income level is considered highly correlated, as indicated in Table 5.3. The marginal effect shows that individuals with high income are more likely to experience life satisfaction, and this effect is substantial compared to demographic variables. Interestingly, higher material well-being, measured by meeting basic needs, appears to have a more significant impact on life satisfaction than income alone. Even when estimating these two indicators separately with controlled demographics, meeting basic needs is deemed more crucial than being at the top of the income scale, marking a noteworthy result.

Social capital, a complex and multidimensional concept capturing various forms of social interactions, was included in the model. Drawing on Bourdieu's (1984) contributions, social capital involves creating networks that offer value to members by providing access to social resources within the network. According to social capital theory, social relationships are key sources of development and contribute to the accumulation and characteristics of human capital. This concept gained popularity through Putnam's seminal works (Putnam et al., 1994; Putnam, 1995, 2000). Putnam defines social capital as "features of social organization such as networks, norms, and social trust that facilitate coordination and cooperation for mutual benefit" (Putnam, 1995). Therefore, variables reflecting trust among society members, trust in institutions, and active participation in volunteer organizations were added to the model. As expected, an increase in institutional trust is positively correlated with higher life satisfaction. Interpersonal trust is also positively correlated with individual life satisfaction levels. Individuals participating in at least one volunteer organization report higher life satisfaction compared to the base category of no active membership in any volunteer organization. The positive and strong correlation between the dimensions of social capital and life satisfaction reveals that social capital is associated with purpose and satisfaction in life and engaging the community and society helps increase life satisfaction. Not only income but also voluntary active participation in an organization increases life satisfaction. This demonstrates that coming together for a purpose and solidarity are related to individuals' subjective well-being. Additionally, as individuals' interpersonal trust, i.e., their trust in other people they live within society, increases, their life satisfaction also increases, highlighting the importance of living in an inclusive community. Finally, trust in institutions increases the likelihood of individuals having higher life satisfaction. Therefore, how individuals relate to and communicate with the state's institutions and government, how they find solutions to their questions and problems, how the government organizes daily life, and the extent to which institutions are democratic are crucial. In essence, perceiving life satisfaction solely as an economic phenomenon is a narrow perspective. The relationship between the individual and both other individuals and the state should be considered as an important variable, and attention should be paid to this when formulating policies.

TABLE 5.3   Regression coefficients and marginal effects

	Model (1) Base model	Model (2) Extended model	Model (2) Marginal effects
Demographic variables			
Age (base <=25)			
25–40	−.115***	−.054	−0.009
	(.035)	(.036)	(0.006)
41–65	−.2***	−.172***	−0.029***
	(.037)	(.038)	(0.006)
>=65	−.058	−.114**	−0.019**
	(.051)	(.052)	(0.009)
Sex (base: male)			
Female	−.011	.001	0.000
	(.021)	(.021)	(0.004)

TABLE 5.3   Regression coefficients and marginal effects (*cont.*)

	Model (1) Base model	Model (2) Extended model	Model (2) Marginal effects
Religiosity (base: Not religious			
Religious	.127***	.081***	0.014***
	(.023)	(.023)	(0.004)
Children (base: no child)			
Having child/children	.163***	.169***	0.029***
	(.025)	(.026)	(0.005)
Education level (base: primary school)			
High School	.13***	.095***	0.016***
	(.024)	(.025)	(0.004)
University	.313***	.223***	0.037***
	(.029)	(.03)	(0.005)
Graduate	.379***	.257***	0.043***
	(.045)	(.046)	(0.007)
Employment status (base: full-time employee)			
Part-time employee	.006	.066*	0.011*
	(.037)	(.038)	(0.006)
Self-employed	−.03	0	0.000
	(.031)	(.032)	(0.005)
Retired/pensioned	−.127***	−.128***	−0.022***
	(.039)	(.04)	(0.007)
Housewife not otherwise employed	−.04	−.03	−0.005
	(.034)	(.035)	(0.006)
Student	.095*	.071	0.011
	(.052)	(.053)	(0.008)
Unemployed	−.401***	−.304***	−0.054***
	(.037)	(.038)	(0.007)
Other	−.436***	−.348***	−0.063***
	(.084)	(.087)	(0.017)
Income level (base: low)			
Middle	.66***	.493***	0.091***
	(.022)	(.022)	(0.004)
High	1.32***	1.071***	0.169***
	(.045)	(.045)	(0.006)

TABLE 5.3   Regression coefficients and marginal effects (*cont.*)

	Model (1) Base model	Model (2) Extended model	Model (2) Marginal effects
Material well-being			
Material well-being (base: low)			
Moderate		.288***	0.071***
		(.093)	(0.023)
High		.87***	0.203***
		(.091)	(0.023)
Very high		1.665***	0.335***
		(.092)	(0.023)
Social capital			
Institutional trust (base: low)			
Moderate		.252***	0.049***
		(.038)	(0.008)
High		.627***	0.111***
		(.041)	(0.008)
Very high		.757***	0.129***
		(.066)	(0.011)
Interpersonal trust			
Moderate		.367***	0.073***
		(.077)	(0.017)
High		.584***	0.110***
		(.078)	(0.017)
Very high		.824***	0.147***
		(.089)	(0.018)
Active membership (base: no active membership)			
Active member		.133***	0.022***
		(.022)	(0.004)
Macro-level variables			
gdppc		4.182***	0.700***
		(.403)	(0.067)

TABLE 5.3   Regression coefficients and marginal effects (*cont.*)

	Model (1) Base model	Model (2) Extended model	Model (2) Marginal effects
women representation		1.364*** (.15)	0.228*** (0.035)
unemployment		.491*** (.058)	0.082*** (0.010)
Constant	Yes	Yes	Yes
Country Fixed Effect	Yes	Yes	Yes
Observations	80189	80189	80189

Note: Standard errors are in parentheses. *** $p < .01$, ** $p < .05$, * $p < .1$
Original equilibrated weights from the World Values Survey were used. To calculate standard errors, we use the linearized method. Marginal effects refer to dy/dx for factor levels as the discrete change from the base level
SOURCE: AUTHORS' CALCULATION

Finally, we added country-level macro variables to examine the relationship between aggregate indicators and individual-level life satisfaction. All macro-level indicators, including GDP per capita, unemployment rate, and the representation of women in parliament, exhibit a positive correlation with increased life satisfaction. Women's representation in the parliament has a relatively higher correlation with higher life satisfaction. Even this variable added to the model to measure country-level gender equality, it can be accepted as the proxy of general democratic conditions. Among these indicators, country-level income per capita emerges as the most impactful factor, even when considering variations at the country level. These findings present a contradiction: when examining life satisfaction and income levels at a country level (see Table 5.1), it appears that the income scale does not fully explain the variations in life satisfaction, aligning with the Easterlin results. However, upon extending the analysis, both individual-level variables and macro-level gross domestic product per capita continue to be recognized as the most influential factors, along with material well-being, under the findings of Veenhoven. If both Easterlin and Veenhoven are correct, what should we do? It appears that we need to explore a new paradigm that not only considers material well-being but also provides an environment for all people to realize their capabilities and functioning across the world, not in a single country or a group of countries. But how?

4   The Pursuit of Happiness in a Capitalist Economy and
       Circular Economy

It is crucial to highlight that, in the 21st century, income remains a fundamental aspect of global life satisfaction analysis. Nevertheless, delving into other
determinants such as trust within the community and individual trust in institutions reveals their equal significance in explaining variations in life satisfaction. It is important to recognize that, while understanding the relationship
between both national-level and individual-level income and life satisfaction is
vital, there is a potential risk of committing the ecological fallacy when studying life satisfaction and happiness. Reports like the World Happiness Report
aim to amalgamate individual-level happiness to offer a numerical overview of
a country's overall life satisfaction and happiness levels. Nonetheless, both life
satisfaction and happiness are subjective, individual variables, and attempting
to derive an aggregate level may not be practically feasible. A detailed overview
of the country sample and the associated characteristics, including a list of
included countries and a summary of the number of individuals per country,
can be found in Appendix/Table 5.4

   And now, the question arises as to whether the capitalist world economy
genuinely prioritizes individual life satisfaction. Unfortunately, the answer
appears to be negative. In the empirical literature, there is limited research on
the relationship between capitalism and life satisfaction. For instance, studies
like Easterlin (2009) predominantly concentrate on the transition from socialism to capitalism, specifically in Eastern Europe during the 1990s. Similarly,
Frijters et al. (2004a, 2004b) focus on individual political changes in countries
such as East Germany, Russia, or other Eastern European nations during their
transition processes at specific points in time.

   What about historical capitalism? While capitalism undeniably contributes
to life satisfaction to some extent, it also gives rise to enduring crises such as climate change and fosters inequalities in income, gender, and regional levels. In
Wallerstein's historical analysis of capitalism as a social system, he asserts that
within a capitalist world economy, the fundamental economic mechanisms
supporting the capitalist mode of production hinge on the commodification
of everything, capital accumulation, and proletarianisation. Moreover, the system emphasizes productivity, and modernization, including the expansion of
firms and changes in state structures favouring the capitalist mode of production (Chase-Dunn and Grimes, 1995). On an individual level, transitioning from
socialism to capitalism characterizes a country's shift in its state organization.
However, from a broader perspective, the international division of labour has
already established a hierarchy among countries, unless a country positions
itself as an external area, which is exceptionally challenging in the 21st century

(Wallerstein, 1995). Consequently, a shift in our viewpoint is imperative. We exist in a capitalist society, and this system aims to ensure life satisfaction or happiness as a means to enhance productivity, alleviate inequality, sustain continuous capitalist accumulation, and address climate change for planetary preservation, all while promoting increased production and consumption of commodities.

Capitalism is currently at a crossroads, facing threats such as climate change, health crises, and economic challenges. These issues significantly impact human happiness and well-being, signalling the need for a paradigm shift. The outdated growth-centric paradigm and the human-centric sustainable human development paradigm should transition to one that encompasses planetary boundaries.

The concept of the circular economy provides tools to address these challenges, potentially enhancing people's happiness. However, in the literature, Kirchherr et al. (2017) delineated conceptual differences in the understanding of the circular economy, identifying 114 different definitions. In this study, starting from the numerous distinct circular economy definitions, some commonly repeated and emphasized key terms stand out. The most frequently used concepts within the circular economy framework are identified as 'recycling, reuse, and reducing' (Ghisellini, 2015). While certain circular economy designs formulate policies within the capitalist system, focusing on the production side and creating policies for recycling, reusing, and reducing their primary goal is not immediately aimed at increasing human well-being. Instead, they strive to ensure the regenerative capacity of the capitalist mode of production with higher ethical standards and an eco-friendly approach (Clube and Tennant, 2020; Geissdoerfer et al., 2017). Nevertheless, as discussions on the circular economy gain popularity, there is a growing divergence in understanding what circularity entails. It is believed that reconciling these differences in understanding, without overlooking interdisciplinary interactions, will pave the way for rapid progress in designing the structure of this circular system.

In her acclaimed book, 'Doughnut Economics: Seven Ways to Think Like a 21st-Century Economist,' Raworth (2017) presents a groundbreaking approach to production and redistribution, going beyond the circular economy's focus on recycling or reusing. She advocates for a transformative shift in economic theory, departing from the traditional circular flow diagram, redefining the roles of various entities—especially households, commons, society, earth, and power—and changing the overarching goal from economic growth to designing, redistributing, and creating for regeneration. Doughnut Economics is envisioned as a compass for human prosperity in the 21st century, aiming to fulfil the needs of all people within the ecological limits of the living planet. The Doughnut model consists of two concentric rings: a social foundation to ensure that no one falls short of life's essentials and an ecological ceiling to prevent humanity from collectively surpassing the planetary boundaries safeguarding Earth's life-supporting systems. This configuration creates a doughnut-shaped space that is both ecologically secure and socially equitable—a space conducive to human thriving. Various studies have already explored the link between the Doughnut model and life satisfaction, including works by Murray et al. (2017), Nademi and Khochiani (2024), and Zsolnai et al. (2023). Raworth's proposition for redistribution, as detailed in Doughnut Economics, implies a paradigm shift in economic theory. Policymakers might contemplate enacting measures that target income inequality, guarantee access to essential resources, and foster conditions conducive to widespread well-being. Exploring the ideas laid out in Doughnut Economics can serve as a framework for policy design. This involves not only redefining economic goals beyond mere growth but also integrating social and ecological dimensions, aiming for a delicate equilibrium between human needs and planetary boundaries.

Making the incorporation of the new ecological paradigm into economic decision-making a top priority is essential for policymakers. This requires recognizing the interconnectedness of planetary boundaries, human well-being, and economic prosperity. Policies should be realigned to promote sustainable practices that acknowledge and respect these intricate relationships. Given the global scale of challenges, including climate change, health crises, and economic instability, policymakers should advocate for international collaboration as well. Encouraging shared solutions and coordinated efforts can have a more significant impact in addressing these multifaceted issues. Moreover, future research should focus on designing policies that connect and bridge life satisfaction and the circular economy.

References

Abdallah, S., Thompson, S., and Marks, N. (2008). Estimating worldwide life satisfaction. Ecological Economics, 65(1), 35–47.

Beja, E. L. (2014). Income growth and happiness: Reassessment of the Easterlin Paradox. International Review of Economics, 61, 329–346.

Bjørnskov, C., Dreher, A., and Fischer, J. A. (2008). Cross-country determinants of life satisfaction: Exploring different determinants across groups in society. Social Choice and Welfare, 30, 119–173.

Blanchflower, D. G., and Bryson, A. (2024). The female happiness paradox. Journal of Population Economics, 37(1), 1–27.

Boyce, C. J., Brown, G. D., and Moore, S. C. (2010). Money and happiness: Rank of income, not income, affects life satisfaction. Psychological science, 21(4), 471–475.

Boes, S., and Winkelmann, R. (2010). The effect of income on general life satisfaction and dissatisfaction. Social Indicators Research, 95, 111–128.

Bourdieu, P. (1984). Distinction: A social critique of the judgement of taste. Translated by Richard Nice. Cambridge, MA: Harvard University Press.

Brundtland, G. H. (1985). World Commission on Environment and Development. Environmental Policy and Law, 14(1), 26–30.

Easterlin, R. A. (2009). Lost in transition: Life satisfaction on the road to capitalism. Journal of economic behavior & organization, 71(2), 130–145.

Chase-Dunn, C., and Grimes, P. (1995). World-Systems Analysis. Annual Review of Sociology, 21, 387–417. http://www.jstor.org/stable/2083416.

Cheng, E. W., Chung, H. F., and Cheng, H. W. (2023). Life satisfaction and the conventionality of political participation: The moderation effect of post-materialist value orientation. International Political Science Review, 44(2), 157–177.

Cheung, F., and Lucas, R. E. (2015). When does money matter most? Examining the association between income and life satisfaction over the life course. Psychology and aging, 30(1), 120.

Clube, R. K., and Tennant, M. (2020). The Circular Economy and Human Needs Satisfaction: Promising the radical, delivering the familiar. Ecological Economics, 177, 106772.

Diener, E., Lucas, R. E., and Oishi, S. (2002). Subjective well-being: The science of happiness and life satisfaction. Handbook of positive psychology, 2, 63–73.

Easterlin, R. A. (2003). Explaining happiness. Proceedings of the National Academy of Sciences, 100(19), 11176–11183.

Easterlin, R. A. (1974). Does economic growth improve the human lot? Some empirical evidence. In David, R. and Reder, R., (Eds.), Nations and Households in Economic Growth: Essays in Honor of Moses Abramovitz, New York: Academic Press, https://doi.org/10.1016/B978-0-12-205050-3.50008-7.

Easterlin, R. A. (1973). Does money buy happiness? The Public Interest, 30, 3–10.

Frey, B. S. (2010). Happiness: A revolution in economics. MIT Press.

Frijters, P., Haisken-DeNew, J. P., and Shields, M. A. (2004a). Money does matter! Evidence from increasing real income and life satisfaction in East Germany following reunification. American Economic Review, 94(3), 730–740.

Frijters, P., Haisken-DeNew, J. P., and Shields, M. A. (2004b). Investigating the patterns and determinants of life satisfaction in Germany following reunification. Journal of Human Resources, 39(3), 649–674.

Gamble, A., and Gärling, T. (2012). The relationships between life satisfaction, happiness, and current mood. Journal of Happiness Studies, 13, 31–45.

Geissdoerfer, M., Savaget, P., Bocken, N. M., and Hultink, E. J. (2017). The Circular Economy—A New Sustainability Paradigm? Journal of Cleaner Production, 143, 757–768.

Gelman, A. (2008). Scaling regression inputs by dividing by two standard deviations. Statistics in medicine, 27(15), 2865–2873.

Ghisellini, P., Cialani, C., ve Ulgiati, S. (2016). A review on circular economy: the expected transition to a balanced interplay of environmental and economic systems. Journal of Cleaner Production, 114, 11–32.

Graham, C. (2005). The economics of happiness. World economics, 6(3), 41–55.

Haerpfer, C., Inglehart, R., Moreno, A., Welzel, C., Kizilova, K., Diez-Medrano, J., Lagos, M., Norris, P., Ponarin, E. and Puranen, B. (2022). World Values Survey Wave 7 (2017–2022) Cross-National Dataset. Version: 4.0.0. World Values Survey Association. DOI: doi.org/10.14281/18241.18.

Kapteyn, A., Smith, J. P., and Soest, A. V. (2010). Life Satisfaction. International Differences in Well-Being.

Kamilcelebi, H. (2023). Veenhoven vs. Easterlin in Happiness Economics: Does Economic Growth Increase Happiness? Journal of Economic Policy Research, 10(2), 691–720.

Kirchherr, J., Reike, D., and Hekkert, M. (2017). Conceptualizing the circular economy: An analysis of 114 definitions. Resources, conservation and recycling, 127, 221–232.

Layard, R. (2005). Happiness: Lessons from a New Science, New York: The Penguin Press.

Lipietz, A. (1990). The Rise and Fall of the Golden Age: An Historical Analysis of Post-war Capitalism in the Developed Market Economies. Money, Finance and Trade Reform of WIDER/UNU. Helsinki: Clarendon-Oxford UP.

Machalek, R., and Martin, M. (2015). "Sociobiology and Sociology: A New Synthesis." International Encyclopedia of the Social & Behavioral Sciences: Second Edition, March, 892–98. https://doi.org/10.1016/B978-0-08-097086-8.32010-4.

Masuda, Y. J., Williams, J. R., and Tallis, H. (2021). Does life satisfaction vary with time and income? Investigating the relationship among free time, income, and life satisfaction. Journal of happiness studies, 22, 2051–2073.

Murray, A., Skene, K., and Haynes, K. (2017). The circular economy: an interdisciplinary exploration of the concept and application in a global context. Journal of Business Ethics, 140, 369–380.

Nademi, Y., and Khochiani, R. (2024). The Pursuit of Happiness in a Circular Economy. Journal of the Knowledge Economy, 1–28.

Ortiz-Ospina, E. and Roser, M. (2017). "Happiness and Life Satisfaction" Published online at OurWorldInData.org. Retrieved from: https://ourworldindata.org/happiness-and-life-satisfaction [Online Resource].

Pavot, W., and Diener, E. (2008). The satisfaction with life scale and the emerging construct of life satisfaction. The journal of positive psychology, 3(2), 137–152.

Pittau, M. G., Zelli, R., and Gelman, A. (2010). Economic disparities and life satisfaction in European regions. Social Indicators Research, 96, 339–361.

Perelman, M. (2007). The End of the Golden Age of Capitalism. In The Confiscation of American Prosperity. New York: Palgrave Macmillan, pp. 17–29.

Putnam, R. D. (2000). Bowling alone: The collapse and revival of American community. Simon and Schuster.

Putnam, R. D. (1995). Bowling Alone: America's Declining Social Capital. Journal of Democracy 6 (1): 65–78. https://doi.org/10.1353/JOD.1995.0002.

Putnam, Robert D., Leonardi, R. and Nanetti, Y. R. (1994). "Making Democracy Work," December. https://doi.org/10.1515/9781400820740.

Raworth, K. (2017). Doughnut economics: seven ways to think like a 21st-century economist. Chelsea Green Publishing.

Sen, A. (1999) Development as Freedom. New York: Alfred A. Knopf.

Todaro, Michael P., and Smith, C. S. (2012). Economic development 12th edition. USA: Princeton.

United Nations. Report of the World Commission on Environment and Development: Our Common Future. United Nations, 1987.

Zsolnai, L., Ócsai, A., Kovacs, G., Kelemen, K., and Valcsicsak, Z. (2023). Wellbeing Policies for Countries and Cities. In Value Creation for a Sustainable World: Innovating for Ecological Regeneration and Human Flourishing (pp. 285–307). Cham: Springer International Publishing.

Veenhoven, R., & Vergunst, F. (2014). The Easterlin illusion: Economic growth does go with greater happiness. International Journal of Happiness and Development, 1(4), 311–343.

Veenhoven, R. (1989). National wealth and individual happiness. Understanding economic behaviour, 9–32.

Verme, P. (2011). Life satisfaction and income inequality. Review of Income and Wealth, 57(1), 111–127.

Yin, R., Lepinteur, A., Clark, A. E., and D'ambrosio, C. (2023). Life satisfaction and the human development index across the world. Journal of Cross-Cultural Psychology, 54(2), 269–282.

Wallerstein, I. M. (1995). Historical capitalism with capitalist civilization. Verso.

Appendix

TABLE 5.4   List of the countries

Country	Freq.	Percent	Cum.
ARG	916	1.14	1.14
ARM	1202	1.50	2.64
AUS	1649	2.06	4.70
BGD	1198	1.49	6.19
BOL	1985	2.48	8.67
BRA	1607	2.00	10.67
CAN	3997	4.98	15.66
CHL	961	1.20	16.85
CHN	2822	3.52	20.37
COL	1498	1.87	22.24
CYP	891	1.11	23.35
CZE	1180	1.47	24.82
DEU	1464	1.83	26.65
ECU	1187	1.48	28.13
EGY	1104	1.38	29.51
ETH	1218	1.52	31.03
GBR	2024	2.52	33.55
GRC	1135	1.42	34.96
GTM	1109	1.38	36.35
IDN	3164	3.95	40.29
IRQ	1172	1.46	41.76
JOR	1190	1.48	43.24
JPN	1155	1.44	44.68
KAZ	1125	1.40	46.08
KEN	1219	1.52	47.60
KGZ	1173	1.46	49.07
KOR	1245	1.55	50.62
LBN	1200	1.50	52.11
LBY	1111	1.39	53.50
MAR	1200	1.50	55.00
MDV	1003	1.25	56.25
MEX	1639	2.04	58.29
MMR	1198	1.49	59.79

TABLE 5.4   List of the countries (*cont.*)

Country	Freq.	Percent	Cum.
MNG	1625	2.03	61.81
MYS	1312	1.64	63.45
NGA	1208	1.51	64.95
NIC	1199	1.50	66.45
NLD	1581	1.97	68.42
NZL	856	1.07	69.49
PAK	1868	2.33	71.82
PER	1378	1.72	73.54
PHL	1200	1.50	75.03
ROU	1092	1.36	76.39
RUS	1712	2.13	78.53
SGP	1948	2.43	80.96
SRB	940	1.17	82.13
SVK	1168	1.46	83.59
THA	1426	1.78	85.37
TJK	1189	1.48	86.85
TUN	1163	1.45	88.30
TUR	2309	2.88	91.18
UKR	1193	1.49	92.67
URY	967	1.21	93.87
USA	2507	3.13	97.00
VNM	1200	1.50	98.49
ZWE	1207	1.51	100.00
Total	80189	100.00	

SOURCE: AUTHORS' CALCULATION BASED ON WVS, WAVE 7 DATA

The Relationship between Economic Policy and Happiness: a Crosscut of Public Policy and Well-Being

Burcu Türkcan

Happiness as a qualitative notion has been tried to measure by quantitative methods during the last decades. Although it's hard to measure all aspects of happiness, the quantification of this issue has been a useful approach for both determining the situation and forming an effective policy. Macroeconomic factors like inflation, unemployment and income inequality; and microeconomic factors like income, wealth and consumption have always had direct influences on people's lives. Hence, measuring happiness with such quantitative notions has provided efficient insights for policy formation. A successful economic policy design can also provide overall happiness for the whole society. Thus, there is a reciprocal relationship between happiness and economic policy. In this context, the main purpose of this study is to show the pros and cons of different economic policy types in terms of happiness. Thus, after a brief introduction, measurement methods of happiness are examined in the first section. The second section is devoted to the related literature to be able to shed light on the nexus between economic policy and happiness. Lastly, economic policy types and their possible effects on happiness are classified. Since this classification is the first for the related literature, it is expected to make a significant contribution.

1 Introduction

The question of 'What is happiness?" has been one of the main enquiries of humankind since ancient times. Philosophers have tried to find a good way of defining this subject for life and the afterlife. Aristotle was the first one to give a proper definition of happiness by calling it "Eudaimonia". He defined happiness as "The activity of the soul as to the virtue." (Helliwell et al., 2023: 3). Following Aristotle, many other philosophers searched for the definition of happiness. However, they were always conducting their discourses and research in a qualitative notion. It was, of course, arising because of the nature of this concept. However, in the modern age, humankind has been trying to develop better ways of defining happiness with quantitative methods.

The afford of measuring happiness has been on the agenda for just last few decades. With the rise of quantitative methods and technological break-throughs to collect and store data, there have emerged some measurement methods and indexes showing the happiness levels of people and societies. Although it is still hard to measure all aspects of happiness, the quantifica-tion of this issue has become a useful tool for both determining the situation and forming an effective policy. Hence, quantitative expressions of happiness have provided data for both researchers and policymakers. Happiness indexes and methods have created a database for policy formation processes and also, they have created an ease to evaluate policy outcomes. As Stiglitz et al. (2018) underlined "What you measure affects what you do."

At this point, there has been an ongoing discussion about the basic deter-minants of happiness. Surely, happiness as a term has a wider meaning than material standard of living (by covering education, health, security, social support, freedom etc.). However, it is widely accepted that income level and wealth have always been basic determinants of happiness. What is more is that the direct impacts of economic downturns on people's happiness have been observed through global crises, several times. Macroeconomic factors like inflation, unemployment and income inequality have always had direct influences on individuals' and societies' lives. In this manner, measuring hap-piness with quantitative methods has provided efficient insights for both gov-ernments and supranational institutions like the United Nations (UN).

As a sub-branch of public policy, economic policy formation is surely an important act for both voters and politicians. A successful design of an eco-nomic policy can provide overall happiness for the whole society and hence it brings about the continuity of government administrations. Moreover, there is a public policy dilemma about happiness during economic crises. During hard times, economic policy may serve as a bitter pill to swallow, and a trade-off may arise between happiness and economic deliverance during these times. In this context, there is a critical relationship between economic policy and hap-piness. Following this fact, the main purpose of this study is to show the pros and cons of different economic policy types in terms of happiness. The related literature exhibits a general overview of this relationship, but it seems that there is an urgent need for a deeper understanding of today's complex world. Hence, in this study, after a brief introduction to economic policy and happi-ness relationships, measurement methods of happiness are examined in the first section. The second section is devoted to the related literature to be able to shed light on the developments in this topic. Lastly, economic policy types and their possible effects on happiness are classified. Since this classification is the first for the related literature, it is expected to contribute by providing a useful tool for both researchers and policymakers.

2   Measurement Methods of Happiness: Ongoing Efforts to Find a Better Tool for Quantification

Stiglitz et al. (2018) underlined that "What you measure affects what you do." Hence measuring happiness has been in the spotlight of researchers since the second half of the 20th century. One of the very first attempts at measuring happiness was a Gallup Poll Survey including the direct question of "How happy would you say that you are?". This type of survey resided on respondents' feelings and was used in the related literature during the 1950s. Then Cantril (1965) suggested a more complicated survey called "Self-Anchoring Striving Scale" which included hopes and fears apart from personal feelings. It was applied in 14 countries across the World. This survey has produced a rating ranging from 0 (the worst possible life) to 10 (the best possible life). It also resided on personal feelings and opinions and hence, it had the same subjective perspective with Gallup Poll Survey (Easterlin, 1974: 90–91). However, the Gallup poll-type survey and the Self-anchoring striving survey have been important because they were the first attempts at quantifying happiness. In the following years, these methods have been developed by emerging methods and tools. Emerging attempts have enhanced the understanding of happiness from a wider perspective. Several new dimensions have been added to measurements and the definition of happiness has also evolved as to the research area and perspective. In this manner, it is seen that some studies call happiness as quality of life and some others call as subjective well-being.

In this context, apart from the survey methods, some other experimental methods have also been developed to measure the level of happiness. One of them is the Experience Sampling Method (ESM). In this method, respondents should carry a handheld computer to give responses to a set of questions whenever they are asked during the day (or days). The questions were about their initial level of happiness, the people that they engaged in and the activities that they made just before the questions arose. The basic reason why this method has been developed was to reduce cognitive biases. However, it was costly to apply to a large sample and getting complete feedback from respondents was not easy. Hence, another method has been enhanced the Day Reconstruction Method (DRM). In this method, respondents filled out diaries in which their actions and intensity of feelings took place (Powdthavee, 2007: 56–57). This method was simpler for respondents but harder to transcript for researchers.

All these psychology-based surveys and experiments have been enhanced by the methodologies of other social disciplines. Since happiness has several dimensions in people's lives, it directly affects the socioeconomic conditions of regions and nations. Hence, some national and global efforts have emerged in the 21st century and they have become commonly-held on the global scale. The U.S. Gallup-Sharecare Well-Being Index is one of the most-known national happiness measurement attempts. It surveys 500 Americans every day since 2008. It includes 6 dimensions of well-being as: (1) present life condition and anticipated life condition (life evaluation dimension), (2) daily feelings and mental well-being (emotional health dimension), (3) job satisfaction and workplace conditions (work environment dimension), (4) physical well-being to continue a full life (physical health dimension), (5) engaging in behaviours affecting physical conditions (healthy behaviour dimension), and (6) feeling safe and satisfied within a community (basic access dimension) (GALLUP, 2024). This happiness measurement attempt has been widened to the global scale by the Gallup Global Emotions Report. It is also based on a Gallup poll-type survey. It tries to quantify feelings and emotions. It excludes economic indicators and only focuses on intangibles. In this survey, there are two types of questions positive experience index questions and negative experience index questions. Positive experience questions include the terms about well-being—resting in a day, being treated with respect by other people, smiling a lot during a day, doing something interesting and experiencing various positive feelings. Moreover, negative experience questions include feeling physical pain, worrying about something, feeling sadness, having stress and feeling anger during the day. All the scores from these questions are used to form a positive experience index and a negative experience index, ranging from 0 to 100 (GALLUP, 2023).

A macro-regional attempt to measure happiness is the OECD (The Organisation for Economic Co-Operation and Development) Centre on Well-Being Reports. OECD Centre on Well-Being lists 11 elements of current well-being as: income and wealth, work and job quality, housing, health, knowledge and skills, environmental quality, subjective well-being, safety, work-life balance, social connections, and civic engagement. Also, resources for future well-being are counted down as: natural capital, economic capital, human capital and social capital (OECD, 2024). OECD publishes annual data about well-being with all dimensions for 37 OECD. Its methodology relies on both subjective data (Gallop poll-type survey questions) and objective socio-economic indicators (Carpentier, 2023: 8).

Another attempt to measure happiness levels across countries is the Happy Planet Index (HPI). It tries to quantify sustainable well-being in terms of efficient use of environmental resources. The focus of this calculation is catching the nexus between environmental sustainability and personal well-being. In this manner, it has three basic dimensions across questions: well-being (in terms of feelings, physical exercising and health conditions), life expectancy (in terms of the average number of years a person is expected to live) and ecological footprint (in terms of average hectares of land per person required to sustain typical consumptions patterns). It uses traffic lights to show how well countries score on each factor and the index score ranges from 0 to 100 (happyplanetindex.org).

Global Happiness Council (GHC) has been formed as another effort for happiness measurement. It is a global network of academicians working on happiness concept. GHC has created the Global Happiness and Well-being Policy Report (GHWPR) which is thought to support the Global Dialogue for Happiness and to be complementary to World Happiness Reports. GHWPR captures 5 dimensions of happiness: education, work, health, vulnerable populations and digital technologies (GHC, 2022).

In addition to all these measurement methods, it is sure that the most-known universal measurement is the World Happiness Report. It has been published since 2013, regularly. It focuses on nations' happiness and creates a de facto comparison across them. It relies on the idea that happiness is a term used to define life satisfaction. In this sense, it underlines six factors determining the life satisfaction of people: income, health, social support, having a sense of freedom to make key life decisions, generosity, and the absence of corruption (Helliwell et al., 2023: 6).

All the happiness measurement efforts exhibit the rising importance of individual and societal happiness for economic development story. The main idea behind all these efforts is measuring the happiness level to take effective actions. Happier nations are more productive, safer and future-oriented. Hence, increasing happiness and sustaining higher levels of happiness are key subjects of today's governments. Moreover, happiness is an important indicator to be able to observe the outcomes of public policies. If public policies—especially economic policies—are effective, then people become happier. So, it can be also perceived as an indirect measure of the effectiveness of economic policies. Consequently, there is a reciprocal relationship between happiness and economic policy formation/implementation.

3   What Does Research Tell Us? Empirical Findings for the Nexus
        Between Economic Policy and Happiness

Happiness subject is a relatively new research area for economists. Although
well-being has been identified through income, wealth and utility, their definition of happiness is relatively new. Defining happiness with today's understanding and trying to understand its role and effects on the economy and society
date back only the second half of the 20th century. Very first studies defined
happiness in terms of income and wealth and what is more interesting is that
this narrow view has taken attention until the 1990s. Some studies—especially
conducted in the USA until the 1990s—have suggested that income increases
the happiness level. In those studies, there was an implicit assumption suggesting "income buys happiness". However, some other studies have tried to underline the fact that income does not always bring happiness. Easterlin (1974) was
the first economist to point out this reality. He reported that income does not
always increase happiness level since there are numerous other indicators of
happiness and sometimes, they may overcome the importance of income.
Hence, emerging methods of measuring happiness since the mids of 1990s,
propose a wider understanding of both which determinants bring happiness
and how are the cross-correlations between them (Veenhoven, 1995: 301). In
this context, Frey and Stutzer (2000) have classified the factors determining the
level of happiness as (1) personality and demographic factors (2) microeconomic
and macroeconomic factors, and (3) institutional conditions in an economy and
society. Today, it is widely accepted that happiness cannot be degraded only to
income and hence mankind should have a wider perspective to measure it.

There is also another strand of discussion about happiness in the literature.
Should happiness be handled with a utilitarian approach or an egalitarian
approach? The utilitarian approach suggests that the happiness level should
be increased for more people. In other words, as the number of happy people
increases, it is good for the economy. However, the egalitarian approach underlines that this is not the destination and providing happiness for the whole
society is the critical point. Egalitarians suppose that inequality of happiness
causes lower levels of happiness for the whole. People tend to compare themselves with other people and if some groups or communities are happier than
others, this will be discomfortable for the rest of the society. Hence, an effective policy should provide both a higher number of happy people and an equal
distribution of happiness across society. Sometimes, the utilitarian approach
and egalitarian approach are perceived like they suggest opposite opinions,
but they feed each other (Ott, 2005).

In this manner, the utility term is thought to be directly linked to happiness. Vilfredo Pareto (1909) has developed the cardinal utility term to identify choice behaviours as to price and budget constraints. Jeremy Bentham (1952) has enlarged the understanding of individual optimal utility choice with the proposition that society's welfare can be represented simply as the sum of utilities of different individuals. In the following years, Hirschman (1973) suggested that others' income is also a determinant of a person's happiness level. The existence of richer people may create an information effect on poorer people and may give hope and belief about their future welfare. This may increase the expectations about subjective well-being. Consequently, it can be said that the utilitarian approach started with Pareto, was enlarged by Bentham and evolved through an egalitarian approach by Hirschman.

Those studies have brought about the idea that happiness is an efficient ingredient for economic progress. In this context, the first attempts at linking utility and economic growth were of course from Barro (1990) and, Barro and Sala-I Martin (1992). They tried to exhibit the role of fiscal policy on economic growth and utility. In this manner, Barro (1990) conducted a survey of 98 countries between 1960–1985 period. Empirical results have proved that as expenditures on non-productive government expenditures increase, economic growth decreases but utility may increase. In the following years, some other empirical studies have emerged on this topic. Ram (2009) has analysed 145 countries from 1995 to 2007. Empirical results have underlined that there was no significant relationship between government spending and happiness but there was a positive relationship between income and happiness. Akay et al. (2012) analysed Germany, and they found that taxes positively affect subjective well-being. As another significant empirical study, Oishi et al. (2012) applied an analysis of 54 countries in 2007. They have detected that progressive taxes are positively related to subjective well-being. Moreover, Grimes et al. (2016) analysed 35 countries between the years of 1981–2012. Empirical results have shown that distortionary taxes are associated with higher levels of subjective well-being. From another perspective, Dao (2017) analysed 183 countries during 1990–2016. Empirical results have underlined that government spending affects happiness only in the short-run and there is a direct linkage between government size in economics and happiness. Also, Eklou and Fall (2020) have conducted an analysis of 13 European countries and the 1980–2007 period. They have investigated that fiscal consolidations hurt individual well-being. As one of the most recent empirical studies, Rizkallah (2023) has conducted a panel data analysis for 18 MENA countries for the 2012–2016-time span. Results have indicated that there is a negative relationship between non-distortionary taxes and economic happiness. It is also evident that there is a positive relationship between public revenues and economic happiness (Rizkallah, 2023: 271).

Apart from the studies searching for the relationship between fiscal policy and happiness, some other studies have focused on the nexus between monetary policy tools, their outcomes and happiness. In this manner, Clark and Oswald (1994) have analyzed by using the British Household Panel Study and have found that unemployment and happiness had a negative relationship during the 1990s. Di Tella et al. (2001) has conducted an analysis of 12 European countries and the USA between 1975 and 1991 by using the Euro-Barometer Survey Series. Their empirical results have shown that people are happier when inflation and unemployment are lower. In another study, Di Tella and MacCulloh (2007) used again Euro-Barometer data and found that interest rates have a negative impact on happiness because higher interest rates cause higher inflation and hence unemployment. Headey et al. (2008) have used household economic data from Australia, Britain, Germany, Hungary and the Netherlands. The empirical results have exhibited that wealth had a positive impact on happiness and also its impact is greater than income. Bjorjlund and Freeman (2008) have detected that there was no decrease in average happiness in response to an increase in unemployment in Sweden. However, Ruprah and Luengas (2011) have conducted a subjective well-being survey for Latin America, and they have investigated that both inflation and unemployment decrease well-being. Blanchflower et al. (2014) have also used the Eurobarometer Survey Series for European countries between the 1975–2013 period. They have found that both unemployment and inflation lower happiness, but the impact of unemployment is more than inflation. In a more recent study, D'Ambrosio et al. (2020) used a panel survey for German, called German Socio-Economic Panel which dates to 1984. Empirical findings have underlined that permanent income and wealth are better indicators of life satisfaction than current values of these variables.

After evaluating some important empirical findings about the effects of fiscal and monetary facts and policies on the happiness level, then it is critical to discuss the findings about alternative economic policies, sustainability and happiness. In this sense, Priem et al. (2000) have investigated the relationship between industrialization and happiness in China, Hong Kong and the USA. They have found a positive and significant relationship. Leigh and Wolfers (2006) have used the International Social Survey Programme and the World Values Survey results to analyse the relationship between the Human Development Index and happiness. They have investigated a positive correlation between human development and happiness. However, Blanchflower and Oswald (2005) have had a different result for Australia. Their analysis had exhibited that Australia had high levels of human development however citizens' average happiness was not so high. So, it seems that again results may differ as to time and country, as in fiscal and monetary impacts on happiness. Inglehart et al. (2008) analysed 52 countries between 1981 and 2007. They have investigated that under the human development approach social tolerance, democratization and free choice significantly increase happiness levels. Tsai (2009) conducted analyses of 76 countries in the 1990s. Empirical results have proved that openness has a positive impact on happiness. Roka (2020) have analysed the relationship between the human development index and its drivers with happiness level. Empirical results have proved that there is a positive correlation between the Human Development Index (HDI) and happiness from 2008 to 2016 for 120 countries. What is more is that results have shown that while higher income, economic growth rate, government health expenditures and food increase happiness level; lower life expectancy decreases it. In one of the most recent studies, Khasanah and Suryanto (2023) investigated the relationship between HDI, air pollution and happiness. They have found that while there is a negative correlation between air pollution and happiness index; there is no significant relationship between HDI and happiness level for 9 Asean countries during 2015–2019.

4   The Crosscut of Economic Policy and Happiness

The development of the happiness concept and the related literature imply that there is a close relationship between public policy and happiness. Today, public policy is defined as the combination of policy tools to reduce market failures and reorganize behaviours of social actors. In this sense, today's public policy opinion is far from the understanding of financial resources' redistribution. In current understanding, public policy organizes necessary environmental and institutional conditions to sustain developmental processes (Vercammen, 2011). As a sub-branch of public policy, economic policy directly affects people's lives through disposable income, employment, future wealth and expectations. It is observed that economic policy choices of nations change the happiness levels of countries and in turn, happiness levels determine the sustainability paths of countries/regions. The current success of achieving higher levels of happiness is not the unique target of nations today. If the relevant happiness level cannot be sustained in the long run, many problems arise such as security, migration, poverty and life expectancy. Consequently, the current happiness agenda of the contemporary world is twofold. First, measuring the happiness levels of countries/regions truly. And second, proposing effective economic policies to increase and sustain the current happiness in the long run.

However, designing an effective policy needs a systematic approach. In this context, deficiencies and externalities should be identified; possible outcomes of arrangements should be specified, and promising policy alternatives should be designed (Hirschauer et al., 2015: 648). Such a systematic designation, of course, needs a wide understanding of the pros and cons of the planned public policy. Here, the true measurement of happiness plays a critical role. Schwarz and Starck (1999) underline that happiness (well-being) measurement has some biases since it mainly depends on subjective evaluations. Hence, forming economic policies as to current forms of happiness indexes should need extra caution. However, today's happiness measurement methods are comprehensive and multidimensional. Hence, some caution is necessary, but a pessimistic view is unnecessary. Defining happiness as a public policy component has been an important progress in designing sustainability policies.

If we turn back to the true measurement of happiness for the right economic policy issue, it is critical to define microeconomic and macroeconomic factors affecting happiness levels. There is a consensus about these factors in the related literature. Macroeconomic factors can be listed as: GDP (Gross Domestic Product) per capita, unemployment, inflation, taxes, government expenditures and future expectations about macroeconomic trends (Barro, 1990; Barro and Sala-I Martin, 1992; Clark and Oswald, 1994; Frey and Stutzer, 2000; Di Tella et al., 2001; Blanchflower et al., 2014; Rizkallah, 2023). Moreover, microeconomic factors can also be counted as follows: household income, other households' income, wealth and consumption (Hirschman, 1973; Headey et al., 2008). Both microeconomic and macroeconomic factors determine together the overall happiness level in an economy. Here we may underline that an individual's happiness and society's happiness are in a reciprocal relationship. With a utilitarian approach, as more individuals are happy, society will be happier (Ott, 2005). And with a deductive approach, as society becomes happier, individuals will be happier. Hence, economic policies—and of course all types of public policies—should be designed by considering this reality. However, with an egalitarian view, if inequality exists in a society, then this will create unhappiness among citizens (Ott, 2005). So, creating a higher number of happy people cannot be the only solution for overall well-being and happiness. GDP per capita is a good example of this issue. When a country achieves higher rates of GDP per capita growth—namely economic growth—may increase the happiness level of the country. But we cannot say that GDP per capita growth will increase overall happiness. Sometimes it is seen that there is no significant relationship between GDP per capita growth and happiness level (Easterlin, 1974). Here, the critical point is the inequality across people. If income distortions occur in the society—which can be directly observed through the GINI coefficient—, then people will compare themselves with richer citizens and this will create negative expectations for the future and unhappiness for the present. Consequently, economic policies should be designed by considering sustainability issues. Several empirical studies have exhibited that there is a positive and significant relationship between HDI and happiness (Please see Leigh and Wolfers, 2006; Inglehart et al., 2008; Roka, 2020; Khasanah and Suryanto, 2023). Hence, economic policies should support human development dimensions by being in good cooperation with other public policies.

As a general division, economic policy can be divided into fiscal policy, monetary policy and alternative policies (Stiglitz and Rosengard, 2015; Case et al., 2012). Empirical studies have proved that all types of economic policies are effective in happiness levels. Table 6.1 summarizes the impacts of different economic policies with their both tools and outcomes. Also, it classifies their impacts on happiness as positive and negative.

TABLE 6.1   Impacts of economic policies on happiness

Impact on happiness	Fiscal policy	Monetary policy	Alternative policies
Positive	*Tools* Nonproductive government expenditures Progressive taxes Distortionary taxes	*Tools* Low interest rate	*Tools* Openness to trade Industrialization Investments on human development
	Outcomes Overall increase in government expenditures	*Outcomes* High employment Low inflation	*Outcomes* Economic growth Sustainable development
Negative	*Tools* Fiscal consolidation Nondistortionary taxes	*Tools* High interest rate	*Tools* Trade barriers High government size in the economy
	Outcomes The overall decrease in government expenditures Income inequality	*Outcomes* High unemployment High inflation Income inequality	*Outcomes* Corruption and the informal economy Inefficient management of resources Income inequality

SOURCE: TABLE 6.1 HAS BEEN CONSTRUCTED BY THE AUTHOR AS TO THEORETICAL AND EMPIRICAL LITERATURE'S EVIDENCE

5   Conclusion

Happiness is a multidimensional issue that has been discussed since Aristotle's early works. Aristotle has created the term "Eudaimonia" to define happiness. Eudaimonia is simply defined as "the activity of the soul as to the virtue" (Helliwell et al., 2023: 3). In ancient Greek, Sokrates and Platon had also ratiocinate about happiness. However, philosophers were not on the side of measuring its level. They were discussing the meaning of happiness for life and death. However, modern age has brought about quantification issue. As mankind has evolved through the Age of Mass-Production,[1] quantity has become more important. In this manner, firstly psychologists and then, sociologists and economists have tried to quantify the happiness levels of individuals and societies. Some of them have defined happiness as subjective as well—and some others defined it as life satisfaction. Economists are generally on the side of higher utility and welfare when the subject is defining happiness. All these approaches have come together in attempts at happiness measurement methods and quantifying happiness has become a global attempt in the 21st century. Several multidimensional happiness measurement methods have emerged. Gallup Global Emotions Report, OECD Well-Being Report, Happy Planet Index, Global Happiness and Well-Being Policy Report, and World Happiness Report are the most famous and commonly-held global measurement affords of happiness. All these affords have provided new outlooks for the issue and provided data for the researchers and policymakers. Today, happiness is on the agenda of public policies, and it is especially a dimension of economic policies from the axes of formation, implementation and outcome evaluation.

Economics as a science, tries to allocate scarce resources most efficiently to people's unlimited needs and wants. In this manner, four questions are asked. (1) What is to be produced? (2) How is it to be produced (3) For whom is it to be produced? (4) How are these decisions made? (Stiglitz, 1986: 11). Since all these questions are important for society, it is critical to design the most efficient public policies for all. Economic policies—as a sub-branch of public policies—try to design economies and societies for higher welfare and better well-being. They have different determinants and impacts as to their types.

---

1   Rostow's Stages of Economic Growth Theory suggests that every society experiences same development path. They start with the Traditional Society Stage and reach to the Age of Mass Consumption by passing through the sages of the Preconditions to Take Off, the Take Off and the Drive to Maturity. At the age of mass consumption, a high standard of material living is attained by the courtesy of mass production. And such an economy can be defined as a welfare state (Rostow, 1960).

They can be in the forms of fiscal policies, monetary policies and alternative policies. Each policy type has its tools and outcomes. Hence, the formation and implementation of economic policies are critical issues for regions and nations. If ineffective policy actions are taken, then economic and societal targets will not be able to be attained. There are numerous examples of policy failures in the economic history. As an example, Window Tax introduced in England in 1696 under the Act of Making Good the Deficiency of the Clipped Money. At that time windows were luxury goods and rich people were trying to impress each other by showing how many windows their houses had. Hence, rich houses were endowed with lots of big windows. Since at those times, income statement was not under the full control of the government, income tax was not an option to increase government revenues with the help of the fiscal policy. Hence, policymakers thought that if they would put high taxes on windows, then they would be able to get indirect tax from wealthier people and this would create a fair tax distribution across society. However, something unforeseen happened. Individuals who built houses avoided buying windows as they got more expensive and then, more and more houses became dark. The policy implementation was unsuccessful at the end (Stiglitz, 1986: 17). Another example of ineffective economic policy implementation can be given from modern times. Greece experienced a debt crisis in the last quarter of 2009, due to the spillover effects of the global financial crisis. However, the roots of the Greek debt crisis have dated back to the introduction of the Euro in the Eurozone. With the adoption of the Euro, Greece has experienced inflationary pressures. What is more is that although Greece has provided credits from the European Union, government expenditures were net designed well, and funds created more consumption rather than more production (Manolopoulos, 2011). Similar examples of ineffective policy design and implementation have been in turn for many other countries such as Turkiye, the US, Argentina etc. What is more, is that most of the international economic crises have occurred due to the wrong management of economic policies. The Great Depression, Oil Shocks and The Global Financial Crisis are the most prominent examples of wrong economic management.

All bad experiences of wrong economic policies have created an understanding of the characterization of a good policy. In this sense, a well-designed economic policy has several dimensions including a fair income distribution, less market failures, smaller size of informal economy, higher welfare, more effective production patterns, more environmental awareness and sustainability in the long run (Stiglitz, 1986). And, happiness covering utility, well-being, life satisfaction and expectations, is one of the fundamentals of today's economic policy design. It directly affects individuals' and societies' behaviours, and it is also affected by economic situations and policy outcomes. Hence, there is a reciprocal relationship between happiness and economic policy.

Sustainability has become a global approach with the emergence of the Sustainable Development Goals of the United Nations (UN, 2024). Today, as humankind, we have a wider perspective on the sustainability of our globe. Resources are scarce and the world is approaching its limits (Meadows et al., 2004). When the sustainability goals are taken into account,[2] all of them serve the well-being and happiness of humankind. And happiness brings fairness and efficiency to all. In this sense, it is important to increase and sustain high levels of happiness with the right economic policy tools.

In this chapter, happiness measurement methods are summarized and an outlook for the relationship between economic policy and happiness is given. This relationship is detailed as to the types of economic policies and their impacts on happiness. To the best of our knowledge, this is the first classification attempt in the literature. Hence, we hope to contribute to the related literature and also, we hope to provide a toolkit for policymakers and researchers. Theoretical and empirical studies show that fiscal consolidations, non-distortionary taxes, high interest rates, trade barriers, and large government size are bad economic policy tools for happiness. On the other hand, nonproductive government expenditures like health and education expenditures, progressive taxes, distortionary taxes, low interest rates, openness to trade, industrialization and investments in human development components are good economic policy tools. As to the outcomes of economic policies, it is seen that high unemployment, high inflation, overall decrease in government expenditures, income inequality, corruption, informal economy and inefficient management of resources affect happiness in negative ways. What is more, is that all types of bad economic policies create income distortions and lead to negative impacts on sustainable development. To sum up, a well-designed economic policy—it doesn't matter which type it is—will lead to a higher level and fair distribution of happiness across society. Higher rates of happiness in turn will contribute to the sustainable development path. Happier countries—like individuals—manage their resources in more efficient ways, produce more and invest in the future smarter.

Today's governments and policymakers face hard challenges like increasing environmental degradation, massive natural disasters, pandemics, migration (due to wars and climate changes), food security, cybersecurity, decreasing biodiversity, and waste management. Economic crises have become more

---

2   For more information about Sustainable Development Goals, please visit https://sdgs.un.org /goals.

severe and global. Countries and regions are closely linked to each other through trade, tourism and international agreements. Hence, the collapse of a country's economy spreads all over the world. Today, any country can be isolated. Hence, well-designed and resistant economic policies are critical for the whole. Not just for preventing crises but also for getting over crises, countries need good policy designs. Since happiness is one of the main subjects of individuals—hence societies—and since its level is affected by both the tools and outcomes of economic policies, today's policymakers need to evaluate their actions and possible outcomes. A better world can be created by good policy design. This is not only for the happiness of the current global society but also for the next generations.

References

Akay, A., Bargain, O., Dolls, M., Neumann, D., Peichl, A. and Siegloch, S. (2012). Happy taxpayers? Income taxation and well-being. IZA Discussion Paper No. 6999: 1–34.

Barro, R. J. (1990). Government spending in a simple model of endogenous growth. Journal of Political Economy 98(5): 103–125.

Barro, R. J. and Sala-I-Martin, X. (1992). Public finance in models of economic growth. The Review of Economic Studies. 59(4): 645–661.

Bentham, J. (1952). The Philosophy of Economic Science. In Werner Stark, (ed.), Jeremy Bentham's Economic Writings, Vol. I. London: Published for the Royal Economic Society by George Allen and Unwin, pp. 81–119.

Bjorjlund, A. and Freeman, R. (2008). Searching for Optimal Inequality/incentives. NBER Working Paper No. 14014.

Blanchflower, D. G. and Oswald, A. J. (2005). Happiness and the human development index: the paradox of Australia. Australian Economic Review 38: 307–18.

Blanchflower, D. G., Bell, D. N. F., Montagnoli, A. and Moro, M. (2014). The happiness trade-off between unemployment and inflation. Journal of Money, Credit and Banking 46(2): 117–141.

Cantril, H. (1965). The pattern of human concerns. New Brunswick, New Jersey: Rutgers Univ. Press.

Carpentier, E. (2023). The economics of happiness: a brief review. Intersect 16(3): 1–27.

Case, K. E., Fair, R. C. and Oster, S. M. (2012). Principles of economics. Tenth Edition. Pearson. The USA.

Clark, A. E. and Oswald, A. J. (1994). Unhappiness and unemployment. Economic Journal 104 (424): 648–659.

D'Ambrosio, C., Jantti, M. and Lepiteur, A. (2020). Money and happiness: income, wealth and subjective well-being. Social Indicators Research 148:47–66.

Dao, T. K. (2017). Government expenditure and happiness: direct and indirect effects. Master of Arts in Development Studies, The Hague, The Netherlands, pp. 1–62.

Di Tella, R. and MacCulloh, R. (2007). Happiness, contentment and other emotions for central banks. NBER Working Paper Series. No.13622.

Di Tella, R., MacCulloch, R. J. and Andrew, J. O. (2001). Preferences over inflation and unemployment: evidence from surveys of happiness. American Economic Review 91 (1): 335–341.

Easterlin, R. A. (1974). Does economic growth improve the human lot? Some Empirical Evidence. In (P. A. David and M. W. Reder eds) Nations and Households in Economic Growth: Essays in Honour of Moses Abramowitz. New York and London: Academic Press, pp. 89–125.

Eklou, K. and Fall, M. (2020). The (subjective) well-being cost of fiscal policy shocks. IMF Working Paper No. 20/5.

Frey, B. S. and Stutzer, A. (2000). Happiness, economy and institutions. The Economic Journal 110: 918–938.

GALLUP. (2024). How does the U.S. Gallup-share care wellbeing index work?. https://news.gallup.com/poll/128186/gallup-healthways-index-work.aspx.

GALLUP. (2023). Gallup global emotions 2023. https://www.gallup.com/.

GHC. (2022). Global happiness and well-being policy report. New York. USA. https://www.happinesscouncil.org/.

Grimes, A., Ormsby, J., Robinson, A. and Wong, S. (2016). Subjective wellbeing impacts of national and subnational fiscal policies. Motu Working Paper, No. 16–05, pp. 1–38.

Happy Planet Index. https://happyplanetindex.org/.

Headey, B., Muffels, R. and Wooden, M. (2008). Money does not buy happiness: or does it? A reassessment based on the combined effects of wealth, income and consumption. Social Indicators Research 87: 65–82.

Helliwell, J. F., Layard, R., Sachs, J. D., De Neve, J.-E., Aknin, L. B. and Wang, S. (2023). World happiness report 2023. https://worldhappiness.report/ed/2023/.

Hirschauer, N., Lehberger, M. and Musshoff, O. (2015). Happiness and utility in economic thought—Or: what can we learn from happiness research for public policy analysis and public policy making? Social Indicators Research 121: 647–674.

Hirschman, A. O. (1973). The changing tolerance for income inequality during economic development. Quarterly Journal of Economics 87: 544–566.

Inglehart, R., Foa, R., Peterson, C., and Welzel, C. (2008). Development, freedom, and rising happiness: a global perspective (1981–2007). Perspectives on Psychological Science 3(4): 264–285.

Khasanah, L. and Suryanto. (2023). The impact of air pollution on the happiness index of ASEAN communities. IOP Conference Series: Earth and Environmental Science, Volume 1165, 8th International Conference on Climate Change (8TH-ICCC) 17/11/2022–18/11/2022 Bangkok, Thailand.

Leigh, A. and Wolfers, J. (2006). Happiness and the human development index: Australia is not a paradox. The Australian Economic Review 39(2): 176–84.

Manolopoulos, J. (2011). Greece's 'odious' debt: The looting of the Hellenic Republic by the Euro, the political elite and the investment community. London: Anthem Press.

Meadows, D., Randers, J. and Meadows, D. (2004). Limits to Growth: The 30-Year Update. Chelsea Green Publications. First Edition. The USA.

OECD. (2024) Measuring well-being and progress: well-being research. https://www.oecd.org/wise/measuring-well-being-and-progress.htm.

Oishi, S., Schimmack, U. and Diener, E. (2012). Progressive taxation and the subjective well-being of nations. Psychological Science 23(1): 86–92.

Ott, J. (2005). Level and equality of happiness in nations: does greater happiness for a greater number imply greater inequality in happiness? Journal of Happiness Studies 6.

Pareto, V. (1909). Manuel d'économie politique. Paris: Giard and E. Brière.

Powdthavee, N. (2007). Economics of happiness: a review of literature and applications. Chulalongkorn Journal of Economics 19(1): 51–73.

Priem, R. L., Love, L. G. and Shaffer, M. (2000). Industrialization and values evolution: the case of Hong Kong and Guangzhou, China. Asia Pacific Journal of Management 17: 473–492.

Ram, R. (2009). Government spending and happiness of the population: additional evidence from large cross-country samples. Public Choice 138(3–4): 483–490.

Rizkallah, W. W. A. (2023). The impact of fiscal policy on economic happiness: evidence from the countries of the MENA region. Review of Economics and Political Science 8(4): 271–289.

Roka, D. (2020). The effect of human development on happiness: a comparative study of UN member states. International Journal of Science and Business 4(4): 61–78.

Rostow, W. W. (1960). The stages of economic growth—a non-communist manifesto. Cambridge University Press. New York, Port Chester, Melbourne, Sydney.

Ruprah, I. J. and Luengas, P. (2011). Monetary policy and happiness: preferences over inflation and unemployment in Latin America. The Journal of Socioeconomics 40: 59–66.

Samuelson, P. A. (1947). Foundations of economic analysis. Harvard University Press.

Schwarz, N. and Strack, F. (1991). Evaluating one's life: a judgement model of subjective well-being. In Subjective Well-being: An Interdisciplinary Perspective, ed. Fritz Strack, Michael Argyle, and Norbert Schwarz, 27–47. Oxford, UK: Pergamon Press.

Stiglitz, J., Fitoussi, J. and Durand, M. (2018). Beyond GDP: measuring what counts for economic and social performance, OECD Publishing, Paris.

Stiglitz, J. E. (1986). Economics of the public sector. W. W. Norton & Company. New York & London.

Tsai, M.-C. (2009). Market openness, transition economies and subjective wellbeing. Journal of Happiness Studies 10: 523–539.

UN (United Nations). (2024). The 17 Goals. https://sdgs.un.org/goals.

Veenhoven, R. (2021). Daily happiness: How well we feel most of the time. In H. L. Meiselman (Ed.), Emotion Measurement, Second edition (pp. 773–793). Academic Press.

Veenhoven, R., Dumladag, D., and Gokdemir, O. (2021). Does spending make us happy? The role of consumption on life satisfaction. International Journal of Business and Applied Social Science (IJBASS) 7(10): 37–48.

Veenhoven, R. (1995). World database of happiness. Social Indicators Research 34: 299–313.

Vercammen, J. (2011). Agri-environmental regulations, policies, and programs. Canadian Journal of Agricultural Economics 59(1): 1–18.

CHAPTER 7

The Happiness Agenda: Examining the Meeting Point of Political Strategies and Economic Realities

Eylül Kabakçı Günay

One of the principal factors contributing to the disparities in prosperity among nations is income differentials. Extensive research indicates that an increase in a nation's income level is associated with enhanced welfare and development. Nevertheless, the augmentation of life satisfaction and, consequently, happiness among individuals requires more than just an increase in income level. There exists a robust correlation between happiness and economic development. For economic development to materialize, it is imperative that, alongside income growth, improvements are also made in social, cultural, and political spheres. However, in mainstream (neoclassical) economics, the emphasis is predominantly placed on the significance of income growth, essentially equating to economic enlargement. This situation presents a dilemma regarding whether the objective is to augment happiness or merely to achieve an increase in income. This study aims to underscore that happiness can be achieved not solely through enhancements in economic indicators but also via the implementation of suitable policy strategies, and to share evidence supporting this stance.

1   Introduction

Numerous constructs within the social sciences are devoted to elucidating the well-being of individuals, encompassing subjective well-being, happiness, pleasure, life satisfaction, quality of life, and adaptation. The universal aspiration to infuse life with positive emotions propels endeavours to comprehend and elucidate human well-being, yet research posits that this phenomenon is too intricate and multi-dimensional to be solely attributed to material resources (Güler & Dönmez, 2011: 39). Notwithstanding, happiness is a concept that has garnered extensive scholarly attention in recent years, with the social sciences striving to elucidate its underpinnings. Deliberations on happiness evoke several queries: the current state of individual happiness, comparisons with historical happiness levels, variations in life satisfaction across different societies, the measurability of happiness, determinants of happiness, and the correlation between happiness and living conditions. These questions, albeit challenging, are critically significant, with personal relevance to each individual seeking answers.

In contemporary discourse, life satisfaction and happiness are underscored as pivotal areas of investigation within the social sciences, including "mainstream" economics. Social scientists commonly advocate for the enhancement of objectively quantifiable well-being indicators, such as GDP per capita, to augment economic welfare. Economists posit that economic growth leads to an increase in GDP per capita, which in turn enhances individuals' welfare levels through development. Yet, the question arises whether individuals perceive themselves as happy based on economic objective measurement methodologies.

Within the literature on happiness economics, inquiries into how objectively defined and measurable concepts such as economic growth, unemployment, inflation, and institutional variables influence well-being, which is inherently subjective, have gained prominence. The measurement of happiness and the identification of indicators prompting individuals to self-identify as 'happy' pose significant challenges. This discourse raises the question of whether reliable comparisons exist that can definitively demonstrate the presence of happiness.

To this end, economists explore the impact of economic factors on the pursuit of happiness. This study discusses research on the relationship between income and happiness, focusing on the World Happiness Report by the United Nations, the Global Happiness Index, Gross National Happiness, the Better Life Index, and the Happy Planet Index prepared by the OECD, among others. Emphasis is placed on measurement and evaluation methodologies for assessing happiness. The conclusion drawn from examining these methodologies indicates that while happiness is not exclusively evaluated concerning income in measured countries, the existence of happiness transcends mere income. A secondary objective of this study is to ascertain which variables, beyond income, contribute to the measurable quality of happiness, given its subjective nature.

2   The Relationship between Income, Economic Growth and Happiness

The annual average income of a nation's populace is regarded in the economic scholarly discourse as a principal indicator of that nation's welfare level. For over five decades, income, alternatively referred to as Gross Domestic Product (GDP), has been the predominant metric utilized to assess the progression of a country's economic activities (Costanza et al., 2009: 3).

GDP serves a function analogous to that of an electricity meter for a household, quantifying the flux of goods and services generated within an economy (Constanza, 2009). The Nobel Prize-winning economist Kuznets has issued cautions against the direct correlation of Gross Domestic Product with national welfare (Kuznets, 1934). Despite its original intent, Gross Domestic Product has diverged to become erroneously perceived as a measure of human advancement, thereby becoming the primary objective for states globally. The endeavour to augment GDP inherently seeks to enhance economic growth, as nations aspire to elevate their economic growth levels, thereby increasing income levels, boosting production, and ultimately providing their citizens with a life of higher welfare. Within this discourse, economists typically posit that the fulfilment of individuals' needs correlates with an increase in their happiness levels. Consequently, national economic policies are formulated to promote growth, enhance production, elevate per capita income levels, and ultimately achieve development. Nevertheless, the universally acknowledged truth that individuals harbour divergent views on what constitutes happiness (even though there might be near-universal consensus on the contribution of love or social participation to happiness) implies a plurality of perspectives. Various conditions facilitate the emergence of happiness; for instance, an individual might equate happiness with fame, raising offspring, improving social status, or material wealth. Therefore, in the realm of economic literature, happiness is predominantly associated with income. Former United Nations Secretary-General Ban Ki-moon has characterized happiness as neither an inconsequential concept detached from seriousness nor a luxury but rather a profound yearning shared by all humanity. According to him, happiness should be an inalienable right, accessible to everyone.

The prerequisite for increasing the level of income is the stimulation of economic growth. Economic growth is delineated as the augmentation in the quantity of goods and services produced within a country over time, or the sustained increase in real Gross Domestic Product over time (Yıldırım et al., 2008:18). Economic growth is deemed the solitary pathway to perpetually elevate the living standards of a nation's inhabitants. Hence, one of the fundamental macroeconomic objectives for all countries is the swift realization of economic growth (Ünsal, 2009:15). To measure economic growth, economists rely on GDP data, which reflects the aggregate income of all individuals within an economy. For instance, the present GDP of the United States exceeds its 1950 level by more than threefold, and its real per capita GDP is double that of its 1950 level (Mankiw, 2010:214). This scenario emerges as a significant stride towards welfare and development. It is imperative to elucidate the distinction between economic growth and development in this context. Development transcends mere increases in production and per capita income to encompass the transformation and modernization of the economic and socio-cultural framework of an underdeveloped society. Alongside the rise in per capita national income, development entails structural transformations such as shifts in the efficiency and quantities of production factors, and an increase in the industrial sector's contribution to national income and exports, forming the core elements of development. Growth, for the sake of clarification, represents a change that is predominantly quantitative rather than qualitative. An economy's growth can be conceptualized as the enhancement of production and per capita income (Han & Kaya, 2013:2). Therefore, it can be said that increasing economic growth, which is one of the main goals of macroeconomists, is not sufficient on its own to increase development or, in other words, the level of welfare. However, when it comes to happiness, a more complex relationship is encountered. It can be said that an increase in income created only by economic growth or living in a developed country does not make individuals happy.

Upon existing literature, it becomes evident that there is an extensive body of work examining the empirical relationship between material welfare and happiness. These studies commonly accept the premise that attaining happiness is a key life goal and that income is one of the most significant means to achieve happiness. This situation suggests a strong association between happiness and wealth/income; however, according to the happiness-income paradox, this is not always the case. A prominent figure in discussions on the relationship between happiness and income is Richard Easterlin. In his seminal work, "Does Economic Growth Improve the Human Lot? Some Empirical Evidence", Easterlin (1974) pioneered the interrogation of the relationship between income and happiness. He posited that while there is a strong positive correlation between income and happiness within a country, this correlation becomes weak or even nonexistent in international comparisons or long-term analyses. This phenomenon has been termed the Easterlin paradox and has been extensively debated by economists, psychologists, and social scientists.

Easterlin's (1974) study was conducted across three principal dimensions. He sought to answer the question: "Is higher income necessary for greater happiness?" The first dimension examined differences in happiness levels between wealthy and poor individuals in the United States. Secondly, he conducted an international comparison to explore the relationship between countries' average happiness levels and their Gross National Product (GNP) sizes. Finally, he

FIGURE 7.1   Happiness and real GDP per capita, USA, (1973–2004)

SOURCE: A. E. CLARK, P. FRIJTERS, VE M. A. SHIELDS RELATIVE INCOME, HAPPINESS,
AND UTILITY: AN EXPLANATION FOR THE EASTERLIN PARADOX AND OTHER PUZZLES,
JOURNAL OF ECONOMIC LITERATURE, 2008

performed a time-series analysis exclusive to the United States, investigating
changes in the relationship between happiness and income levels over the
years. In the primary dimension of his study, comparing groups, he found that
wealthy individuals were, on average, happier than those considered poor.
Among individuals with an annual income below $3,000, 29% described
themselves as very happy, compared to 56% of those with an annual income
above $15,000. Conversely, 13% of individuals earning less than $3,000 annually reported being unhappy, whereas only 4% of those earning more than
$15,000 stated the same. These data indicate a positive correlation between
income and happiness (Easterlin, 1974:100–109). Similar to Easterlin's findings,
a review of studies examining the relationship between happiness and income
generally finds a statistically significant but weak relationship between material well-being, expressed in terms of welfare or income, and happiness
(Schurer & Yong, 2016:2). The weak nature of this relationship stems from the
difference between short-term and long-term periods. While a stronger positive correlation exists between income and happiness in the short term, this
relationship weakens over the long term.

According to Figure 7.1, between 1973 and 2004 in the United States, real
GDP per capita nearly doubled, yet there was no observed trend of increase in
happiness levels. In other words, the increase in income did not bring about
an increase in happiness. This situation has prompted a more detailed examination of the relationship between income and happiness. While there are
views attributing the increase in happiness beyond a certain level of living to
factors such as friendships and good family life rather than income; there are
also perspectives emphasizing the significant role of income comparisons,

expectations, and adaptation factors in explaining this paradox (Richard Layard 2005, Robert E. Lane 2000, Bruno S. Frey & Alois Stutzer 2002 in Veenhoven & Dumludağ, 2015:46–51).

In another prominent study titled "Happiness and Growth the World Over: Time Series Evidence on the Happiness-Income Paradox," Easterlin and Angelescu (2009) present compelling evidence that contradicts the conventional wisdom linking long-term income growth to increases in happiness levels. Their comprehensive analysis spans 37 countries, categorized into three distinct groups: 17 developed, 9 developing, and 11 transition economies. This classification facilitates a nuanced examination of the happiness-income relationship across varying economic landscapes.

The study meticulously analyses time series data, ranging from 12 to 34 years, to investigate the dynamics of happiness about income changes. The findings uniformly reveal that despite short-term fluctuations in happiness levels corresponding to immediate income variations—attributable to macroeconomic conditions—there is no evidence of a sustained positive relationship between happiness and income growth in the long term. This observation emphatically reinforces the validity of the Easterlin Paradox, which posits that while short-term analyses may show a positive correlation between income and happiness, such a relationship dissipates over extended periods.

At the heart of this paradox lies the concept of "hedonic adaptation," a psychological phenomenon where individuals' happiness levels eventually return to their baseline despite significant positive or negative changes in their circumstances. This implies that the temporary uplift in happiness experienced upon achieving certain gains does not translate into a permanent increase in well-being. The study's inability to establish a significant long-term relationship between GDP growth and happiness across 37 countries, regardless of their development status, underscores the complexity of the happiness-income nexus and challenges the notion that economic prosperity is a straightforward pathway to societal well-being.

Easterlin and Angelescu's (2009) research offers a critical perspective on the pursuit of economic growth as a means to enhance happiness, suggesting that factors beyond income—such as social relationships, quality of work-life, and environmental conditions—play pivotal roles in determining overall happiness. This paradigm shift calls for a broader evaluation of what constitutes success for individuals and nations alike, advocating for policies and practices that prioritize holistic well-being over mere economic expansion.

In a study conducted by Daniel Kahneman and another Nobel laureate economist, Angus Deaton, the question of "How much income is optimal for maximizing our happiness in daily life" was explored. This research discerned that emotional well-being and life satisfaction have distinct relationships with income. The concept of emotional well-being was examined through the analysis of over 450,000 responses to a survey conducted among 1,000 American citizens during 2008–2009. The findings indicated that an annual income of $75,000 was optimal for maximizing daily happiness, with any additional income not contributing to an increase in the level of happiness in daily life (Kahneman & Deaton, 2010:16489). This survey was organized by the Gallup organization and contributed to the creation of the Gallup-Healthways Well-Being Index. Furthermore, this study evaluates personal welfare from two different perspectives: Emotional Well-Being and Life Evaluation. Questions related to emotional well-being focused on assessing a variety of emotions experienced the previous day, such as happiness, pleasure, anger, sadness, stress, and anxiety. To measure Life Evaluation, Cantril's Self-Anchoring Scale was employed, wherein individuals were asked to rate their satisfaction with life on a scale from 0 to 10, with 0 indicating no satisfaction with life and 10 indicating the highest level of satisfaction (Kahneman and Deaton, 2010:1). Thus, it can be stated that for individuals with an income above a certain amount, the formula for happiness becomes indifferent to additional income. It is also a reality that the scarcity of income exacerbates the impact of existing adverse conditions.

TABLE 7.1   Average percentage of people who reported a lot of sadness and worry yesterday, by income group and (%)

	Income < 1000$/Month			Income ≥ $3000/Month		
	No	Yes	Difference	No	Yes	Difference
Weekend Vacation	46.6	44.5	−2.1	22.3	17.1	−5.2
Divorced	44.3	50.5	6.2	20.5	24.4	3.9
Alone	44	58.9	14.9	20.5	31.5	11
Chronical Headache	38	69.5	31.6	18.9	38.4	19.5
Asthma	33.1	40.8	7.8	18	21.6	3.6

SOURCE: KAHNEMAN & DEATON, 2010: 16492 "HIGH INCOME IMPROVES EVALUATION OF LIFE BUT NOT EMOTIONAL WELL-BEING"

In the table, two groups are considered: those with incomes below 1000 dollars per month and those with incomes above 3000 dollars per month. Do you have bad expectations from life for these groups? The question was posed. As can be seen, the expectations of the poor group are more negative than the other group under every special situation. The negative expectations of some who experience negative situations such as asthma, divorce and loneliness appear to be significantly exacerbated by poverty; Even the benefits of the weekend were observed to be less among people in the lower income group. Similar results are valid for stress and positive affect (Kahneman & Deaton, 2010: 16492).

In parallel with this economic literature, there are also many studies in the psychology literature showing that happiness is strongly dependent on personality traits and other subjective outcomes such as family and personal relationships (Schurer & Yong, 2016:3). For example, according to Lyubomirsky, people have control over only 40% of their happiness level, no matter what they do. According to Lyubomirsky, happiness is affected by the following factors:

1.   50% Genetic Predisposition
2.   10% External Factors
3.   40% Our Actions and Thoughts (Lyubomirsky, 2008:225).

3   Measuring the Happiness

Happiness is influenced not only by income but also by the environmental factors one is exposed to and genetic predisposition. In this context, how happiness is measured becomes a subject of curiosity. Under this topic, the methods used to measure happiness and how these methods are developed will be discussed. Among these methods, the most used in the literature include the World Happiness Report's World Happiness Index, Gross National Happiness, the Better Life Index prepared by the OECD, and the Happy Planet Index. This section will focus on how the most common methods of measuring happiness are constructed.

WORLD HAPPINESS INDEX: The World Happiness Index is released in World Happiness Report every year, prepared and published annually by the United Nations, and utilizes the Gallup World Poll for its calculations. It stands as the most frequently used index in international comparisons, incorporating a composite of six factors: GDP per capita, social support, healthy life expectancy, freedom to make life choices, generosity, and perception of corruption. As we will notice, many of the factors that related to the political decisions and implications, directly or indirectly. For example, freedom to make life choices and perception of corruption are directly related to political and governmental issues. To reveal the existence of the factor of corruption that kind of question has arisen on the Gallup world pool: "Is corruption widespread throughout the government or not" and "Is corruption widespread within businesses or not?" Do people trust their governments and have trust in the benevolence of others? Another factor that we need to correlate with political strategies is the freedom to make life choices. The question is "Are you satisfied or dissatisfied with your freedom to choose what you do with your life?" This also includes Human Rights. Inherent to all human beings, regardless of race, sex, nationality, ethnicity, language, religion, or any other status. Human rights include the right to life and liberty, freedom from slavery and torture, freedom of opinion and expression, the right to work and education, and many more. Everyone is entitled to these rights without discrimination. According to the latest report released in 2023, Finland is ranked as the happiest country in the world. This index provides a comprehensive measure of well-being and happiness across countries, offering insights into how economic, social, and governance factors contribute to the quality of life. In 2023, the first 5 ranking belongs to Finland, Denmark, Iceland, Israel and the Netherlands, respectively (WHR, 2023).

GROSS NATIONAL HAPPINESS: This index, calculated for the first time by the Kingdom of Bhutan, attracted the attention of the whole world. This concept, introduced by Bhutanese King Jigme Singye Wangchuck in 1972, is Gross National Happiness (GNH). King Wangchuck said that when comparing countries with each other, the gross national happiness value should be considered rather than the gross national product. While creating this index value, happiness is considered a multidimensional concept.

TABLE 7.2 Weights of gross happiness index components

Factors	Weight (%)
Health	14
Ecological diversity and resilience	12
Community vitality	12
Cultural diversity and resilience	10
Living standards	11
Time use	10
Psychological wellbeing	12
Good governance	9
Education	10

As examined in Table 7.2, the most weight was given to health among the variables. This is followed by psychological well-being, ecological diversity and social vitality. Thus, it can be said that the index was shaped on the basis that health is the only concept that will make a person feel happy. The weight of living standards that can be associated with income is around 11%.

According to the 2022 GNH Index reveals that 48.1% of individuals aged 15 and older were deemed happy, marking an increase from 40.9% in 2010 to 48.1% in 2022. In the same year, it was found that the other 51.9% of the population in Bhutan were categorized as not yet happy, suggesting that they are missing certain factors and conditions necessary for well-being.

BETTER LIFE INDEX: The Better Life Index aims to engage citizens in discussions concerning the measurement of societal welfare and to facilitate a more informed and active participation in the policy-making process that shapes all our lives. Particularly since the 2000s, defining welfare solely in terms of income does not accurately reflect the well-being of individuals, societies, and even nations. Hence, this index, which adopts a more comprehensive approach to welfare, examines the areas in which individuals are happier. With this index, countries can develop policies regarding criteria where they lag and implement practices that maximize the welfare of their citizens (Akar, 2014: 2).

According to OECD (2023), 11 topics within the index are currently based on one to three indicators. Within each topic, the average of the indicators is calculated with equal weights. This index, comprising 11 criteria, compares the welfare of 35 OECD countries individually for each criterion. Moreover, the index, initially covering 35 countries, was revised in 2012, expanding the set of countries to 38. Non-OECD member countries such as Brazil, Russia, and South Africa were added to the index. The countries included in the most recent update of the index are Australia, Austria, Belgium, Canada, Chile, the Czech Republic, Denmark, Estonia, Finland, Greece, Hungary, Iceland, Ireland, Israel, Italy, Japan, Korea, Latvia, Luxembourg, Mexico, the Netherlands, New Zealand, Norway, Poland, Portugal, Slovakia, Slovenia, Spain, Sweden, Switzerland, Turkey, the United Kingdom, the United States, and non-OECD members Russia, Brazil, and South Africa. The 11 criteria featured in the index are Housing (housing expenses), Income (household net adjusted disposable income, household financial wealth), Jobs (employment rate, long-term unemployment rate, personal earnings), Community (quality of social support networks), Education (education level, years of education), Environment (air pollution, water quality), Civic Engagement (voter turnout, policy engagement), Health (life expectancy), Life Satisfaction, Safety (crime rate), and

Work-Life Balance (working hours). For each criterion, countries are assigned a value ranging from 0 to 10.

HAPPY PLANET INDEX: The Happy Planet Index is an index calculated and published annually by the New Economics Foundation, a UK-based think tank. According to this index, it measures sustainable well-being for everyone. In doing so, it attempts to assess how successful nations are in achieving long, happy, and sustainable lives. In the research covering 140 countries, none of the G8 countries have ranked within the top 30 in this ranking. Costa Rica, a small tropical country, has ranked first in this ranking for the third time, establishing superiority over Western economies (Jeffrey, 2016). Western countries, often seen as the standard of success, do not rank highly in the Happy Planet Index. Instead, many countries in Latin America and the Asia-Pacific region, with much smaller ecological footprints, guide other countries by providing high life expectancy and well-being. The Happy Planet Index (2023) provides nations with a guiding compass and demonstrates that it is possible to live good lives without imposing any cost on the world. When calculating the Happy Planet Index, four variables are considered: well-being, life expectancy, inequality of outcomes, and ecological footprint.

4   The Happiness and Political Pathway

In an endeavour to reconcile the lofty aspirations of political visions with the tangible constraints of economic systems, the discourse on the "Happiness Agenda" offers a profound re-evaluation of success metrics within contemporary society. This paradigmatic shift advocates for a transition from conventional economic indicators, such as Gross Domestic Product (GDP), towards a more holistic assessment of well-being, epitomized by innovative metrics like Bhutan's Gross National Happiness index. These indices challenge the prevailing orthodoxy by questioning the extent to which economic prosperity translates into enhanced collective well-being, thus prompting a re-examination of the underlying assumptions of economic policy and its impact on societal happiness. Beyond mere economic prosperity, the well-being and contentment of citizens are essential indicators of a flourishing society. To achieve this, policymakers must employ a range of strategic initiatives that address various facets of human experience.

One of the fundamental objectives pursued by nations in their developmental agenda is to enhance the well-being of their citizenry. In this context, the populace harbours expectations encompassing the augmentation of their purchasing power, the accessibility of educational and healthcare services, and the assurance of residing in an environment characterized by freedom and safety, all of which are facilitated through the implementation of strategic policies and legislative measures by their governments. At the core of these aspirations lies the pursuit of happiness. While happiness is influenced by a multitude of personality-specific and psychological factors, it is feasible to cultivate a generalized state of contentment, or at the very least, a sense of satisfaction, through the enactment of efficacious policies. The fundamental approach to comprehending this potential involves delineating the nexus between happiness and fundamental human needs, the unfulfillment of which precipitates distress and adversity. When looking at the definition of needs, they are depicted as phenomena that bring happiness and pleasure when met, and sorrow and sadness when not met. The most common approach to defining and systematizing human needs is to refer to Maslow's Hierarchy of Needs. The Hierarchy of Needs Theory is a theory related to human psychology that was proposed in a study published by the American psychologist Abraham Maslow in 1943 and has since been developed further. Maslow examined needs in five basic categories, approached them hierarchically, and stated that once the needs at the bottom were met, individuals would move towards the needs in the next category above. According to this hierarchy of needs, individuals start with basic needs, meet their needs in certain categories, move on to the next phase, try to satisfy their needs in that category in a pyramid shape, and then move to a higher category. However, other needs emerge only after the needs at one level are met to a certain extent. For the next need to emerge, it is not necessary for the previous need to be completely satisfied (as cited in Onaran, 1981). While the most basic needs of individuals are at the lowest level, needs become more complex as one moves up the layers. An individual cannot become aware of a higher need without satisfying the essential and fundamental needs at the bottom. In today's economic order, for physical needs to be met, individuals need to be above a certain income level. Income, however, appears as a concept that satisfies basic needs but loses its exchange capability as one moves up the steps according to Maslow's hierarchy of needs. Moreover, Maslow (1943) also explains that some needs placed later in the sequence can emerge earlier under certain conditions.

As governments produce policies aimed at providing the basic level in Maslow's hierarchy of needs, they will create a basis where the citizens of that country can be happy.

As we noticed, the first step in the pyramid is physiological needs like food, shelter, and clothing. To meet these needs as public needs to follow a policy. Policy implementations are one of the most important parts of the spread of

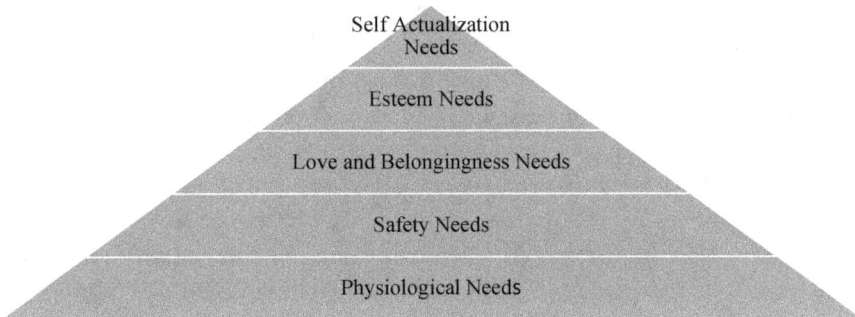

FIGURE 7.2 Maslow's hierarchy of needs
SOURCE: OXFORD POVERTY AND HUMAN DEVELOPMENT INITIATIVE
(OPHI), 2024

mass happiness in society. Now we will investigate the policy recommendations for the governments after meeting the physiological needs of the people.

One of the required steps that must be taken by the government to implement policies may be considered an investment in mental health services.
Accessible and affordable mental health services are crucial for individuals
grappling with stress, anxiety, and depression. By allocating resources towards
counselling, therapy, and support groups, policymakers can provide the necessary support structures for enhancing mental well-being. Another crucial component of the happiness policy is the promotion of work-life balance. Modern
life often demands a delicate equilibrium between professional responsibilities
and personal fulfilment. Policies such as flexible working hours, telecommut-
ing options, and parental leave enable individuals to strike a healthier balance,
fostering higher levels of life satisfaction. Also, social support programs can be
helpful to strengthen society's bonds. Building strong community ties is par-
amount for fostering social cohesion and mutual assistance. Initiatives such
as community centres, volunteer opportunities, and neighbourhood projects
facilitate social connections, reducing feelings of isolation and bolstering overall happiness. As we mentioned before, for happiness income carries an incon-
trovertible importance. Addressing income inequality through progressive
taxation and social welfare policies ensures a fairer distribution of resources.
Studies suggest that beyond a certain threshold, additional income yields
diminishing returns on happiness, emphasizing the importance of equitable
wealth distribution. Also, education systems that prioritize holistic development, including emotional intelligence and resilience, contribute significantly
to individual happiness. Furthermore, lifelong learning opportunities empower

individuals to pursue their passions, fostering a sense of fulfilment and purpose. Environmental factors play a significant role in shaping individual and collective well-being, while the state of well-being of individuals can, in turn, influence their relationship with the environment Protecting the environment is not only crucial for future generations but also for current well-being. Clean air, water, and access to natural spaces have been linked to improved mental health. Policies promoting renewable energy, sustainable transportation, and conservation efforts thus contribute to a happier and healthier populace. Social injustice has profound effects on individual and collective happiness, contributing to a range of negative outcomes like psychological distress, damage to social cohesion and trust and political disengagement. So eradicating systemic discrimination and injustice is imperative for fostering an inclusive society. Social justice initiatives build trust, cooperation, and social cohesion, laying the groundwork for collective happiness and well-being.

By implementing a combination of these strategies, policymakers can create environments conducive to individual and collective happiness. Prioritizing well-being alongside economic growth is essential for building a more fulfilling and prosperous society. Ultimately, the pursuit of happiness lies at the heart of effective governance and societal progress.

One of such policies is Universal Basic income. The examination of Universal Basic Income (UBI)[1] within this context provides a critical lens through which the implications of such a policy on happiness can be assessed. Through a comparative analysis of case studies, this investigation scrutinizes the traditional presumption that economic security is a panacea for discontent, thereby illuminating the nuanced relationship between financial stability and subjective well-being. Concurrently, policy initiatives aimed at enhancing work-life balance, such as the implementation of flexible work arrangements and robust family support systems, exemplify the complex interplay between economic efficiency and personal satisfaction. These varied approaches across jurisdictions yield a diverse array of outcomes, offering valuable insights into the formulation of policies that promote a more harmonious and fulfilling life.

Furthermore, endeavours aimed at community building, encompassing the development of communal spaces and the facilitation of local events, underscore the significance of social connectivity in the pursuit of happiness. Such initiatives not only engender a sense of belonging but also represent a strategic alignment of economic development objectives with the enhancement of social bonds. Additionally, the acknowledgement of mental health

---

1   https://www.undp.org/sites/g/files/zskgke326/files/migration/cn/UNDP-CH-Universal
    -Basic-Income-A-Working-Paper.pdf.

services as essential economic investments illuminates the reciprocal relationship between a society's psychological well-being and its economic vitality. Prioritizing mental health not only yields direct benefits in terms of increased productivity and reduced healthcare costs but also serves as a foundational pillar for a thriving society.

The proposition to integrate well-being education into educational curricula suggests a transformative shift towards equipping individuals with the competencies necessary for emotional resilience and happiness. This pedagogical evolution holds the promise of long-term economic benefits by cultivating a workforce that is not merely intellectually prepared but also emotionally adept. In parallel, the interconnection between environmental policies and subjective well-being invites an exploration of how sustainable practices and access to natural environments contribute to psychological upliftment, thereby challenging us to conceive of economic models that are supportive of both ecological sustainability and human contentment.

In the era of digital technology, the influence of social media and technological advancements on well-being has emerged as a critical area of inquiry. The formulation of policies aimed at mitigating the negative repercussions of digital interconnectedness, while leveraging technology to enhance quality of life, reflects the intricate balance between innovation and well-being. Moreover, discussions surrounding economic inequality and its impact on societal happiness emphasize the detrimental effects of stark disparities, advocating for the implementation of policies that promote social equity.

Lastly, the role of cultural engagement in shaping subjective well-being highlights the necessity of supporting cultural initiatives that contribute to the collective quality of life. Such cultural endeavours, often impeded by economic limitations, underscore the imperative for political strategies that recognize and nurture the value of cultural participation in fostering a contented and cohesive society.

Collectively, these elements of the "Happiness Agenda" craft a narrative that transcends conventional dichotomies between political objectives and economic realities. This discourse invites a recalibration of societal priorities towards a vision where the pursuit of happiness and well-being is central to our collective ambition, advocating for a reimagined framework that aligns economic policies with the enrichment of human life.

5   Conclusion

For many years, the goal of increasing income, seen as the key to economic development and progress, has remained important. However, developments in behavioural economics and research aimed at understanding whether this goal is truly as significant as assumed have led to a departure from its traditional definition. It has shifted from being seen as the ultimate concept for humanity's development, increasing well-being, and ultimately achieving happiness, to being recognized merely as a necessary component. Studies aimed at understanding the nature of income traditionally considered the key to individual happiness, have been promising. They have illuminated the path to the correct understanding for social scientists. For example, as the number of individuals suffering from incurable diseases increases in a society, GDP will rise due to increased production for healthcare purposes, but societal well-being will deteriorate.

Contrary to the common belief that low-income levels lead to unhappiness or that happiness increases proportionally with income, our study has shown otherwise. It has been observed that even in high-income countries, very high levels of happiness are not achieved, and in poor countries with low-income levels, such as Bhutan, more than half of the population identifies themselves as happy. Thus, based on data on poverty, human development, happiness, and individual well-being, it can be concluded that happiness cannot be entirely viewed as a phenomenon dependent on the quality of life through country comparisons made within the framework of poor countries.

As a result of studies aimed at understanding the nature of happiness, various measurement methods have been developed by international economic organizations. It has been observed that countries with the highest incomes are not always classified as the happiest countries. In this context, it can be said that there is no universally agreed-upon definition or approach to happiness. Consequently, we can say that happiness is not a concept that changes only depending on income. Studies on the multidimensional nature of happiness have shown that policymakers also have important duties. For happiness to have a sustainable and ongoing quality, regulations must be made to ensure education, health, morality, and safety in society. Eradicating systemic discrimination, ensuring justice, and providing a respectful attitude and positive externalities to disadvantaged groups another important components for political implementations.

References

Akar, S. (2014). Türkiye'de daha iyi yaşam endeksi: OECD ülkeleri ile karşılaştırma, Journal of Life Economics, 1, pp. 1–12.

Carbonell, A. F. (2005). Income and well-being: an empirical analysis of the comparison income effect. Journal of Public Economics 89 (2005) 997–1019. https://bse.eu/sites/default/files/ReferenceIncome.pdf.

Clark, A. E., Frijters, P., and Shields, M. A. (2008). Income, happiness, and utility: an explanation for the Easterlin paradox and other puzzles, Journal of Economic Literature.

Costanza, R., Hart, M., Posner, S. and Talberth, J. (2009). Beyond GDP: The need for new measures of progress. Pardee Papers, Boston University Press.

Coşkun, S. and Tireli, M. (2008). Avrupa Birliğinde Yoksullukla Mücadele Stratejileri ve Türkiye. Nobel, Ankara.

Easterlin, R. (1974). Does economic growth improve the human lot? some empirical evidence. In: David, R. and Reder, R., Eds., Nations and Households in Economic Growth: Essays in Honor of Moses Abramovitz, Academic Press, New York.

Easterlin, R. A. and Angelescu, L. (2009). Happiness and growth the world over time series evidence on the happiness-income paradox, IZA Discussion Papers, No. 4060, Institute for the Study of Labor (IZA), Bonn, https://nbn-resolving.de/urn:nbn:de:101:1-20090327277.

Frey, B. S. and Stutzer, A. (2002). What can economists learn from happiness research? Journal of Economic Literature, Vol. 40, No. 2. pp. 402–435.

Güler, M. and Dönmez, A. (2011). İyi olma hali bağlamında uyum düzeyi kuramı ve hedonik döngü. Türk Psikoloji Yazıları, Haziran 2011, 14 (27), 38–45.

Han, E. and Kaya, A. A. (2013). Kalkınma Ekonomisi Teori ve Politika, 8. Baskı Nobel Akademik Yayıncılık Ankara.

Happy Planet Index, (2023). https://happyplanetindex.org/ Access Date: 01.03.2024.

Jeffrey, K., Wheatley, H. and Abdallah, S. (2016). The Happy Planet Index 2016, A global index of sustainable wellbeing, New Economics Foundation.

Kruskal, J. B. and Wish, M. (1991). Multidimensional Scaling, United States of America: Sage Publications.

Kahneman, D. and Deaton, A. (2010). High income improves the evaluation of life but not emotional well-being. PNAS | September 21, 107 (38): 16489–16493.

Kahneman, D. (2003). Maps of bounded rationality: psychology for behavioural economics. The American Economic Review, 93(5): 1449–1475.

Kahneman, D. and A. B. Krueger (2006). Developments in the measurement of subjective well-being. Journal of Economic Perspectives, Vol. 20.

Kuznets, S. (1934). "National Income, 1929–1932", National Bureau of Economic Research, Inc. https://www.nber.org/books-and-chapters/national-income-1929-1932.

Lyubomirsky, S. (2008). Nasil Mutlu olunur? (Gülfer Göze, Trans.). Istanbul, Turkey: Kapital Medya Hizmetleri.

Mankiw, G. (2010). Makroekonomi. Efil Yayınları, Ankara.

Maslow, A. H. (1943). A theory of human motivation. Psychological Review, 50(4), 370–396. https://doi.org/10.1037/h0054346.

New Economic Foundation (2016). The Happy Planet Index. http://happyplanetindex .org/.

OECD, (2023). https://www.oecdbetterlifeindex.org/ Access Date: 29.02.2024.

Schurer, S. and Yong, J. (2016). Happiness, income and heterogeneity, The Singapore Economic Review, 61(3).

Ünsal, E. (2009). Makroiktisat. İmaj Yayınları Ankara.

Veenhoven, R. and Dumludağ, D. (2015). Iktisat ve Mutluluk: Bugün Daha Mutlu Muyuz? Chapter 11 in: Dumladağ, D., Gökdemir, O., Neyse, L. & Ruben, E. (Ed.), İktisatta Davranışsal Yaklaşımlar (Behavioral Approaches In Economics), Imge Kitabevi, Ankara Turkey, 201–230.

Yıldırım, K. (2008). Makro Ekonomi, Ed. Kemal Yıldırım, 9. Baskı, Ankara, Seçkin Yayıncılık.

GNH, (2022). https://ophi.org.uk/policy/bhutan-gnh-index/ Access Date: 29.02.2024.

WHR, (2023). https://worldhappiness.report/ed/2023/.

CHAPTER 8

Political Systems, Stable Democracies and Happiness

Necmettin Çelik

Improving life satisfaction or happiness is a primary goal for governments, regardless of their economic and political systems. On the other hand, happiness is mainly associated with the economic welfare of individuals as well as other demographic and psychological factors. However, the impacts of economic welfare on happiness vary across different political systems. In essence, economic welfare is aa but insufficient for overall happiness, and understanding the political context is essential. In other words, happiness cannot be understood without considering the political regime types of governments. To explore this relationship, a study investigated the linkage between political systems and happiness. By examining the happiness levels of countries using World Happiness Rankings and analyzing their democratic statutes, the study aimed to understand whether democracy and freedom contribute to higher levels of happiness. The findings revealed a positive relationship between a country's level of democracy and its happiness level. As democracy increases, happiness tends to rise gradually. However, democracy alone is not a sufficient determinant of happiness. The presence of ongoing, stable, and mature democratic practices is more critical than merely having a democratic system. Although there are a few exceptional cases, overall, the evidence suggests that stable democratic institutions play a vital role in fostering happiness. For this reason, democratic practices, especially in democratic but unhappy countries, should be strengthened through human development, education and economic development channels.

1 Introduction

Improving the well-being, happiness, or welfare of citizens is a priority for all governments, regardless of their economic systems. It is related to the economic and political tasks of governments. However, it is understood that this task is not easy, considering that almost half of the countries are unhappy.[1] This is because, happiness, which could be determined by several factors such as indicators like satisfaction with life, health, or psychological state of mind (Singh *et al.*), depends on various internal and external determinants. In literature, mental, emotional, and physical health, social, cultural, or environmental harmony, and the welfare of individuals (Singh *et al.*) are generally accepted as priority internal determinants of happiness. However, these individual conditions are associated with external determinants in society, such as economic welfare or economic development.

On the other hand, as a key determinant of rapid economic growth and economic development in both exogenous and endogenous growth models, technological improvement is strongly associated with human capital. In other words, economic growth and development depend on technological improvements, which are mainly determined by human capital accumulation (Solow, 1956; Romer, 1990). This linkage is explained through various terms and channels, such as knowledge, knowledge externalities, innovation, and R&D activities. These channels are directly related to higher labour productivity, which in turn leads to greater development levels. These findings align with the research of Barro (2001) and Hanushek (2013). At this juncture, happiness becomes crucial, as it is closely tied to labour productivity. In other words, happiness can be considered a positive determinant of labour (factor) productivity or human capital accumulation. Studies by Sharifzadeh and Almaraz (2014), Oswald *et al.* (2015), DiMaria *et al.* (2020), and Bellet *et al.* (2023) indicate a positive relationship between happiness and labour productivity at both the firm level and the macro level. Consequently, the relationship between happiness and economic development is reciprocal: as the development level increases, so does the level of happiness (Zagorski *et al.*, 2010; Clark and Senik, 2011; Veenhoven and Vergunst, 2014; Kanaujiya and Maurya, 2022), and vice versa (Loubser and Steeneakmp, 2016). It is related to the theory of absolute utility which posits that additional income contributes to long-term happiness (Hagerty and Veenhoven, 2003). In essence, increased purchasing power leads to greater long-term happiness.

Indeed, Figure 8.1 shows that there is a positive relationship between the development level and the happiness level of countries. On the other hand, 98 percent of high-income countries are happy, and the deviation between their minimum and maximum index values is quite small. Similarly, 100 percent of low-income countries are unhappy. This supports the hypothesis that

---

1   According to the Happiness Index of the Global Economy, 46% of the world's countries are relatively unhappy in 2002.

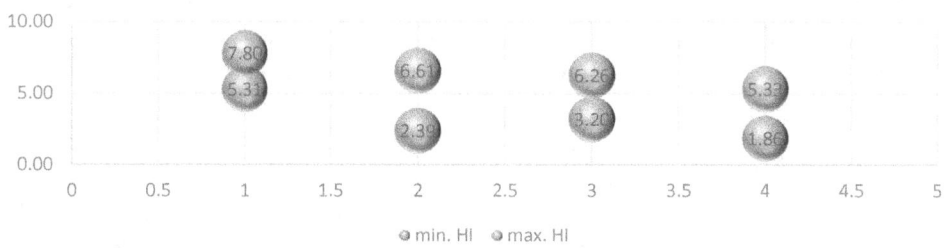

FIGURE 8.1 Minimum–maximum values of happiness index (HI) in terms of development level of countries (2022)
SOURCE: HTTPS://WWW.THEGLOBALECONOMY.COM/RANKINGS/HAPPINESS/,
ACCESS DATE: 11.02.2024

as countries' income levels increase, their happiness level also increases. In other words, there is a positive relationship between the development level of countries and the level of happiness. On the other hand, happiness deviation or gap is small in top countries where almost everyone is happy or no one is unhappy (Helliwell *et al.*, 2023).

However, the deviation between the minimum and maximum happiness index values is higher in upper-middle-income countries than in lower-middle-income countries and lower-income countries. On the other hand, 53 percent of upper-middle-income countries are just happy. It shows that happiness cannot be explained solely by income level and purchasing power. In other words, the linkage between income and happiness is weakening, especially in upper-middle-income countries. Firstly, this finding is consistent with the very weak correlation coefficient, as measured by Paleologou (2002), between income and democracy in middle-income countries. Secondly, according to Easterlin (1974), the highest-income countries are happier than the lowest-income countries on average, but these happiness differences are not consistently supported at the international level. Finally, researchers such as Shin (1980), Kenny (2007), Schimmel (2009), Easterlin (2017), and Kundu *et al.* (2024) indicate that increased income does not necessarily lead to increased happiness, or income may not universally accept as a determinant of happiness. It is called by Easterlin Paradox in the literature.

For this reason, happiness cannot be explained by economic conditions alone, or without considering the political tasks and aspects of governments. At this juncture, the idea that regime types can affect happiness levels comes to the fore. This is because individual happiness is intricately linked to the overall happiness of society. When democratic norms and values—such as civil liberties, political equality, independence of the judiciary, freedom of expression, and the right to vote—are expanded, the happiness level of society tends to rise. Consequently, democracy emerges as a crucial determinant of happiness, functioning as a political object. In simpler terms, people experience freedom in all aspects of their lives due to democratic norms and values. These include "freedom of expression," "freedom of belief," "rule of law," "voice and accountability," and "trust in the delivery of government power." Over the long term, these democratic principles contribute to higher levels of happiness (Helliwell and Huang, 2008; Inglehart and Ponarin, 2013; Berggren and Bjornskov, 2020; Paleologou, 2022; Graafland, 2023). In essence, democracy leads to happiness by choice (Potts, 2016). Empirical findings from studies by Inglehart and Klingemann (2000), Helliwell (2006), Dorn *et al.* (2007), Inglehart *et al.* (2008), Owen *et al.* (2008), Helliwell and Huang (2008), Ott (2010), Ott (2011), Orviska *et al.* (2011), Rode *et al.* (2013), Potts (2016), Paleologou (2022), Liu *et al.* (2023), and Kundu *et al.* (2024) also underscore that happiness is positively affected by various components of democracy, including the electoral process, freedom, quality of government (good governance), and fair and inclusive institutions.

Indeed, 84 percent of happy countries are governed by democratic regimes. On the other side, half of democratic countries are not happy.[2] It can be expressed that democracy is necessary but insufficient for happiness. This mismatch may be related to specific governance problems in democratic countries. Therefore, the impacts of regime types and political events must be investigated as potential determinants of happiness, as well as economic development.

In this chapter, the impacts of regime types and specific political change events on happiness levels are quantitatively investigated. Accordingly, in the first stage, the sub-types of political systems were defined. Secondly, the relationship between regime types and happiness was discussed quantitatively. Thirdly, the negative impacts of specific political change events, especially in 26 democratic but unhappy countries, on their happiness were discussed as exceptional cases. Finally, policy proposals were developed on how countries can ensure full and stable democracies for higher happiness.

---

2   The happiness levels of 88 percent of autocratic countries are above the world average contrary to expectations. It is inconsistent with the argument that democracy leads to greater happiness. However, 7 of 9 countries with anocracy status have high development levels and purchasing powers. On the other hand, they have political stability or there are no specific political change events in their recent histories. Therefore, autocratic countries with high incomes and stable political histories can also be happy. This means that high income and political stability may be more important factors for a happy society than types of political regimes.

2   Regime Types and Happiness

While examining the relationship between regime types and happiness, democratization or political regime scores of the countries, which are coded by the Polity IV Project, were used. Polity IV project is a study aimed at coding the authority characteristics of countries using various indicators for comparative and quantitative analysis. In the project, democracy is accepted as a governance that includes three essential elements based on eleven indicators. Accordingly, mature or stable democracies are defined as countries where political participation is unrestricted, open and fully competitive, executive recruitment is elective, and barriers to the chief executive are substantial while autocracies are defined as countries in which competitive political participation is sharply restricted or suppressed, chief executives are chosen from among political elite, and there are few barriers to the exercise of power (Marshall and Jaggers, 2007). Polity IV scores are coded from 10 (full democracy) to –10 (autocracy). Accordingly, democracies consist of two subcategories; full democracy is coded 10, and democracy is coded 6 and 9 while autocracies consist of three subcategories; open anocracy is coded 1 and 5, closed anocracy is coded 0 and –5, and anocracy is coded –6 and –10.

According to the political regime scores of 129 countries with happiness index in the world, as can be seen from Table 8.1 and Table 8.2, these contain a summary and detailed statistics about countries' level of income, happiness and political regime respectively, 66 percent of the countries are governed by democracy, classified as full democracy or democracy, while 34 percent are governed by autocracy, classified as closed anocracy, open anocracy, or anocracy. When the relationship between regime types and happiness levels is examined, it is seen that 84 percent of democracies are happy, while only 55 percent of democracies are unhappy. On the other hand, as democratic values increase, the level of happiness also increases. Accordingly, it can be argued that democracies are happier, or that democracy is one of the crucial political determinants of happiness, but it cannot be argued that autocracies are unhappier. In other words, a remarkably strong linkage between democracy and happiness could be interpreted as happiness being attributed to democracy; or that democracy largely reflects happiness (Inglehart, 2009).[3] This suggests that there could be a strong relationship between democracy and happiness.

---

3   This linkage, also, could be spurious because of the strong relationship between the level of democracy and the level of economic development. Indeed, income has a positive impact on happiness especially in high-income countries (Paleologou, 2022), but this idea does not apply to upper-middle-income countries without happiness or lower-middle-income countries with happiness.

TABLE 8.1   The number of happy and unhappy countries in the different political regimes

	Full Democracy (Polity IV: 10)	Democracy (Polity IV: 6 to 9)	Open Anocracy (Polity IV: 1 to 5)	Closed Anocracy (Polity IV: −5 to 0)	Anocracy (Polity IV: −10 to −6)	Total
Happy	33 (100 %)	26 (50 %)	3 (14 %)	1 (7 %)	7 (88 %)	70 (54 %)
Unhappy	0 (0 %)	26 (50 %)	18 (86 %)	13 (93 %)	2 (22 %)	59 (46 %)
Total	33 (26 %)	52 (40 %)	21 (16 %)	14 (11 %)	9 (7 %)	129

Note: Numbers indicate the number of happy or unhappy countries while ratios in parentheses ( ) indicate the share of them in their political regime types
SOURCE: HTTPS://WWW.THEGLOBALECONOMY.COM/RANKINGS/HAPPINESS/, ACCESS DATE: 11.02.2024

TABLE 8.2   The countries' income. Happiness and political regime levels and statuses

Nu.	Countries	Happiness index value	Happiness status	Income status	Polity IV score	Political regime status
1	Finland	7.80	Happy	High Income	10	Full Democracy
2	Denmark	7.59	Happy	High Income	10	Full Democracy
3	Israel	7.47	Happy	High Income	10	Full Democracy
4	Sweden	7.40	happy	High Income	10	Full Democracy
5	Netherlands	7.40	happy	High Income	10	Full Democracy
6	Norway	7.32	happy	High Income	10	Full Democracy
7	Switzerland	7.24	happy	High Income	10	Full Democracy
8	Luxembourg	7.23	happy	High Income	10	Full Democracy
9	New Zealand	7.12	happy	High Income	10	Full Democracy
10	Austria	7.10	happy	High Income	10	Full Democracy
11	Australia	7.09	happy	High Income	10	Full Democracy
12	Canada	6.96	happy	High Income	10	Full Democracy
13	Ireland	6.91	happy	High Income	10	Full Democracy
14	USA	6.89	happy	High Income	10	Full Democracy
15	Germany	6.89	happy	High Income	10	Full Democracy
16	Belgium	6.86	happy	High Income	8	Democracy

TABLE 8.2   The countries' income. Happiness and political regime levels and statuses (*cont.*)

Nu.	Countries	Happiness index value	Happiness status	Income status	Polity IV score	Political regime status
17	Czechia	6.85	happy	High Income	8	Democracy
18	UK	6.80	happy	High Income	10	Full Democracy
19	Lithuania	6.76	happy	High Income	10	Full Democracy
20	France	6.66	happy	High Income	9	Democracy
21	Slovenia	6.65	happy	High Income	10	Full Democracy
22	Costa Rica	6.61	happy	Upper Middle Income	10	Full Democracy
23	Singapore	6.59	happy	High Income	−2	Closed Anocracy
24	Romania	6.59	happy	High Income	9	Democracy
25	United Arab Emirates	6.57	happy	High Income	−8	Anocracy
26	Uruguay	6.49	happy	High Income	10	Full Democracy
27	Slovakia	6.47	happy	High Income	10	Full Democracy
28	Saudi Arabia	6.46	happy	High Income	−10	Anocracy
29	Estonia	6.46	happy	High Income	10	Full Democracy
30	Spain	6.44	happy	High Income	10	Full Democracy
31	Italy	6.40	happy	High Income	10	Full Democracy
32	Mexico	6.33	happy	Upper Middle Income	8	Democracy
33	Chile	6.33	happy	High Income	10	Full Democracy
34	Poland	6.26	happy	High Income	10	Full Democracy
35	Panama	6.26	happy	High Income	9	Democracy
36	Nicaragua	6.26	happy	Lower Middle Income	9	Democracy
37	Latvia	6.21	happy	High Income	8	Democracy
38	Bahrain	6.17	happy	High Income	−10	Anocracy
39	Guatemala	6.15	happy	Upper Middle Income	8	Democracy
40	Serbia	6.14	happy	Upper Middle Income	8	Democracy
41	Kazakhstan	6.14	happy	Upper Middle Income	−6	Anocracy
42	Japan	6.13	happy	High Income	10	Full Democracy
43	Cyprus	6.13	happy	High Income	10	Full Democracy

TABLE 8.2   The countries' income. Happiness and political regime levels and statuses (*cont.*)

Nu.	Countries	Happiness index value	Happiness status	Income status	Polity IV score	Political regime status
44	Croatia	6.13	happy	High Income	9	Democracy
45	El Salvador	6.12	happy	Lower Middle Income	8	Democracy
46	Brazil	6.12	happy	Upper Middle Income	8	Democracy
47	Hungary	6.04	happy	High Income	10	Full Democracy
48	Honduras	6.02	happy	Lower Middle Income	7	Democracy
49	Argentina	6.02	happy	Upper Middle Income	8	Democracy
50	Uzbekistan	6.01	happy	Lower Middle Income	−9	Anocracy
51	Malaysia	6.01	happy	Upper Middle Income	6	Democracy
52	Portugal	5.97	happy	High Income	10	Full Democracy
53	South Korea	5.95	happy	High Income	8	Democracy
54	Greece	5.93	happy	High Income	10	Full Democracy
55	Mauritius	5.90	happy	High Income	10	Full Democracy
56	Thailand	5.84	happy	Upper Middle Income	7	Democracy
57	Mongolia	5.84	happy	Lower Middle Income	10	Full Democracy
58	Kyrgyzstan	5.83	happy	Lower Middle Income	7	Democracy
59	Moldova	5.82	happy	Lower Middle Income	9	Democracy
60	China	5.82	happy	Upper Middle Income	−7	Anocracy
61	Vietnam	5.76	happy	Lower Middle Income	−7	Anocracy
62	Paraguay	5.74	happy	Upper Middle Income	9	Democracy
63	Montenegro	5.72	happy	Upper Middle Income	9	Democracy

TABLE 8.2   The countries' income. Happiness and political regime levels and statuses (*cont.*)

Nu.	Countries	Happiness index value	Happiness status	Income status	Polity IV score	Political regime status
64	Jamaica	5.70	happy	Upper Middle Income	9	Democracy
65	Bolivia	5.68	happy	Lower Middle Income	7	Democracy
66	Russia	5.66	happy	Upper Middle Income	4	Open Anocracy
67	Colombia	5.63	happy	Upper Middle Income	7	Democracy
68	Bosnia and Herz.	5.63	happy	Upper Middle Income	5	Open Anocracy
69	Domin. Rep.	5.57	happy	Upper Middle Income	8	Democracy
70	Ecuador	5.56	happy	Upper Middle Income	5	Open Anocracy
71	Peru	5.53	unhappy	Upper Middle Income	9	Democracy
72	Philippines	5.52	unhappy	Lower Middle Income	8	Democracy
73	Bulgaria	5.47	unhappy	Upper Middle Income	9	Democracy
74	Nepal	5.36	unhappy	Lower Middle Income	6	Democracy
75	Armenia	5.34	unhappy	Upper Middle Income	5	Open Anocracy
76	Tajikistan	5.33	unhappy	Low Income	−3	Closed Anocracy
77	Algeria	5.33	unhappy	Lower Middle Income	2	Open Anocracy
78	Indonesia	5.28	unhappy	Upper Middle Income	9	Democracy
79	Albania	5.28	unhappy	Upper Middle Income	9	Democracy
80	R. of Congo	5.27	unhappy	Lower Middle Income	−4	Closed Anocracy

TABLE 8.2   The countries' income. Happiness and political regime levels and statuses (*cont.*)

Nu.	Countries	Happiness index value	Happiness status	Income status	Polity ivPolitical score	regime status
81	Somalia	5.27	unhappy	Low Income	5	Open Anocracy
82	North Macedonia	5.25	unhappy	Upper Middle Income	9	Democracy
83	Venezuela	5.21	unhappy	Upper Middle Income	4	Open Anocracy
84	Laos	5.11	unhappy	Lower Middle Income	−7	Anocracy
85	Georgia	5.11	unhappy	Upper Middle Income	7	Democracy
86	Ukraine	5.07	unhappy	Lower Middle Income	6	Democracy
87	Guinea	5.07	unhappy	Low Income	4	Open Anocracy
88	Ivory Coast	5.05	unhappy	Lower Middle Income	4	Open Anocracy
89	Gabon	5.03	unhappy	Upper Middle Income	3	Open Anocracy
90	Nigeria	4.98	unhappy	Lower Middle Income	4	Open Anocracy
91	Cameroon	4.97	unhappy	Lower Middle Income	−4	Closed Anocracy
92	Mozambique	4.95	unhappy	Low Income	4	Open Anocracy
93	Iraq	4.94	unhappy	Upper Middle Income	3	Open Anocracy
94	Morocco	4.90	unhappy	Lower Middle Income	−4	Closed Anocracy
95	Iran	4.88	unhappy	Upper Middle Income	−7	Anocracy
96	Senegal	4.86	unhappy	Lower Middle Income	7	Democracy
97	Mauritania	4.72	unhappy	Lower Middle Income	−2	Closed Anocracy
98	Burkina Faso	4.64	unhappy	Low Income	0	Closed Anocracy
99	Namibia	4.63	unhappy	Upper Middle Income	6	Democracy

TABLE 8.2   The countries' income. Happiness and political regime levels and statuses (*cont.*)

Nu.	Countries	Happiness index value	Happiness status	Income status	Polity IV score	Political regime status
100	Turkey	4.61	unhappy	Upper Middle Income	9	Democracy
101	Ghana	4.61	unhappy	Lower Middle Income	8	Democracy
102	Pakistan	4.56	unhappy	Lower Middle Income	7	Democracy
103	Tunisia	4.50	unhappy	Lower Middle Income	7	Democracy
104	Niger	4.50	unhappy	Low Income	6	Democracy
105	Kenya	4.49	unhappy	Lower Middle Income	9	Democracy
106	Sri Lanka	4.44	unhappy	Lower Middle Income	5	Open Anocracy
107	Uganda	4.43	unhappy	Low Income	−1	Closed Anocracy
108	Chad	4.40	unhappy	Low Income	−2	Closed Anocracy
109	Cambodia	4.39	unhappy	Lower Middle Income	2	Open Anocracy
110	Benin	4.37	unhappy	Lower Middle Income	7	Democracy
111	Gambia	4.28	unhappy	Low Income	−5	Closed Anocracy
112	Bangladesh	4.28	unhappy	Lower Middle Income	4	Open Anocracy
113	Mali	4.20	unhappy	Low Income	5	Open Anocracy
114	Egypt	4.17	unhappy	Lower Middle Income	−4	Closed Anocracy
115	Togo	4.14	unhappy	Low Income	−2	Closed Anocracy
116	Jordan	4.12	unhappy	Upper Middle Income	−2	Closed Anocracy
117	Liberia	4.04	unhappy	Low Income	6	Democracy
118	India	4.04	unhappy	Lower Middle Income	9	Democracy

TABLE 8.2   The countries' income. Happiness and political regime levels and statuses (*cont.*)

Nu.	Countries	Happiness index value	Happiness status	Income status	Polity IV score	Political regime status
119	Madagascar	4.02	unhappy	Low Income	3	Open Anocracy
120	Zambia	3.98	unhappy	Lower Middle Income	7	Democracy
121	Tanzania	3.69	unhappy	Lower Middle Income	−1	Closed Anocracy
122	Comoros	3.55	unhappy	Lower Middle Income	9	Democracy
123	Malawi	3.50	unhappy	Low Income	6	Democracy
124	Botswana	3.44	unhappy	Upper Middle Income	8	Democracy
125	DR Congo	3.21	unhappy	Low Income	5	Open Anocracy
126	Zimbabwe	3.20	unhappy	Lower Middle Income	4	Open Anocracy
127	Sierra Leone	3.14	unhappy	Low Income	7	Democracy
128	Lebanon	2.39	unhappy	Upper Middle Income	6	Democracy
129	Afghanistan	1.86	unhappy	Low Income	2	Open Anocracy

Note: Full Democracy is coded by 10, Democracy is coded between 6 and 9, Open Anocracy is coded between 1 and 5, Closed Anocracy is coded between 0 and −5, and Anocracy is coded between −6 and −10.

Income statuses of countries are classified as World Bank thresholds values for the countries' 2022 GNI per capita values. Accordingly, the values below $1,085 are labeled with low income, the values between $1,086 and $4,255 are labeled by lower middle income, the values between $4,256 and $13,205 are labeled by upper middle income, the values above $13,205 are labeled by high income

SOURCE: IT IS COMPILED BY POLITY4, THE GLOBAL ECONOMY AND WORLD BANK DATABASES

However, 46 percent of the world's countries are unhappy, and almost half of them are governed by democracy. On the other hand, 26 of the 52 democratic countries are unhappy. This may seem to support Inglehart and Ponarin's (2013) argument that happiness cannot be explained without considering other factors that are at least equally important, or that the high correlation between democracy and happiness does not reflect the fact that democracy makes people happy. Thus, it may cast doubt on the argument that democracies are happier, but it does not. It is about the stability and maturity of democratic practices. Since all the 33 countries governed by full democracy are happy, the problem lies with the unstable or immature democracies rather than the nature of democracy itself.[4]

Specific political change events that negatively affect democratic norms and values, or lead to instability, can hinder happiness in democratic countries. For this reason, democratic countries experiencing special political change events such as autocratic backsliding,[5] coup d'état, executive auto-coups (or autogolpe), state failure, or direct foreign military regime change intervention cannot be recognized as full or stable democracies. They are unstable or immature democracies. Stable democracy refers to a democratic governance that generally exhibits considerable staying power and the capacity to endure without great changes frequently (Eckstein, 1961). Therefore, during these specific periods of political regime change, countries often struggle to uphold the necessary conditions for democracy accurately. For instance, failed states and occupied territories find it challenging to protect democratic rights and conditions when their sovereignties are in doubt. Conversely, new governments or executives may not prioritize safeguarding democratic norms and values during coup d'état or executive auto-coup periods. Ultimately, autocratic backsliding processes undermine democracy. In summary, countries experiencing adverse special political change events cannot be unequivocally accepted as democratic, even if they exhibit democratic features. In fact, countries that fall in the middle in terms of their political regimes such as democracies, open anocracy and closed anocracy, are more likely to experience political instability (Goldstone and Ulfelder, 2004). It is related to arguments of democratic-elit or demo-elite theory about why some countries have experienced a breakdown of evolving democracy. Accordingly, the absence of relative autonomy of elites from the state, media, justice and bureaucracy which are considered struggles for the development of democratic norms and values (Etzioni-Halevy, 1990)

---

4   Special polity change events include autocratic backsliding (a five-point or greater change toward more autocratic authority that forcibly replaces an established regime), executive auto-coups or *autogolpe* (a five-point or greater change in regime authority initiated by a ruling executive), revolutionary change (a forcible ouster of an established regime and its wholesale replacement by a radically different regime authority and ruling elite), state failure (the total or near-total collapse of central authority affecting more than fifty percent of state territory), and coup d'etat (a military or military-backed forcible ouster of an established executive with little or no change in regime authority). Detailed information is available at: The Polity IV Country Report 2006 Series (systemicpeace.org)

5   Autocratic backsliding or adverse regime change means a situation includes an unexpected and sharp shift from democratic norms to autocratic rules which could be caused by coups d'tats, executive auto-coups, and collapse of state authority or state failure (Goldstone and Ulfelder, 2004).

may be a potential cause of instability or breakdown of democracy in these countries.

For this reason, investigating the stability and maturity levels of democracies is crucial for understanding the unhappy situations in these countries and establishing the correct relationship between democracy and happiness. Table 8.3 includes special political change events that occurred in 26 democratic countries experiencing unhappiness. Among these, 21 out of 26 countries have faced events such as autocratic backsliding, coup d'état, executive auto-coups (or autogolpe), interruptions, and/or interregnum processes. These events were often triggered by state failure or direct foreign military regime change interventions in their recent histories.

Specifically:

- INTERREGNUM PROCESS CAUSED BY DIRECT FOREIGN MILITARY REGIME CHANGE INTERVENTION (1990–2004): Lebanon experienced direct foreign military intervention during this period.
- INTERREGNUM PROCESS CAUSED BY STATE FAILURE: Sierra Leone (1997–2001), Comoros (1995), and Liberia (1990–1995) faced interregnum processes due to state failure.
- COUP D'ÉTATS OR EXECUTIVE AUTO-COUPS: Several countries, including Sierra Leone, Comoros, Zambia, Benin, Kenya, Niger, Tunisia, Pakistan, Ghana, Turkey, Senegal, Albania, Indonesia, Nepal, Philippines, Peru, Liberia, and Bulgaria, witnessed at least one coup d'état or executive auto-coup. Many of these events led to autocratic backsliding.
- UKRAINE: The ongoing conflict environment in Ukraine has contributed to an increasing worry level (Helliwell *et al.*, 2023).
- MALAWI: Although Malawi does not have a long and stable democratic history, it also faces challenges.

In summary, understanding the impact of these special political change events is essential for assessing the true state of democracy and its relationship with happiness. Therefore, these countries do not have stable or mature democracies.

In this context, the specific political change events that occurred in 21 out of 26 democratic countries can be considered as the political reasons behind their unhappy situations. In other words, these countries lack stable and mature democracies. Consequently, the argument that stable and mature democracy, rather than mere democracy, is the primary political determinant of happiness holds strong.[6] Notably, while mature and stable democracies tend to be happier, democracies lacking these qualities are often unhappier

---

6 This argument is not valid for 5 countries that are Botswana, India, Namibia, Georgia, and North Macedonia. These democratic countries have not experienced any special adverse

TABLE 8.3 Special political change events in the democratic but unhappy countries

Country name	Special political change events	Explanation
Lebanon	available	interruption process caused by State Failure between 1975 and 1989 interregnum process caused by Direct Foreign Military Regime Change Intervention between 1990 and 2004
Sierra Leone	available	autocratic backsliding in 1967 executive auto-coups or *autogolpe in 1971* coup d'etats in 1968, 1991, 1996, and 1997 interregnum process caused by state failure between 1997 and 2001
Malawi	available	Short and instable democratic history (1994–today)
Comoros	available	coup d'etat in 1976 executive auto-coups or *autogolpe in 1976* *interregnum process caused by state failure in 1995* autocratic backsliding in 1999
Zambia	available	executive auto-coups or *autogolpe in 1968 and 1996*
Benin	available	autocratic backslidings in 1963 and 1972 coup d'etats in 1963 and 1970
Kenya	available	executive auto-coups or *autogolpe (1966)*
Niger	available	coup d'etat in 1974, autocratic backsliding in 1996, executive auto-coups or *autogolpe in 2009*
Tunisia	available	coup d'etat in 1987
Pakistan	available	autocratic backslidings in 1958, 1977 and 1997 coup d'etat in 1999
Ghana	available	coup d'etats in 1966, 1978 and 1979 autocratic backslidings in 1972 and 1981
Turkey	available	coup d'etat in 1960 autocratic backslidings in 1971 and 1980
Senegal	available	autocratic backsliding in 1962
Ukraine	available	Russia-Ukraine Conflict since 2014
Albania	available	executive auto-coups or *autogolpe in 199)*
Indonesia	available	autocratic backsliding in 1957 coup d'etat in 1966

TABLE 8.3   Special political change events in the democratic but unhappy countries (*cont.*)

Country name	Special political change events	Explanation
Nepal	available	autocratic backsliding in 1960
		executive auto-coups or *autogolpe in 2002*
Philippines	available	executive auto-coups or *autogolpe in 1972*
Peru	available	autocratic backslidings in 1948, 1962 and 1968
		coup d'etats in 1962 and 1975
		executive auto-coups or *autogolpe in 1992*
Liberia	available	coup d'etat in 1980
		interregnum process in 1990–1995 caused by state failure
Bulgaria	available	coup d'etat in 1989
Botswana	not available	-
India	not available	-
Namibia	not available	-
Georgia	not available	-
North Macedonia	not available	-

SOURCE: IT IS COMPILED FROM "SYSTEMIC PEACE POLITY IV DATABASE" BY THE AUTHOR.
DETAILED INFORMATION IS AVAILABLE AT: HTTPS://WWW.SYSTEMICPEACE
.ORG/POLITY/POLITY4.HTM, ACCESS DATE: 24.02.2024

than even autocracies. These findings align with the research by Dorn *et al.* (2007) and Inglehart and Klingemann (2000), which highlight that the impact of democracy on happiness is more pronounced in countries with a democratic tradition, and stable democracies are more likely to experience higher levels of happiness.

Finally, seven non-democratic countries (UAE, Saudi Arabia, Bahrain, Kazakhstan, and China)[7] experience happiness despite their non-democratic

political change events in their recent history, but they are unhappy. Therefore, their unhappy situations cannot be explained by political determinants.

7   This argument is not valid for 7 countries. Accordingly, the happiness levels of Uzbekistan and Vietnam are above the world average, even though their democracy and income levels are low. On the other hand, the happiness levels of North Macedonia, Georgia, Namibia and Botswana are below the world average, even though their democracy and income levels are high as well as they have political stability. Therefore, the happy situation of Uzbekistan

status. However, they share common traits: upper or upper-middle income and political stability. This suggests that the stability and maturity of political regimes play a more significant role in happiness than the specific type of regime. Furthermore, stable democratic practices consistently lead to higher levels of happiness. In other words, it is the main finding of this chapter that there is a strong and positive relationship between stable democracies and happiness. If countries can achieve higher levels of democracy, they can also achieve higher levels of happiness over time. For this reason, democratic practices, especially in democratic but unhappy countries, should be strengthened.

Achieving stable democracy is not a simple or easy process, especially for democratic countries that have experienced adverse political change events in their recent history. Because they are faced with dynamics that hinder democratic deepening, such as coup d'etats, executive auto-coups, or state failure. However, they should focus on and apply the economic, political, and cultural determinants of stable democracy. Accordingly, in the conclusion part, policy proposals regarding the transition process from democracy to stable democracy are discussed from different perspectives.

3   Conclusion

Happiness has been extensively studied by various disciplines and scientists over time. It is intricately linked to several domains, including economics, business, politics, and physiology, in terms of both its determinants and consequences. Notably, the happiness of citizens represents a fundamental goal for governments, regardless of their regime types. However, achieving a genuinely happy society requires a deep understanding of the factors that influence happiness. Surprisingly, nearly half of the world's countries experience unhappiness. In this context, economic determinants of happiness take centre stage, particularly in economic literature. The relationship between happiness and economic growth and development is widely acknowledged as a primary economic objective for governments. Essentially, as happiness levels rise, so do economic performance and development, often leading to increased labour productivity and vice versa. Because, the process of rapid economic growth and economic development is essentially shaped by factor productivity, which is related to the happiness level of labour. Various empirical studies show that there is a positive and statistically significant relationship between labour

---

and Vietnam as well as the unhappy situation of North Macedonia, Georgia, Namibia and Botswana cannot be explained by their political and economic conditions.

productivity and labour happiness. Therefore, achieving higher levels of happiness is a vital goal, especially for developing and underdeveloped countries. On the other hand, as income or purchasing power increases, thanks to rapid economic growth performance, the level of happiness also increases. This phenomenon holds across both highly developed and underdeveloped nations, although happiness disparities are more pronounced in upper-middle-income countries. However, it is essential to recognize that happiness cannot be solely explained by economic conditions. Political determinants play a crucial role. This insight sheds light on the Easterlin Paradox, which highlights why various empirical studies find no statistically significant relationship between income and happiness. In summary, understanding the intricate interplay between economic and political factors is essential for promoting genuine happiness.

In the realm of political literature, the notion that political regime types can significantly impact happiness levels has gained prominence. Democracy is often associated with happier societies due to several factors: freedom of expression and belief, fair and inclusive institutions, the rule of law, good governance, voice and accountability, and adherence to democratic norms and values. Essentially, as democracy expands within a society, happiness tends to increase. Remarkably, approximately 84 percent of democratic countries worldwide experience happiness. However, there exists a paradox: nearly half of the unhappy countries are also governed by democracy, and conversely, half of the democratic countries are unhappy. These exceptional cases challenge the straightforward argument that democracies inherently lead to greater happiness. Instead, the critical factor lies in the stability and maturity of democracy itself. Consider the exceptional cases, including Lebanon, Sierra Leone, Comoros, Zambia, Benin, Kenya, Niger, Tunisia, Pakistan, Ghana, Turkey, Senegal, Albania, Indonesia, Nepal, Philippines, Peru, Liberia, Bulgaria, Ukraine, and Malawi. These countries have recently undergone specific political changes or events that disrupted democratic norms and values, rendering them immature and unstable democracies. When we exclude these cases, a clear pattern emerges stable and mature democracies indeed contribute to happier societies. In essence, democracy remains one of the most crucial political determinants of happiness. However, there are five exceptional democratic countries—Botswana, India, Namibia, Georgia, and North Macedonia—that defy this claim. Despite the absence of recent adverse political change events, they grapple with unhappiness. This complexity underscores the multifaceted relationship between democracy and happiness.

From this perspective, particularly in unstable democratic countries, the focus should be on practices that strengthen the stability of their democratic regimes, ultimately contributing to greater happiness. In other words, these countries must establish secure functioning, stable democracies. Notably, stable democracy is closely associated with human development, cultural progress, and economic growth. Firstly, we need to delve into the human development theory of democracy. The interplay between human development, freedom, and democracy is crucial. As human development expands, so does the desire for freedom and awareness of its importance. This, in turn, exerts higher pressure to establish and preserve democratic norms and values. Researchers like Welzel and Inglehart (1999) have highlighted this mutual relationship. For unstable democratic countries, the initial focus should be on the human development process. This involves enhancing the quality of education at all stages and fostering a democratic culture. Thanks to these improvements, democratic regimes can create democratic elites and societies that maintain the stability of democracy.

Secondly, the relationship between democracy and economic growth is non-linear (Barro, 1999); however, it is argued that democracy is associated with economic growth mutually. For this reason, democratic countries can achieve rapid growth rates and thus strengthen their democracies, if they focus on increasing effective public investments, especially in tertiary education and technological infrastructure. Indeed, as the level of economic development of countries increases, their chances of sustainability of democracy also increase according to Lipset's Thesis (Wucherpfennig and Deutsch, 2009). It is about the strong linkage between the level of economic development and the process of modernization, including economic and political rights acquisitions. During the modernization process, industrialization, urbanization, and deepening education processes can be highly associated with democracy, considering that a high level of education is a sufficient condition for democracy (Lipset, 1959). On the other hand, as international economic relations between fully democratic countries and democratic countries increase, cultural and diplomatic relations may also increase. Later, as economic and cultural relations expand, democratic culture can become widespread in society. Therefore, democracies can turn into stable and mature democracies by ensuring economic, cultural and human development. Thus, in the long run, a higher level of happiness can be achieved with a lower happiness gap in unstable democracies. In summary, democratic countries should focus on their modernization and development process for a higher happiness level, and their priorities should be deepening education and democratic culture to cover all groups of society.

Finally, functionalism is one of the most important factors that cause instability in democracies along with state-led discrimination and bad neighbourhoods. Democratic countries should therefore avoid factionalism by creating formal and informal institutions that encourage political parties to seek support from various social groups to gain power (Goldstone and Ulfelder, 2004). In other words, formal and informal democratic institutions must be created to limit the dominance of certain elite groups. On the other hand, in establishing stable democracies, unifying domestic policies against disadvantaged groups, peaceful international policies especially against neighbours and liberal economic policies may be preferred.

References

Barro, R. J. (1999). Determinants of democracy. Journal of Political Economy 107(S6): 158–183.

Barro, R. J. (2001). Human capital and growth. The American Economic Review 91(2): 12–17.

Bellet, C. S., De Neve, J. E. and Ward, G. (2023). Does employee happiness have an impact on productivity? Management Science.

Berggren, N. and Bjornskov, C. (2020). Institutions and life satisfaction. In: K. L. Zimmerman (ed.) Handbook of Labor, Human Resources and Population Economics. Research Institute of Industrial Economics, pp. 1–48.

Clark, A. and Senik, C. (2011). Will GDP growth increase happiness in developing countries? IZA Institute of Labor Economics, Discussion Paper Series No. 5595.

DiMaria, C. H., Peroni, C. and Sarracino, F. (2020). Happiness matters Productivity gains from subjective well-being. Journal of Happiness Studies 21(1): 139–160.

Dorn, D., Fischer, J. A., Kirchgässner, G. and Sousa-Poza, A. (2007). Is it culture or democracy? The impact of democracy and culture on happiness. Social Indicators Research 82: 505–526.

Easterlin, R. A. (1974). Does economic growth improve humans' lot? Some empirical evidence. In Nations and households in economic growth. Nations and Households in Economic Growth (1974): 89–125.

Eckstein, H. (1961). A Theory of Stable Democracy. USA: Center of International Studies, Woodrow Wilson School of Public and International Affairs, Princeton University.

Etzioni-Halevy, E. (1990). Democratic-elite theory: Stabilization versus breakdown of democracy. European Journal of Sociology / Archives Européennes de Sociologie 31(2): 317–350.

Graafland, J. (2023). On Rule of Law, Civic Virtues, Trust, and Happiness. Applied Research in Quality of Life 18(4): 1–26.

Goldstone, J. A. and Ulfelder, J. (2004). How to construct stable democracies. The Washington Quarterly 28(1): 7–20.

Hagerty, M. R. and Veenhoven, R. (2003). Wealth and happiness revisited—growing national income does go with greater happiness. Social Indicators Research 64: 1–27.

Hanushek, E. A. (2013). Economic growth in developing countries: the role of human capital. Economics of Education Review 37(2013): 204–212.

Helliwell, J. F. (2006). Well-being, social capital and public policy: what's new? The Economic Journal 116(510): C34–C45.

Helliwell, J. F. and Huang, H. (2008). How's your government? International evidence linking good government and well-being. British Journal of Political Science 38(4): 595–619.

Helliwell, J. F., Huang, H., Norton, M., Goff, L. and Wang, S. (2023). World happiness, trust and social connections in times of crisis. World Happiness Report.

Inglehart, R., Foa, R., Peterson, C. and Welzel, C. (2008). Development. freedom, and rising happiness. Perspectives on Psychological Science 3(4): 264–85.

Inglehart, R. and Klingemann, H. D. (2000). Genes, culture, democracy, and happiness. In: E. Diener and E. M. Suh (eds) Culture and Subjective Well-being. The MIT Press, pp. 165–183.

Inglehart, R. F. and Ponarin, E. D. (2013). Happiness and democracy, 1972–2008. Journal of Siberian Federal University Humanities and Social Sciences 8(6): 1097–1106.

Inglehart, R. (2009). Democracy and happiness: What causes what? In: A. K. Dutt and B. Radcliff (eds) Happiness, Economics and Politics Towards a Multi-Disciplinary Approach. Edward Elgar Publishing, pp. 256–270.

Kanaujiya, K. S. and Maurya, N. K. (2022). Does development lead to happiness? IASSI-Quarterly 41(4): 498–515.

Kenny, C. (1999). Does growth cause happiness, or does happiness cause growth? Kyklos 52(1): 3–25.

Kundu, S., Kundu, R. and Chettri, K. B. (2024). Asymmetric effects of democracy and macroeconomic factors on happiness under high and low per capita incomes: A threshold panel analysis. Ecological Economics 216: 108030.

Lipset, S. M. (1959). Some social requisites of democracy: Economic development and political legitimacy. American Political Science Review 53(1): 69–105.

Liu, Y., Wang, L. and Ye, M. (2023). Public participation in democracy, local accountability and happiness: Evidence from rural China. Governance 36(4): 1225–1245.

Loubser, R. and Steenekamp, C. (2017). Democracy, well-being, and happiness: A 10-nation study. Journal of Public Affairs 17(1–2): e1646.

Marshall, M. G. and Jaggers, K. (2007). Polity IV Project: Political Regime Characteristics and Transitions, 1800–2006: Dataset Users' Manual. Centre for Systemic Peace.

Orviska, M., Caplanova, A. and Hudson, J. (2014). The impact of democracy on well-being. Social Indicators Research 115: 493–508.

Oswald, A. J., Proto, E. and Sgroi, D. (2015). Happiness and productivity. Journal of Labor Economics 33(4): 789–822.

Ott, J. C. (2010). Good governance and happiness in nations: Technical quality precedes democracy and quality beats size. Journal of Happiness Studies 11(3): 353–368.

Ott, J. C. (2011). Government and happiness in 130 nations: Good governance fosters higher levels and more equality of happiness. Social Indicators Research 102: 3–22.

Owen, A. L., Videras, J. and Willemsen, C. (2008). Democracy, participation, and life satisfaction. Social Science Quarterly 89(4): 987–1005.

Paleologou, S. M. (2022). Happiness, democracy and socio-economic conditions: Evidence from a difference GMM estimator. Journal of Behavioral and Experimental Economics 101(2022): 1–16.

Potts, J. C. (2016). Democracy and happiness: A true correlation. Journal of Arts and Humanities 5(3): 86–92.

Rode, M., Knoll, B. and Pitlik, H. (2013). Economic freedom, democracy, and life satisfaction. Economic freedom of the world: 2013 annual report. Vancouver: Economic Freedom Network.

Romer, P. M. (1990). Endogenous technological change. Journal of Political Economy 98(5): 71–102.

Schimmel, J. (2009). Development as happiness: The subjective perception of happiness and UNDP's analysis of poverty, wealth and development. Journal of Happiness Studies 10(1): 93–111.

Sharifzadeh, M. and Almaraz, J. (2014). Happiness and Productivity in the Workplace. American Journal of Management 14(4): 19–26.

Shin, D. C. (1980). Does rapid economic growth improve the human lot? Some empirical evidence. Social Indicators Research 8: 199–221.

Singh, S., Kshtriya, S. and Valk, R. (2023). Health, hope, and harmony: a systematic review of the determinants of happiness across cultures and countries. International Journal of Environmental Research and Public Health 20(4): 1–68.

Solow, R. M. (1956). A contribution to the theory of economic growth. The Quarterly Journal of Economics 70(1): 65–94.

Veenhoven, R. and Vergunst, F. (2014). The Easterlin illusion: Economic growth does go with greater happiness. International Journal of Happiness and Development 1(4): 311–343.

Welzel, C. and Inglehart, R. (1999). Analyzing democratic change and stability: A human development theory of democracy. WZB Discussion Paper, No. FS III 99–202.

Wucherpfennig, J. and Deutsch, F. (2009). Modernization and democracy: Theories and evidence Revisited. Living Reviews in Democracy (2009): 1–9.

Zagorski, K., Kelley, J. and Evans, M. D. (2010). Economic development and happiness: Evidence from 32 nations. Polish Sociological Review 169(1): 3–20. https://www.systemicpeace.org/polity/polity4x.htm, Access Date: 24.02.2024.

CHAPTER 9

Analysis of Economic and Political Policies Affecting the Happiness of Individuals: the Example of Turkey

Gökmen Kantar and Nermin Akarçay

The concept of happiness can be considered as an individual feeling good about oneself, and nurturing positive emotions when alone or in relationships with others. As a result of these emotions, the individual tends to approach the environment and events more optimistically and positively. There are numerous factors contributing to happiness, including personal characteristics, as well as variables such as one's surroundings, friends, family, socio-economic status, and the effects of the country and city one lives in. Additionally, economic and political policies implemented in a country have an impact on both its citizens and people residing in other countries. There is a considerable amount of literature on happiness, particularly in recent years, where it has become a subject of intense scientific interest. This study specifically explores the economic influences affecting happiness, focusing on individuals living in Turkey. Factors influencing happiness at the provincial level, such as the quantity of residences, medical facilities, healthcare professionals, and per capita GDP statistics, are employed. As per the findings from the conducted panel Granger causality analysis, significant causal relationships between variables influencing happiness and income have been identified. The importance of this research resides in its methodology., which differs from previous research on income and happiness. Instead of aggregating happiness data, this study creates panel data by separately considering happiness data for each province. Employing the econometric analysis method of Granger causality, the study determines the directions of causality between happiness variables and GDP.

1   Introduction

When defining the concepts of happiness or unhappiness, individuals may have different interpretations based on their existence and identities. The understanding of happiness varies among people, and throughout the existence of the world, millions of individuals have pondered on the precise definition of happiness. Philosophers, over approximately three thousand years, have failed to reach a consensus on what happiness truly is or the methods to attain it. As different concepts of happiness have become more comprehensible over time, some common ground has been reached (Rojas, 2007:5). Widely accepted theories have been developed, such as in economic theory, where achieving a higher income allows individuals to reach a higher indifference curve in consumption choices, ultimately increasing their level of satisfaction. The definition of utility in this context is individually related to the happiness or satisfaction level one feels.

Research findings concerning the correlation between happiness or utility levels and income often produce contradictory results. While it can be argued that people with higher revenue levels are happier than those with less revenue at a specific point in time, the same cannot be said when considering an entire country. The country's income situation may increase over time, but the level of happiness does not necessarily follow suit. The concept of time in this context is dependent on the comparison of average income and happiness levels of countries and is associated with economic growth (Paul and Daniel, 2013:900).

In 1974, Easterlin proposed a paradox in the United States, suggesting that, during a certain time frame, rich individuals were happier than poor individuals. However, this ceased to hold true after World War II, as despite significant increases in income, people's levels of happiness remained at a certain level (Easterlin, 1974:111–118). As individuals' income levels increase, they may find it easier to access the goods and services they desire, potentially increasing their level of happiness. However, as time progresses, and one's income continues to rise, and their habits shift towards luxury consumption, accessing the same services may not bring the same level of happiness. Therefore, a detailed and long-term examination of the relationship between happiness and income may be necessary.

2   Literature Review

In their research, Inkeles (1993) and Veenhoven (1991) contended that there is no straightforward correlation between income and happiness in affluent nations, while there exists a connection between income and happiness in less affluent nations. Di Tella et al. (2003) conducted a study for the European region between 1975 and 1992, focusing on macroeconomic variables, and concluded that GDP and changes in GDP affect the happiness levels of countries. Helliwell et al. (2010, 2017) found in their studies that variables such as per capita revenue, social effort, generosity, healthy life expectancy, and religious affiliation are significantly and positively related to happiness, while poverty-related variables have a significant and negative relationship. Stevenson and Wolfers (2013) found in their research that increases in individuals' and countries' absolute incomes are significantly related to increases in individuals' happiness levels, although the increase in happiness is slower than the increase in income. Wang et al. (2015) conducted research in China and found that regional happiness levels increased when the Gini coefficient was below a certain threshold (0.405), but beyond that point, as inequality increased, happiness levels decreased. Ngamaba et al. (2018) showed in their study that the relate from the Gini coefficient to happiness. That has a positive effect and holds in both developing to less developed countries. Ding et al. (2021) demonstrated in their research on China that income inequality is inversely U-shaped concerning individual well-being. Cuong (2021) surveyed elderly individuals aged 74–85 in Vietnam, concluding that there is a positive impact between money and happiness, especially when retirement pensions are considered as external income. Luo (2021) used a large national panel data set for Germany, revealing that high-income households have a higher quality of life and satisfaction in the long term. Jin and Honk (2022) suggest a negative relationship between income disparity and subjective welfare, particularly related to income, training, and age. They advocate for studies conducted on a spatial basis and country-specific research. Shvalye and Gunatilaka (2022) analysed the relationship between income disparity and happiness, finding that individual-centred income disparity is more effective in both countryside and urbanisation fields. Kundu et al. (2024) used data from 83 countries, suggesting that factors determining life satisfaction and well-being yield different results for high and low-income countries. They found that per capita income does not have a direct relationship with happiness but is effective when combined with other variables.

In studies conducted in Turkey, Köksal and Şahin (2015) utilized data from the life satisfaction research executed by the Turkish Statistical Institute in 2012, revealing that as individuals' perception levels of their situation increase relative to others' welfare levels, the influence of income on happiness decreases. Çirkin and Göksel (2016) investigated the impact of income on various levels of happiness and overall life satisfaction, discovering a notable association with life satisfaction but not with happiness. Menteş (2020) concluded in his study that income has a big impact on happiness but little impact on democracy. Öndeş (2019) emphasized in his research that income, social life, health, and active working conditions increase happiness, while population, individual security, and satisfaction with education decrease happiness levels.

3   Concept of Happiness

Since its existence, humanity has always strived to define, understand, and attain happiness. Happiness is defined as the level of satisfaction felt when it is achieved in conjunction with all desires, complete and continuous. Arıcı (2020:219) describes happiness as the fulfillment of dreams, and ideals, and the satisfaction of the soul and consciousness related to the world and the afterlife, within the framework of religious beliefs. Happiness is the highest motivating factor for humans (Kangal, 2013:44). In this century, happiness has been extensively studied psychometrically by various researchers, comparing it with different dimensions. The "subjective well-being" scale, which evaluates an individual's overall satisfaction with life using five items, is among the most commonly utilized measures globally for assessing happiness. (Tekke, 2020:164–165). High levels of subjective well-being not only benefit individuals but also contribute to the overall well-being of society. Personal who have high subjective well-being make too much effort to engage in activities beneficial to society than those who sometimes seem irresponsible and act selfishly in their pursuit of happiness for their interests. People with high subjective well-being strive to be more useful to society than others (Tov and Diener, 2008).

Another observation related to subjective well-being is that women are predisposed to notify higher phases of happiness than men, which can be described by either women having no fewer life expectations than men or the genetic capacity of women to feel happiness being stronger. However, women also tend to express their unhappiness more than men (Maseide, 2021:7). One of humanity's main goals throughout history has been to lead a better and happier life. In this process, there have been reflections and research on how individuals can be happier over time, aiming to make people happy both individually and publicly and increase contentment in life. The concepts of happiness and life contentment are holistic concepts formed by the influence of many factors. While life satisfaction is defined as sustaining a beautiful and satisfying life with all factors related to life, including economic conditions, security, family ties, friendships, social relationships, health, and many others, happiness is expressed as a state of joy and well-being. Therefore, life contentment and happiness are intertwined concepts embedded in many factors.

Individuals have contemplated how to achieve a healthier life, live more quali-tatively, preserve physical health by exercising, work in jobs where they can earn higher incomes through better education, improve their situations, and increase their quality of life.

In modern times, countries and states have made it an important goal to ensure that people lead satisfied and happy lives following the basic prin-ciples of their constitutions. While the traditional perspective measured the well-being levels of societies by per capita income, nowadays, life satisfaction and happiness have taken over, and public policies in economics, finance, and economic policies have evolved to make people happy and increase their life satisfaction. Many studies and research have been conducted for social wel-fare, happiness, and life satisfaction. One of the prominent ones is the life contentment survey and statistics executed by the Turkish Statistical Institute since 2003 (Akman, 2021:39–40). Although studies on happiness date back to ancient times, it is observed that there has been an increased focus on this subject in recent times.

The intensified research in recent years is attributed to the significant con-tribution of economists to the field, leading to a substantial increase in studies related to happiness (Veenhoven and Dumludağ, 2015:46–51). The concept of happiness has become more crucial in recent years globally and in our country. The studies conducted in this field serve as guiding principles for individuals. In this context, identifying the factors that influence happiness and improving them has become a necessity for people to live a more prosperous life.

3.1   *Life Satisfaction*

In the studies conducted on life satisfaction, research on happiness in the 21st century has gained significant value. Happiness, when examined on a country-by-country basis, has been accepted as a measure of development and well-being. Governments, in shaping public policies, have utilized statistics and data in this field, leading to the establishment of units both nationally and internationally to maintain healthier statistics (Gül, 2017: 21). In contemporary economies, indexes that can replace GDP and measure more dimensions are being reconsidered. The well-being index, one of these, aims to measure indi-viduals' levels of well-being with eleven fundamental components, including health, income, and education indicators, as well as family life, social envi-ronment, and similar factors. The social development index, which focuses on individual development, aims to provide conditions for individuals to rec-ognize their abilities by addressing the needs of individuals in a country and improving their quality of life. Calculating the degree of happiness in societies

involves calculating mortality rates, and additionally, happiness and satisfaction statistics are used to determine individuals' happiness levels (Özdemir,
2019:6601–6602).

Major scales used in measuring happiness include the Cantril Ladder,
World Values Survey, Oxford Happiness Inventory, Eurobarometer Survey,
Life Satisfaction Scale, and Social Survey, all of which are widely used globally
(Aydın, 2020:140). World happiness reports related to this issue are published,
such as the OECD's Better Life Index, which, beyond gross domestic product
and economic data, includes concrete living circumstances and the quality of
life of individuals based on eleven key topics determined by the OECD, including housing data related to place, income statistics, information about profes-
sions, social issues, education year and quality, environmental information,
participation in civil organizations, health, an essential aspect of life, safety,
individuals' satisfaction rates, and work-life and life balance. It is an index
that allows for comparisons between countries (OECD, www.oecdbetterlifein
dex.org). Another report is the World Happiness Report, which measures a
nation's level of happiness by asking a group how happy they are and conducting research, publishing reports on 137 countries (World Happiness Report,
2023, worldhappiness.report).

The Happy Planet Index is a calculation that includes 16 countries ranking high in happiness in various regions of the world (Çevik et al., 2019:189).
For Turkey, the Turkish Statistical Institute (TUİK) addresses factors such as
health, love, success, money, and work as sources of happiness in its annual
life satisfaction statistics (TUİK, 2021:9). Various happiness data are collected
annually, and in some cases, monthly and quarterly periods. Instant data can
also be collected through surveys conducted in provinces and regions, and
these are frequently used in scientific research. The lack of data from certain
countries creates difficulties in conducting analyses and research.

3.2   *Income and Happiness Relationship*

The connectivity between income and happiness has been studied by scientists for decades, and their findings suggest that money does buy happiness,
but it buys less than most people think (Dunn et al., 2011:1). While happiness
used to be a primary focus for psychologists in the past, it has recently cap-
tured the interest of economics, leading to significant interdisciplinary studies between psychology and economics. One of the pioneers in these studies
is Easterlin, whose work dates back to 1974. Economists, following this study
since the 1990s, have conducted research on happiness, examining countries in
different geographies at different times (Frey and Stutzer, 2002: 404). Graham

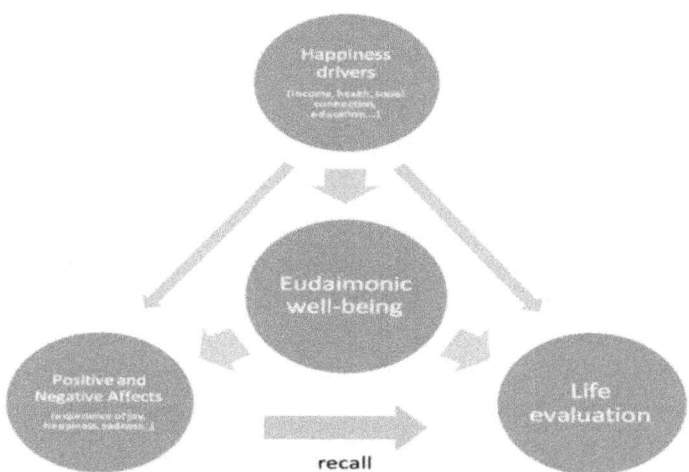

FIGURE 9.1   Determinants of happiness in Japan and the Netherlands:
macro and micro analysis and comparison
SOURCE: TAKAHASHI ET AL., 2018

and Chattopadhyay (2013) investigate demographic and socioeconomic variables, analyzing variations in well-being across genders. They have found that
women in different parts of the world are generally happy, and there is a significant difference between those aged 25 aged and over, educated individuals,
and most of them living in cities. Married women were found to be happier
than married men. Also being married is seen to contribute to happiness as it
provides love, gratitude, and higher household income, suggesting that mar-
riage has a positive impact on human well-being (Graham and Chattopadhyay,
2013: 212–232). Many researchers hold the view that as household income
increases, people's life satisfaction should also increase. This is because with
an increase in income, it becomes possible to live in better housing, access better healthcare, and achieve a higher standard of living. Additionally, income
provides individuals with opportunities to fulfill desires and wishes, leading
to greater satisfaction (Cheung and Lucas, 2015:120–135). In their 2018 study
using micro and macro data in Japan, Takahashi and others developed a discourse on the determinants of happiness. According to them, there is a four-
fold cycle that includes the fundamental concepts of happiness (Takahashi
et al., 2018:124–150).

According to the cyclical model presented in Figure 9.1, three fundamental concepts of happiness are identified. The individual's state of well-being
emerges from various situations related to happiness throughout the life cycle,

considering both positive and negative behaviors. These situations are represented by variables significant in one's life, such as income, health, socialization, and education.

4   Methodology

The analysis utilized annual data for the 81 provinces of Turkey from 2013 to
2021. Per capita gross domestic product (GDPPC), the number of hospitals
(NH), the count of healthcare personnel (HP), and the number of residences
(NR) are abbreviated as key variables. The data was acquired from the official
website of the Turkish Statistical Institute. The panel regression model for the
established equation (9.1) is presented below.

$$GDDPCit = \beta_0 i + \beta_1 NHit + \beta_2 + HPit + \beta_3 NRit + uit \tag{9.1}$$

In Table 9.1, abbreviations, units, data transformations, and database information for per capita GDP, the number of hospitals, healthcare personnel, and
residences for Turkey's 81 provinces during the examined period are presented.
The table includes raw forms of the variables, and in econometric analyses, the
logarithmic forms of all variables were used to obtain full elasticity models.

In Table 9.2, descriptive statistics for the variables, including mean, standard deviation, minimum, and maximum values, are presented. The abbreviations represent per capita GDP (GDPPC, the number of hospitals (NH),
healthcare personnel (HP), and residences (NR). During the specified period,
the minimum value for per capita GDP was approximately 19,368 TRY, and the
maximum value was 153,170 TRY. The minimum number of hospitals recorded

TABLE 9.1   Abbreviations, units, and database information

Variables	Abbreviations	Unit	Data transformation	Database
Gross Domestic Product Per Capita	GDPPC	Turkish Lira, Thousand TL	Logarithmic	TSI
Number of Hospitals	NH	Unit, Building	Logarithmic	TSI
Healthcare Personnel	HP	Number of Personnel	Logarithmic	TSI
Number of Residence	NR	Unit, Housing	Logarithmic	TSI

TABLE 9.2   Descriptive statistics

Variables	Observation	Mean	Median	St. deviation	Minimum value	Maximum value
GDPPC	729	33,610.43	28,381.75	19,367.63	7,603.242	153,169.8
NH	729	19.09722	12	27.60836	1	238
HP	729	1907.156	770	4215.488	111	42268
NR	729	16768.41	6861	32568.1	124	276223

Note: *, ** and *** respectively indicate significance levels of 0.10, 0.05 and 0.01

TABLE 9.3   Correlation analysis

Variables	Correlation coefficients	Probability
LGDPPC	1	
LNH	0.2633***	0.0000
LHP	0.3141***	0.0000
LNR	0.4131***	0.0000

during this period was 1, while the maximum was 238. The minimum number of healthcare personnel was 111, and the maximum was 42,268 individuals. The number of residences ranged from a minimum of 124 to a maximum of 276,223.

In Table 9.3, correlation coefficients between the explanatory variables examined within the scope of the research and the dependent variable are presented. A statistically notable positive correlation exists between per capita GDP (GDPPC) and the quantity of hospitals, healthcare personnel, and residences. Per capita GDP demonstrates correlation coefficients of approximately 0.26, 0.31, and 0.41 with the number of hospitals, healthcare personnel, and residences, respectively. Consequently, it is understood that the log-transformed per capita GDP variable (LGDPPC) has a positive relationship with log-transformed variables LNH, LHP, and LNR, and expectations in the regression model align with these directions.

Panel regression models that consider all effects not observable over time and units are referred to as two-way error component models, while structures that only consider the unit or time dimension are one-way error component models (Balestra and Nerlove 1966, Baltagi 2008; Özer and Çiftçi 2009). Generally, if the sample (country, individual, etc.) is randomly drawn from a

TABLE 9.4   Results of F test for unobservable effects

Testing for unit and time effects	F statistics	Probability	Conclusion
	642.05***	0.0000	Ho is rejected. Unit, time or there are both unit and time effects.
Test for unit effects	F Statistics	Probability	Conclusion
	249.41***	0.0000	Ho is rejected. There are unit effects.
Test of time effects	F	Probability	Conclusion
	1088.82***	0.0000	Ho is rejected. There are time effects.

Note: *, ** and *** respectively indicate significance levels of 0.10, 0.05 and 0.01

large population, there are random effects; if the drawing is done considering specific characteristics, there are fixed effects (Baltagi 2008). For instance, it can be a group of G8 countries or a region, province, etc., and in this case, the inference is limited to the observed N countries, and regions. Thus, it can be said that the behaviour of the examined group is restricted to this. Then, a choice can be made using the fixed effects model (Baltagi 2008; Tatoğlu 2018). However, to determine whether this fixed effects model is one-way or two-way, an F-test, which can be used instead of a Chow test, can be used (Baltagi 2008). Moreover, this test can be used like an ANOVA F-test, as recommended by Moulton and Randolph (1989) (Baltagi 2008, Baltagi et al. 1992, Baltagi and Chang 1996). Table 9.4 presents the results of the F-test to identify whether there are unit, time, or unit and-time effects that are not observable.

Table 9.4 displays the outcomes of the F-test implemented to examine the presence of unit and time effects within the fixed effects model. Upon examining the F-test statistics, the null hypothesis stating the absence of unit and time effects is rejected. At this stage, evidence is found suggesting the presence of unit effects, time effects, or both unit and time effects together. For a more detailed investigation, unit and time effects are individually tested. It can be observed that the null hypotheses stating the absence of only unit effects and the absence of only time effects are rejected. Therefore, it is understood that both unit and time effects coexist.

Table 9.5 presents the findings obtained from the Hausman test. In the fundamental hypothesis of the Hausman test, it is stated that the difference between the coefficients is not systematic. Upon examining the chi-square ($\chi 2$) statistic, it is observed that the fundamental hypothesis is rejected. In this

TABLE 9.5   Results of the Hausman test

χ2 statistics	Probability
975.86***	0.0000

Note: *, ** and *** respectively indicate significance levels of 0.10, 0.05 and 0.01

TABLE 9.6   Prediction results of the two-way fixed effects model (Driscoll-Kraay estimator)

Dependent variable: LGDPPC

Independent variable	Coefficient	Driscoll-Kraay resistant st. errors	t statistics	Probability
LNR	0.3333	0.0902	3.69	0.0050
LHP	2.5979	0.2546	10.2	0.0000
LNH	0.0277	0.0679	0.41	0.6930
Constant	−10.4351	1.5094	−6.91	0.0000

Model information

F İst.	76.72***
Probability (F St.)	0.0000

Diagnostic tests in basic fixed effects model

Different Variance Test	Statistics	Probability
Wo	2.0620***	0.0000

Horizontal Cross-Section Dependence Test	Statistics	Probability
Pesaran CD Test	145.804***	0.0000

Autocorrelation Test	Statistics
Mod. Bhargava vd. Test	0.7966
Baltagi-Wu Test	1.2661

Note: *, ** and *** respectively indicate significance levels of 0.10, 0.05 and 0.01
ii. Due to different variance, autocorrelation, and cross-sectional dependence problems, the Driscoll-Kraay (1998) estimator, which can derive robust standard errors in their presence, was used

case, it can be stated that the random effects estimator is inconsistent, and the fixed effects estimator is not effective (Arı and Zeren, 2011).

According to the findings presented in Table 9.6:

- The chi-square statistic indicates the overall statistical significance of the estimated regression model. In this context, within the specified period, the LNR and LHP variables have a statistically significant effect on the LGDPPC variable.
- A 1% increase in housing numbers brings about a 0.33% increase in per capita gross domestic product values.
- A 1% increase in personnel numbers in Turkey results in a 2.60% increase in per capita gross domestic product values. Therefore, an increase in personnel numbers has a more significant impact than itself.
- Although a positively aligned coefficient estimate was made for the LNH variable indicating hospital numbers, its statistical significance is not confirmed.

TABLE 9.7   Panel Granger causality analysis results

Direction of causality	F statistics	Probability	Conclusion
LHS LGSYH	12.0219***	0.0006	*The main hypothesis is rejected.* From LNY to LGDPPC there is a causality relationship.
LGSYH LHS	2.7219*	0.0995	*The main hypothesis is rejected.* LGDPPC to LNH there is a causality relationship.

Direction of Causality	F Statistics	Probability	Conclusion
LKS LGSYH	23.7538***	0.0000	*The main hypothesis is rejected.* From LNR to LGDPPC there is a causality relationship.
LGSYH LKS	5.6965***	0.0173**	*The main hypothesis is rejected.* From LGDPPC to LNR there is a causality relationship.

TABLE 9.7 Panel Granger causality analysis results (*cont.*)

Direction of Causality	F Statistics	Probability	Conclusion
LPS LGSYH	8.9777***	0.0028	*The main hypothesis is rejected.* LHP to LGDPPC there is a causality relationship.
LGSYH LPS	0.3999	0.5274	*The main hypothesis is rejected.* LGDPPC to LHP there is a causality relationship.

Note: i., *, and *** represent significance levels of 0.10, 0.05, and 0.01, respectively. ii. The default lag length is set to "1"

Table 9.7 presents the results of the panel Granger causality test. The fundamental hypothesis in the test asserts that the excluded variable is not the cause of the dependent variable. The results obtained are as follows:

- The fundamental hypothesis stating that there is no causality relationship from LNH to LGDPPC is rejected. Therefore, there is a causality relationship from LNH to LGDPPC.
- The fundamental hypothesis stating that there is no causality relationship from LGDPPC to LNH is rejected. Thus, it is understood that there is a bidirectional causality relationship between LGDPPC and LNH.
- The fundamental hypothesis stating that there is no causality relationship from LNR to LGDPPC is rejected. Similarly, there is a causality relationship from LGDPPC to LNR. This indicates a bidirectional causal relationship between LGDPPC and LNR.
- The fundamental hypothesis stating that there is no causality relationship from LHP to LGDPPC is rejected. On the other hand, the fundamental hypothesis stating that there is no causality relationship from LGDPPC to LHP cannot be rejected. Thus, it is understood that there is a unidirectional information flow from LHP to LGDPPC.

Moreover, the findings confirm the design of the regression model introduced in Equation (9.1) in terms of the direction of information flow.

5 Conclusion

The concept of happiness is influenced by various factors, not only the psychological and emotional state of individuals. Therefore, definitions of happiness are associated with one's subjective well-being, characterized by a more stable and long-term emotional state, distinct from the instantaneous emotional reactions of individuals. How an individual defines or feels about their well-being is related to how they have experienced various stages of life and how much individual and societal satisfaction they have achieved. In many decisions made by states, whether political or public, the reactions and happiness levels of citizens play a significant role. This is because these reactions are formed by considering different aspects of people's lives, consisting of satisfactions experienced at every moment or, conversely, unfulfilled desires and wishes we refer to as unhappiness. Additionally, these can change for such as age, gender, or income status.

According to the results obtained in this study regarding the health-related variables affecting individuals' happiness, a causality link has been found between variables such as the number of hospitals, healthcare personnel, and housing units in a province and the share of individuals from the gross national income. Thus, there is a bidirectional causality between the number of hospitals and income; the number of hospitals affects income, and incomes also influence the number of hospitals. On the other hand, there is a bidirectional causality relationship between the number of housing units and income; the number of housing units affects the income, and incomes also have an impact on the number of housing units. Finally, it has been concluded that the number of healthcare personnel has an effect on income, but incomes do not affect the number of healthcare personnel.

This research conducted for Turkey not only helps measure the impact of variables related to happiness on the country's income but also assists in measuring how income affects variables related to happiness in the same way. With the collection of data for Turkey over more extended periods, the study can be expanded to conduct a time-series analysis and examine the results. Additionally, it is recommended to develop existing policies and plan new policies by the government to ensure that citizens lead happier and more prosperous lives by considering variables related to their happiness.

References

Akman, S. Ü. (2021). Mutluluk ve Yaşam Memnuniyetinin Belirleyicileri: Türkiye İstatistik Kurumu Yaşam Memnuniyeti Araştırması Üzerine Analizler. *İstanbul Üniversitesi Sosyal Siyaset Konferansları Dergisi.* 81, 35–69.

Arıcı, H. Y. (2020). Mutluluk Tarihi. Türkiye Din Eğitimi Araştırmaları Dergisi, 9, 217–243.

Arı, A. ve Zeren, F. (2011). CO_2 Emisyonu ve Ekonomik Büyüme: Panel Veri Analizi, Yönetim ve Ekonomi Dergisi. 18 (2), 37–47.

Aydın, H. İ. (2020). Mutluluk ve Ekonomi: Yaşam Memnuniyeti Araştırması Üzerinden Bazı Dikkatler. *Current Research in Social Sciences*.6(2), 135–148.

Balestra, P. and Nerlove, M. (1966). Pooling Cross Section and Time Series Data In The Estimation of a Dynamic Model: The Demand for Natural Gas. *Econometrica: Journal of The Econometric Society*, 585–612.

Baltagi, B. H. (2008). Econometric Analysis of Panel Data. (4). Chichester: Wiley.

Baltagi, B. H. and Chang, Y. J. (1996). Testing for Random Individual Effects Using Recursive Residuals. *Econometric Reviews*, *15*(3), 331–338.

Baltagi, B. H., Chang, Y. J. and Li, Q. (1992). Monte Carlo Results on Several New and Existing Tests For the Error Component Model. *Journal of Econometrics*, *54*(1–3), 95–120.

Çevik, N. K., Altınkeski, B. K. and Kantarcı, T. (2019). Mutlu Gezegen Endeksi: Dünyanın En Mutlu Ülkelerinden Panel Veri Bulguları. *Iğdır Üniversitesi Sos Bil Dergisi* Ek Sayı, 181–201.

Cheung, F. and Lucas, R. E. (2015). When Does Money Matter Most? Examining the Association Between Income and Life Satisfaction Over the Life Course. *Psychology and Aging*, 30(1): 120–135.

Cuong, N. V. (2021). Does Money Bring Happiness? Evidence from an Income Shock for Older People. *Finance Research Letters*. (39), 101605.

Çirkin, Z. and Göksel, T. (2016). Mutluluk ve Gelir, *Ankara Üniversitesi SBF Dergisi*, 71(2): 375–400.

Ding, J., Salinas-Jimenez, J. and Salinas-Jimenez, M. (2021). The Impact of Income Inequality on Subjective Well-Being: The Case Of China. *Journal of Happiness Studies*, 22 (2): 845–866.

Dunn, E. W., Gilbert, D. T. and Wilson, T. D. (2011). If Money Doesn't Make You Happy, Then You Probably Aren't Spending İt Right. *Journal of Consumer Psychology*. 21(2), 115–125.

Dünya Mutluluk Raporu (2023). Https://worldhappiness.report/.

Easterlin, R. (1974). Does Economic Growth Improve The Human Lot? Some Empirical Evidence, Nations And Households İn Economic Growth: Essays İn The Honor Of Moses Abramovitz, Academic Press, New York, 89–125.

Easterlin, R. and Angelescu, L. (2009). Dünya Çapında Mutluluk ve Büyüme: Mutluluk-Gelir Paradoksuna İlişkin Zaman Serisi Kanıtları, *IZA Discussion Paper*, (460), 89–125.

Frey, B. S. ve Stutzer, A. (2002). What can the Economist Learn from Happiness Research? *Journal of Economic Literature*, 40 (2): 402–435.

Graham, C., Chattopadhyay, S. (2013). Gender And Well-Being Around The World. *International Journal of Happiness and Development*. 1(2): 212–232.

Gül, S. (2017). Mutluluk Ekonomisi ve Göç Üzerine Bir İnceleme. *Yayımlanmamış Doktora Tezi, Marmara Üniversitesi: Sosyal Bilimler Enstitüsü*, İstanbul.

Helliwell, J. F., Barrington-Leigh, C. P., Harris, A. and Huang, H. (2010). International Evidence On The Social Context Of Well-Being. In: E. Diener, E. Helliwell, J. F. Kahneman, D. (eds.), *International Differences İn Well-Being* (Oxford: Oxford University Press, 291–327.

Helliwell, J. F. Huang, H. and Wang, S. (2017). The Social Foundations of World Happiness, In: J. F. Helliwell, J. F. Layard, R. Sachs, J. (eds.) *World Happiness Report*. New York: Sustainable Development Solution Network. 8–46.

Inkeles A. (1993). Industrialization, Modernization and The Quality of Life. *International Journal of Comparative Sociology*. (34), 1–23.

Jin, J. Hong, S. Y. (2022). Does Income Inequality Affect Individual Happiness? Evidence From Seoul, Korea. *Cities*. (131), 104047.

Kangal, A. (2013) Electronic Journal of Social Sciences. Mutluluk Üzerine Kavramsal Bir Değerlendirme ve Türk Hanehalkı İçin Bazı Sonuçlar, *Elektronik Sosyal Bilimler Dergisi*, 12 (44).

Knight, J. and Gunatilaka, R. (2022). Income Inequality and Happiness: Which Inequalities Matter in China? *China Economic Review*. (72): 101765.

Köksal, O. and Şahin, F. (2015). Gelir ve Mutluluk: Gelir Karşılaştırmasının Etkisi. *Sosyoekonomi Dergisi*. 23(26), 45–60.

Kundu, S., Kundu, R. and Chettri, K. B. (2024) Asymmetric Effects Of Democracy And Macroeconomic Factors On Happiness Under High And Low Per Capita İncomes: A Threshold Panel Analysis. *Ecological Economics*. (216): 108030.

Luo, J. (2021). Happiness Adaptation To High Income: Evidence From German Panel Data, *Economics Letters*, (206), 109995.

Maseide, H. (2021). Income and Happiness. Does the relationship vary with age? *Umea University*, Master Thesis, 1–47.

Menteş, N. (2020). Mutluluk, Gelir ve Demokrasi: Dünya Ülkeleri İçin Yapısal Eşitlik Modeli Önerisi. *İnsan ve Toplum Bilimleri Araştırma Dergisi*. 9(3), 2138–2153.

Ngamaba, K. Panagioti, M. Armitage, C. (2018). Income Inequality and Subjective Well-Being: A systematic Review and Meta-Analysis, *Social Indicators Research: An International and Interdisciplinary Journal for Quality-of-Life Measurement*. 27 (3), 577–596.

OECD (2024). https://www.oecdbetterlifeindex.org/#/11111111111.

Öndeş, H. (2019). Türkiye'de Mutluluk Düzeyini Etkileyen Faktörler: Mekânsal Ekonometri Analizi. *Dokuz Eylül Üniversitesi Sosyal Bilimler Enstitüsü Dergisi*. 21(4), 1039–1064.

Özdemir, Ö. A. (2019). Mutluluk Kavramı ve İktisatta Mutluluk Üzerine Bir İnceleme. *İnternational Social Sciences Studies Journal*, 5(50), 6598–6608.

Özer, M. and Çiftçi, N. (2009). AR-GE Tabanlı İçsel Büyüme Modelleri ve AR-GE Harcamalarının Ekonomik Büyüme Üzerine Etkisi: OECD Ülkeleri Panel Veri Analizi. *Sosyal Ekonomik Araştırmalar Dergisi, 8*(16), 219–240.

Paul, S. and Guilbert, D. (2013). Income–Happiness Paradox İn Australia: Testing The Theories of Adaptation and Social Comparison, *Economic Modelling,* (30), 900–910.

Pavot, W. and Diener, E. (2008). The Satisfaction with Life Scale and The Emerging Construct of Life Satisfaction. *Journal of Positive Psychology,* 3(2), 137–152.

Rojas, M. (2007). Heterogeneity İn The Relationship Between İncome And Happiness: A Conceptual-Referent-Theory Explanation. *Journal of Economic Psychology.* 28(1), 1–14.

Takahashi, Y., Fukushima, S. and Hagiwara, R. (2018). Determinants of Happiness in Japan and the Netherlands: Macro and Micro Analysis and Comparison, *Asia Pacific Review.* 25(1), 124–150.

Tatoğlu, F. Y. (2018). *İleri Panel Veri Analizi: Stata Uygulamalı.* Beta Yayınevi.

Tekke, M. (2020). *Mutluluk.* In book: Etik ve Değerler, https://www.researchgate.net /publication/360157323_Mutluluk.

Tella R. D., MacCulloch R. J., and Oswald A. J. (2001). Preferences over inflation and unemployment: Evidence From Surveys Of Happiness. *American Economic Review.* (91), 335–341.

TUİK, (2021). Yaşam Memnuniyeti Araştırması Raporu, https://data.tuik.gov.tr/Kate gori/GetKategori?p=Gelir,-Yasam,-Tuketim-ve-Yoksulluk-107.

Stevenson B., Wolfers J. (2013). Subjective Well-Being And İncome: Is There Any Evidence Of Satiation? *American Economic Review.* (103), 98–604.

Veenhoven R. (1991). Is Happiness Relative? *Social Indicators Research.* (24), 1–34.

Veenhoven, R. and Dumludağ, D. (2015). İktisat ve Mutluluk. *İktisat ve Toplum Dergisi,* 58, 46–51.

Wang, P. P. and Luo, Z. J. (2018). The Impact of Income Inequality on Individual Happiness: Evidence From China. *Social Indicators Research.* 121 (2), 413–435.

CHAPTER 10

The Quest for International Peace and Security: Is a Happier World Possible through the UN System?

Arif Bağbaşlıoğlu

This study analyzes the importance of international organization and international cooperation in the pursuit of global happiness by focusing on the activities of the UN, the most important institution in this context. The UN's achievements are incomparable to other international organizations within the system of sovereign states. However, the UN Security Council, which is responsible for realizing the UN's main purpose, does not function properly for several reasons, thereby limiting the UN's effectiveness. The main purpose of this study is to review the debates on how to make an international cooperation platform such as the UN, which is critical in the quest for global happiness, more effective.

1 Introduction

Happiness is shifting from being perceived as a purely individual state to an issue that is more related to the global context. This is because the biggest current threat to experiencing happiness, whether individually or societally, is the risks brought about by the globalizing world. Several transboundary problems now hinder people's pursuit of happiness, such as the ecological crisis from climate change, the potential for epidemics to rapidly turn into pandemics, and the pressures and consequences of regional conflicts and wars on the world economy. In today's world of globalized risks and threats, international organizations have an increasing role in establishing and protecting happiness.

The content and intensity of international risks and threats are closely related to changes in the international conjuncture because changes in threat perceptions affect the behaviour patterns of international actors, especially international organizations. Hence, international organizations are in a key position to analyze the understanding of security, which directly reflects the changing agenda and problems of international relations. The United Nations (UN) was established to achieve global happiness and maintain international peace and security.

Shortly after the turn of the millennium, a call emerged from both states and international institutions to use wider measures of well-being, also called happiness, quality-of-life, or beyond GDP indicators, in place of or in addition to gross domestic product. Accordingly, in 2011, the UN General Assembly (2011) adopted Resolution 65/309, "Happiness: towards a holistic approach to development", calling on nations to declare happiness as a fundamental human goal. Since 2013, the UN has celebrated the International Day of Happiness every year on March 20. The UN uses this day to ask that happiness and well-being be included in member states' national plans and public policy objectives (United Nations Regional Information Centre for Western Europe, 2023). In 2015, the UN also launched its 17 Sustainable Development Goals, which seek to end poverty, reduce inequality, and protect the planet. These UN efforts are all significant steps towards achieving global well-being and happiness.

The UN has played a very important role regarding the evolution of a network of specialized international organizations based on the principles of ensuring collective security, peaceful settlement of disputes, and the prohibition of the use of force. Specialized agencies operating within the UN system operate in many areas, from health to communications, from transportation to working life, intending to ensure international peace and security. Through these relatively autonomous specialized agencies, the UN has established international cooperation in many different fields, such as military, political, social, cultural, economic, health, and energy.

The present study analyzes the importance of international organizations and international cooperation in the pursuit of global happiness. To do so, it focuses on the activities of the UN, which is the most important institution in this context. The UN's achievements are incomparable to any other international organization within the system of sovereign states. However, its operations have been hindered by the dysfunctionality of veto powers in the UN Security Council, which is responsible for realizing the UN's main purposes. Thus, the main purpose of the study is to review the debates on how to make international cooperation platforms like the UN more effective, given its regulatory role among states, which is crucial in the quest for global happiness.

2   Globalizing Risks, Happiness and International Organizations

International institutionalization and modernity, which have radically transformed human experiences regarding ways of life and production, have also
affected perceptions of happiness. In contrast to the comparatively static
and closed structures of pre-modern societies, the modern world, which is
dominated by speed and constant change, has destroyed or transformed the
institutions in which people feel safe. Traditional state structures, modes of
production, and worldviews have been replaced by modern nation-states,
industrialization, and capitalism, and a new perspective dominated by secu-
larism and rationality.

Modernity has radically changed human life. In pre-modern societies, both
average human life expectancy and population growth were quite low. The
rapid increase in world population since the 1600s is associated with improvements in welfare due to the Industrial Revolution and reductions in death
rates due to medical advances, especially vaccines (Davis, 2004: 263–277).
According to UN data, the average global lifespan increased from around 47
years in the 1950s to over 70 in the 2000s and is expected to increase further
(UN Department of Economic and Social Affairs Population Division, 2022).
Furthermore, improvements in meeting basic human needs like security,
health, and nutrition are expected to increase people's quality of life and therefore their expectations of happiness.

However, modernity has not brought permanent happiness to human life.
Drawing attention to two different dimensions of modernity, namely the
"opportunity side" and the "dark side", Giddens evaluates the destructive environmental damage from the development of the forces of production in combination with political power, as exemplified by totalitarianism, as two instances
of the dark side of modernity (Giddens, 1991:7–8). Modern society's promise
to produce more and create more prosperous living conditions has resulted in
various risks and threats. Drawing attention to a change in the socio-historical
meaning attributed to the concept of risk, Beck distinguishes between "personal" risks in the past and current global risks that threaten all humanity, such
as nuclear fission or the storage of radioactive waste (Beck, 1992:21).

These risks, which are the biggest threats to human happiness in the modern
world, do not seem preventable by individuals or a single state power. Instead,
given globalized risks and happiness, international organizations now seem
even more important for dealing with advanced technologies, pollution caused
by overproduction and consumption, global warming, and the risk of total war,
including nuclear threats. Within this context, the international organization

with the greatest potential appears to be the UN, through its inclusiveness, areas of expertise and globally accepted legitimacy and capabilities.

3   The UN System

The UN, which was established to maintain international peace and security, has played a critical role in the evolution of international institutionalization through its network of specialized agencies. The UN emerged as a continuation of the alliance established against the Axis Powers during the Second World War. Like the League of Nations (LoN), the UN is a universal organization established by the states that won the war. The UN's main objectives, stated in the UN Charter, are to maintain international peace and security, protect human rights, provide humanitarian aid, and promote international law. Accordingly, the charter lists four interconnected pillars that can only be fully achieved by addressing all together: peace and security, human rights, the rule of law, and development.

The UN system, established through the UN and its affiliated specialized agencies, provides the basic building blocks of today's international system, although it is subject to criticism and debate. The most important reason is that almost all the world's states (193) are UN members, giving it a unique level of representation and legitimacy (Denk, 2015:128). Hence, the UN's establishment and development has been an important development in the history of international organization and international institutionalization. The UN can be considered as reflecting a balance between the idealism of change that the LoN aimed at and conservative realism that was strengthened by conditions during the Second World War (Rüma, 2014:383). Similarly, Bennet and Oliver (2015:71) liken the UN to a new car model with different lines but the same engine. That is, the UN is a revised version of the LoN, with similarities to the LoN, mainly its differences. In particular, the UN Treaty, which was clearly influenced by the USA's diplomatic approach, is more detailed than the LoN Pact was.

The UN's six principal organs are the General Assembly, Security Council, Economic and Social Council, Trusteeship Council, International Court of Justice, and Secretariat. Their powers and interrelations are regulated by the 19 chapters and 111 articles of the UN Charter. Many specialized organizations work under the UN to address various problems, particularly the United Nations Children's Fund, the United Nations Educational, Scientific, and Cultural Organization, the International Labor Organization, the World

Health Organization, and the World Bank. The specialized agencies operating within the UN system operate in many areas, from health to communications, from transportation to working life, to ensure international peace and security. Through its relatively autonomous specialized agencies, the UN has established international cooperation in many different fields, such as military, political, social, cultural, economic, health and energy.

The UN Charter also represents a turning point regarding the rules governing the use of force. Taking into account the unsuccessful LoN experience, the drafters of this text designed a collective security system under the control of the Security Council to ensure the compliance of UN members with the other issues specified in the charter (Vark, 2003:28). The UN's basic rules regarding the use of force, include three complementary security systems within the UN Charter: the security system regulated in Chapters VI and VII; the regional arrangements in Chapter VIII, and the right to individual or collective self-defence in Article 51.

Under the UN system, the maintenance of security and peace is seen as directly proportional to the prevention of violence and wars between states. Within this framework, the use of force is considered illegal, with certain exceptions, under Article 2, paragraph 4 of the UN Charter. This regulation imposes a responsibility on member states to refrain from using or threatening to use force in their international relations against the territorial integrity and political independence of other states or in a way that is incompatible with the purposes of the UN. Furthermore, paragraph 3 of Article 2 requires member states to resolve international disputes by peaceful means in a way that does not harm international peace security and justice. This provision confirms the prohibition on the use of force set out in Article 2 paragraph 4, and emphasizes that disputes should only be resolved by peaceful means (Başeren, 2003:53).

The UN's prohibition of the use of force forms the basis of the international legal understanding, formed in the aftermath of the Second World War, that peace is the essential element to be preserved. Indeed, peace is the first condition required for a happier world.

4   The UN's Role in Ensuring International Peace and Security: Is a More Effective UN Possible?

The UN is the most comprehensive security organization in the current international system, given that its main objective is maintaining international peace and security and that, through its institutional structure and specialized organizations, it operates in security, economy, health, communication, transport and many other technical fields. However, what can be questioned is the UN's success and capability in realizing its objectives.

Here, it is necessary to consider the idea of collective security, which first emerged in Ancient Greece as a means of preventing war between states. However, it was not implemented to achieve global rather than regional peace until the establishment of the LoN. There is a consensus in the literature that certain conditions must be met for the full realization of collective security. In particular, the basic assumption is that the maintenance of peace is in the common interest of all states participating in the collective security system. This basic assumption also determines the necessary conditions for achieving collective security. Hence, the first condition is that each member of a collective security organization should consider the maintenance of peace as the main objective by downplaying its foreign policy objectives and reaching a consensus with other member countries regarding threats to peace. A collective security system will also function more effectively if power is distributed relatively equitably among its members. Conversely, according to Bennett and Oliver (2015:178–179), the presence of a strong state with the capacity to prevent collective action when force is required against an aggressor state or threat will reduce the likelihood of collective action. In addition, if one state is much more powerful than the others within a collective security organization, threats and aggressors may be defined in terms of this state's perceptions and priorities. Hence, it is not very easy to create a collective security organization today. It is clear that the UN system, which has this purpose in theory, cannot fulfil it in practice.

Article 24 of the UN Charter assigns the Security Council primary responsibility for maintaining international peace and security, which is one of the UN's main objectives. According to Doğan (2014: 56), the UN system differs from that of the LoN in emphasizing the right to self-defence rather than collective security with a strong Security Council. The Security Council is composed of fifteen member states, five of which are permanent members. Provisional members are elected for two-year terms on a regional basis. The five permanent members, each with veto power, have become the focus of criticism of the UN system because they symbolize an invisible hierarchy among states and the lack of democracy and justice.

Those who claim that the veto power is necessary generally offer two main justifications. Firstly, it is necessary in an international system with no superior authority that states have that authority, given that they take responsibility for maintaining international peace and security. Secondly, by having a specially authorized executive body, the UN can work rapidly and effectively to maintain international peace and security (Denk, 2015: 185–186).

However, these justifications have not prevented criticisms of the Security Council in practice since the UN's establishment. As part of the UN Security Council's decision-making procedures, the veto reflects the power relations among states in the international conjuncture that emerged after the Second World War. UN Charter Article 2, paragraph 1 states that the organization is built on the principle of sovereign equality. However, the veto power of the permanent members of the Security Council, which takes primary responsibility for ensuring international peace and security, shows that the principle of sovereign equality remains unimplemented in practice.

Nevertheless, it should be acknowledged that the UN's achievements are incomparable to any other organization within the system of sovereign states, including the development of human rights doctrine, prohibition of the use of force, codification of the rules of customary law, the establishment of specialized institutions in many different fields, the establishment of official bodies for settling disputes and disseminating international law. However, the UN's effectiveness is limited by the Security Council, which is responsible for achieving its main purpose due to the veto and the problem of representation.

During the 1990s, the UN Security Council took various decisions allowing member countries or regional organizations to use force[1] and implement the military and political dimensions of the Dayton Peace Agreement in Bosnia.[2] Furthermore, although the UN Security Council did not adopt a resolution authorizing member states to use force in the 1999 Kosovo intervention, the establishment of the Kosovo Force (KFOR) was within the framework of UN Security Council resolutions.[3] These examples demonstrate that the Security Council can undertake missions within the framework of ensuring international peace and security by adopting resolutions permitting the use of force.

However, they also depend on certain developments or factors. The most important of these is the role of the US as a global power in that international

---

1   UN Security Council Resolution 816 of 31 March 1993 authorized both member states and regional organizations, and arrangements of which they were members to take appropriate measures against violators of the prohibition on flights of military aircraft. For the full text of the resolution, see the UN Security Council (1993a). UN Security Council Resolution 836 of 4 June 1993 authorized member states and regional organizations to take necessary measures in safe areas using air power to support UNPROFOR in executing its mandate. For the full text of the resolution, see the UN Security Council (1993b).

2   Security Council Resolutions 1021 of 22 November 1995 and 1031 of 15 December 1995 are of this nature.

3   For the full text of the resolution, see UN Security Council (1999).

conjuncture and the failure of other states with veto power in the Security Council to use this right. In contrast, the UN Security Council has struggled to adopt resolutions permitting coercive measures, specifically regarding various international crises since 2010 in Syria, Ukraine, and, most recently, Afghanistan.

There are many different views on today's international system, such as whether it has evolved into multipolarity, is non-polar, or is moving towards bipolarity again in the medium term. What is certain, however, is that today's international system is not unipolar, whereby a single global power can direct global politics in line with its agenda and interests. In short, considering the above examples of the UN's history, one should no longer have very high expectations regarding the UN's ability to ensure international peace and security because its success depends on the nature of the issue and certain conditions arising from the international conjuncture.

5   UN Reform Debates

Drawing on the legitimacy it gains from the UN Charter, the Security Council has tried to contribute effectively to international peacebuilding (Hurd, 2007: 25). Indeed, according to the UN Charter, the Security Council is the body primarily responsible for maintaining international peace and security. However, not every issue that comes onto its agenda is easily resolved. This is mainly because the Security Council's permanent members, unlike in the General Assembly, have veto power, which they can use whenever a proposed resolution is against their national interests or their opinion about the international system differs from those of other members (Weshler, 2009–2010: 34).

No restrictions or regulations govern when permanent members can use their veto power by casting a negative vote; they are free to vote as they wish, in line with their own views. The Security Council's structure, which grants privileges to the great powers, made sense, at least partially, given the conditions of the period when it was established. According to Erdağ (2014: 11), the Cold War mentality based on balance of power enabled the UN to partially succeed in this mission as a holder of this balance.

Now, in the post-Cold War era, there is a wide consensus among UN members that the Security Council has become an anachronism that no longer reflects current global realities and therefore needs structural reform. The Security Council's structure has attracted increasing criticism with the emergence of new states and centres of power, especially since the Cold War ended (Krasno, 2006: 93–94). The main criticism is that an organization created in the conditions of the post-World War II period maladapted to current conditions. Hence, there have been many different reform proposals from many different sources for transforming its organizational structure to match current conditions. On the other hand, there is also considerable resistance to this restructuring from those seeking to preserve the status quo (Çolak and Köse, 2020: 24).

The first such reform proposal appeared in 1993 in parallel with the global formation of new regional power centres. This initiative, called the "open-ended working group", was implemented by the UN General Assembly. It provides a platform with broad participation in which over 140 UN member states share ideas and suggestions (UN General Assembly, 1994). However, the UN Security Council's permanent members rejected the group's proposals, although they predominantly retained the status quo, because it would remove their veto power. Consequently, the initiative failed.

In March 1997, Malaysian diplomat Ismail Razali proposed the Razali Reform Plan, which planned to increase the number of permanent Security Council members without giving new members veto powers (Lewis, 1997). Despite receiving no positive response for a long time, it was proposed again in 2003 at the initiative of the then UN Secretary-General Kofi Annan. Annan put forward two reform models (A and B). Both distributed seats among four main regions: Africa, Asia-Pacific, Europe, and America. This indicated that Annan preferred a new continental distribution instead of the existing regional groups to determine seat distributions (UN, 2004: 79–81).

Model A proposed adding six new permanent non-veto seats: two each for Africa, Asia, and the Pacific; one each for Europe and the Americas; plus three non-permanent seats. Model B proposed no new permanent seats. Instead, it created a new category of eight four-year renewable-term seats and one new two-year non-permanent (and non-renewable) seat, divided among the major regional areas. For the new category, two seats each were assigned to Africa, Asia-Pacific, Europe, and the Americas. One additional non-permanent seat was assigned to Africa in addition to the existing non-permanent membership seats. Following this proposal, various other proposals were made by different states, but no consensus was reached on any of them.

A focal point of criticism in these debates about reforming the Security Council was the permanent members' veto power is. Nevertheless, the reform proposals seemed to avoid mentioning the abolition of the current permanent membership and its veto power. This was because any reform or change in the UN Charter would be decided by the Security Council itself. However, there is no consensus regarding the structure of the UN Security Council and the elimination of veto powers. Nor does the UN Security Council reflect the

21st-century distribution of power. However, the reform proposals put forward by diplomats and analysts have never addressed the real imbalance between the allocation of UN Security Council seats and military capacity outside the Security Council. Instead, they have sought to address the imbalance between the total number of countries and membership of the UN Security Council, and to discuss the absolute veto power controlled by five countries (Weiss, 2003: 149).

Defenders of veto power argue that without this right it would not be possible to keep the great powers within the system, that the right of veto is a control mechanism against unnecessarily frequent military interventions, and that it generally helps maintain international stability. On the other hand, those who object argue that such power undermines the principle of democratic decision-making and equality of sovereign states, which is one of the most fundamental elements of the UN system. Furthermore, they argue, veto power sometimes prevents effective intervention to prevent war crimes, crimes against humanity, and conflicts. According to Indian diplomat and author Shashi Tharoor, the problem of reforming the UN Security Council is akin to a situation where doctors gathered around a patient agree on the diagnosis but disagree on the prescription (Tharoor, 2011: 397). Nevertheless, adapting the UN Security Council to the realities of today's international politics is crucial in the quest for international peace and security, and a happier world.

6   Conclusion

Although international organizations have become more effective actors in today's international relations, it is also true that states authorize international organizations to a limited extent to achieve certain goals and pay utmost attention to protecting their sovereignty. Hence, it is clear that international organizations are more effective when strong actors within them take responsibility and show political leadership. It should not be forgotten that international organizations are established by international treaties, which are the result of the written will of states. Thus, their success or failure also depends on the will of member states.

Considering the history of global organizations like the LoN and UN, both of which made maintaining international peace and security their main objective, at least in official discourse, we can see that they have succeeded in resolving particular issues so long as certain conditions are met. One of the most important reasons for this success is that, especially in their early years, these organizations faced fewer differences regarding the interests and threat perceptions of those states that could mobilize the organizations. Although the number of proposals and plans indicates that the UN Security Council generally needs reform, there are significant obstacles. In particular, debates over reforming the UN have revealed deep divides between states, NGOs, and other reform advocates. While some seek to strengthen the UN and improve accountability and efficiency, others only seek reform on their terms.

The biggest problem in the functioning of the UN system is the veto power in the Security Council. If this can be overcome, the UN, which prioritizes international peace and security as one of its major goals, will certainly be able to act under its founding philosophy and thereby gain the respect and support of the international community. Because current conditions make it impossible to completely abolish the veto power, the permanent members should be persuaded to adopt a veto system that does not ignore the realities of current international relations. Undoubtedly, this process of persuasion will be difficult. Nevertheless, for a happier world, diplomatic and political authorities must continue their efforts in seeking the most favorable "moment" for reform.

The COVID-19 pandemic and similar international problems have initiated a process in today's international system that is already producing concrete results from discussions on how to make the UN more effective as an international cooperation platform for regulating relations between states. The most important reason is that the current international conjuncture prevents any geopolitical development that would completely abolish the UN system. More importantly, the cost of establishing its replacement would be very high, given that the current system includes 193 countries and has developed specialized institutions like the World Trade Organization, World Bank, World Health Organization, International Labour Organization, International Maritime Organization, and Food and Agriculture Organization, which can establish international regimes and norms in their specific fields.

References

Başeren, S. S. (2003). *Uluslararası Hukukta Devletlerin Münferiden Kuvvet Kullanmalarının Sınırları*, Ankara: Ankara Üniversitesi Basımevi.

Beck, U. (1992). *Risk Society: Towards a New Modernity*, London: Sage Publication.

Bennett, A. L. and Oliver, J. (2015). *Uluslararası Örgütler*, Ankara: BB101 Yayınları.

Çolak, Ö., and Köse, İ. (2020). Birleşmiş Milletler Güvenlik Konseyi'nin Reformu Sorunsalı: İtalya'nın Beklentileri ve Stratejileri, *Gazi Akademik Bakış*, 13(26), 21–48.

Davis, C. J. (2004). *The Human Story: Our History, from the Stone Age to Today*, New York: Harper Perennial.

Denk, E. (2015). *Uluslararası Örgütler Hukuku: Birleşmiş Milletler Sistemi*, Ankara: Siyasal Kitabevi.

Doğan, N. (2014). Birleşmiş Milletler ve Meşru Güç Kullanımı, *Birleşmiş Milletler: BM Sistemi ve Reformu*, ed. Nejat Doğan et al. Ankara: Siyasal Kitabevi.

Erdağ, R. (2014). How Many is Greater than Five: A Comprehensive Model Proposal for the United Nations Security Council, *Alternatives: Turkish Journal of International Relations*, 13(4), 83–95.

Giddens, A. (1991). *The Consequences of Modernity*, Cambridge: Polity Press.

Hurd, I. (2007). *After Anarchy: Legitimacy and Power in the United Nations Security Council*, Princeton and Oxford: Princeton University Press.

Krasno, J. (2006). Legitimacy, Representation and Accountability: A Proposal for U.N. Security Council Reform, *Yale Journal of International Relations*, I (2), 93–100.

Lewis, P. (1997). U.N. Panel Proposes Expanding Security Council to 24 Members, *The New York Times*, *21.03.1997*, https://www.nytimes.com/1997/03/21/world/un-panel -proposes-expanding-security-council-to-24-members.html.

Rüma, İ. (2014). Uluslararası Örgütler, *Küresel Siyasete Giriş: Uluslararası İlişkilerde Kavramlar, Teoriler, Süreçler*, ed. Evren Balta, İstanbul: İletişim Yayıncılık, 371–403.

Tharoor, S. (2011). Security Council Reform: Past, Present and Future, *Ethics in International Affairs*, XXV (4), 397–406.

UN General Assembly (2011). Resolution 65/309, 19 July 2011, https://digitallibrary .un.org/record/715187.

UN Regional Information Centre for Western Europe (2023). Happiness in the Times of War and Climate Change, https://unric.org/en/happiness-in-the-times-of-war -and-climate-change/.

UN (2004). *A More Secure World: Our Shared Responsibility. Report of the High-level Panel on Threats, Challenges and Change*, 02.12.2004, https://www.un.org/peace building/content/more-secure-world-our-shared-responsibility-%E2%80%93 -report-high-level-panel-threats-challenges-and.

UN General Assembly (1994). *Report of the Open-ended Working Group on the Question of Equitable Representation on and Increase in the Membership of the Security Council*. New York: UN, https://digitallibrary.un.org/record/163569?ln=es.

UN Security Council (1993a). Security Council Resolution 816, 31.03.1993, https:// undocs.org/S/RES/816(1993).

UN Security Council (1993b). Security Council Resolution 836, 04.06.1993, https:// undocs.org/S/RES/836(1993).

UN Security Council (1999). Security Council Resolution 1244, 10.06.1999, https:// undocs.org/S/RES/1244(1999).

UN Department of Economic and Social Affairs Population Division (2022). World Population Prospects 2022, https://population.un.org/wpp/Graphs/Demographic Profiles/Line/900.

Vark, R. (2003). The Use of Force in the Modern World: Recent Developments and Legal Regulation of the Use of Force, *Baltic Defence Review*, 2(10), 27–44.

Weiss, T. G. (2003). The Illusion of UN Security Council Reform, *The Washington Quarterly*, XXVI (4), 147–161.

Weshler, J. (2009–2010). The Evolution of Security Council Innovations in Sanctions, *International Journal*, 2009–2010, 65(1), 31–43.

CHAPTER 11

Sociological Understanding of Happiness

Barış Çağırkan

This study investigated the sociological dimensions of happiness, underscoring its multifaceted nature as both an individual and societal phenomenon. By integrating historical and contemporary perspectives, this analysis elucidates how happiness, conceptualised as a state of well-being and contentment, is intricately shaped by personal, social, cultural, economic, and political determinants. While classical philosophers, such as Aristotle, characterised happiness as the ultimate purpose of human existence, contemporary research foregrounds its subjective and objective dimensions, linking it to constructs such as quality of life and social well-being. This study identifies critical determinants, including socioeconomic status, cultural norms, social capital, and interpersonal relationships, as pivotal influences on both individual and collective perceptions of happiness. Moreover, it explores the transformative role of technological advancements, particularly social media, in reshaping social interactions with nuanced implications for well-being, both beneficial and adverse. Adopting a sociological lens, this study examined happiness within a broader framework encompassing structural inequalities, societal trust, and cultural paradigms, integrating these insights to inform evidence-based public policies aimed at enhancing societal welfare. Empirical analyses, including insights from the United Nations' World Happiness Report, were employed to illuminate global patterns and disparities in happiness. The findings underscore that happiness transcends individual experiences and is fundamentally embedded in social structures and cultural milieus. By systematically examining the interconnections between personal well-being and societal conditions, sociology offers a robust framework for addressing inequities and advancing collective happiness as a vital dimension of human existence and a focal point for progressive policymaking.

1   Introduction

Happiness has been a concept of interest to philosophers, psychologists, and sociologists for many years, and almost every branch of social science dealing with individuals, societies, and communities has taken the concept of happiness as the subject of research. When we look at the studies on the concept of happiness, it can be stated that its origins date back to ancient Greece (Veenhoven, 2000). According to Aristotle, the main purpose of human life is happiness, and in his work *"Nicomachean Ethics,"* Aristotle sees happiness as the main goal of most people, whether wise or ignorant, rich, or poor (Cengiz, 2010). Based on Aristotle's statement that "man is a social animal," it is the consideration of social actors only within the social context of being human and being naturally happy. In this context, Aristotle defines the concept of happiness as the main purpose of human life, and all people strive for happiness.

The concept of happiness has been evaluated in two dimensions as an indicator of both individual and social well-being. From the past to the present, both individuals and society/community have been asking, *"How to be happy?"*. This question has always been asked. While the individual dimension of the concept of happiness is evaluated as an indicator of the level of satisfaction that social actors receive from their individual lives, the objective dimension is more related to the scarcity or abundance of the individual's daily living conditions and opportunities. In this context, happiness in its most general sense is synonymous with the quality of life or social well-being of individuals. The high quality of life of the individual and the abundance of opportunities do not indicate what is good in life (Veenhoven, 2009).

The studies have explored the influence of the concept of happiness on happiness from different perspectives, including psychosocial factors, social support, interpersonal relationships, socioeconomic status, social capital, safety, health, and religious affiliation (Omarova & Kenzhakimov, 2023; Adedeji, 2023; Hamzaoglu, 2022). Studies emphasise the importance of understanding the multidimensional nature of happiness and the impact of social and economic factors on individual well-being. Nowadays, the concept of happiness is generally discussed in terms of its economic dimension. The terms quality of life and welfare or social welfare, which are often used, especially by ecologists and sociologists, are related to the level of economic development of the individual's understanding of happiness.

Researchers have examined the impact of the concept of happiness on various aspects, such as psychosocial factors, social support and interpersonal relationships, socioeconomic status, social capital, safety, health, and religious affiliation (Omarova & Kenzhakimov, 2023; Adedeji, 2023; Hamzaoglu, 2022). Studies emphasise the importance of understanding the multidimensional nature of happiness and the impact of social and economic factors on individual well-being. Currently, discussions on happiness generally focus on its economic dimension. The terms quality of life and welfare/social welfare, which are often used, especially by ecologists and sociologists, are related to the level of economic development of the individual's understanding of happiness.

Individuals ascertain their perception of happiness via engaging in different social interactions to uphold their presence within the social hierarchy they belong. The sense of happiness is greatly influenced by social contact among people, families, social groupings, economic situations, and political and cultural frameworks. The study of sociology of happiness, studying within this framework, aims to comprehend and clarify how individuals perceive happiness within their social environments from a sociological point of view. This field of research examines the impact of social and economic environments on individuals' well-being. The research investigates the effects of communities and social institutions on happiness, as well as the effect of cultural values, social practices, interpersonal relationships, and economic situations.

2   The Notion of Happiness

Happiness can be defined as the culmination of all the enjoyable experiences, moments of joy and even the hardships that life presents, or as an assessment of an individual's general contentment with their existence as a whole. Happiness, commonly seen as the ultimate goal, is a state that individuals want to achieve in various ways throughout their whole lives. The idea of happiness can change across individuals, as well as across various cultures, societies, personal beliefs, and life events. Throughout human history, people have discussed happiness with various problems, but they have not agreed upon a clear definition. The concept of happiness has been examined from various perspectives, including the hedonic approach, the eudemonic approach, and the examination of happiness as a positive emotional state (Lomas, 2023). In the social sciences, many disciplinary and interdisciplinary studies have considered the concept of happiness as a research object.

Although the understanding of happiness differs from individual to individual, it is generally believed to have a general standard. Happiness has been discussed in different ways, from the early period when ancient Greek philosophy prevailed through the Enlightenment period to the post-World War II period when the welfare state concept emerged. Seneca, one of the pioneers of Stoic philosophy, wrote in his work '*On the Happy Life*': "The happy person has correct judgements; the person who is happy with everything that happens to him in the current situation, who can adapt to his or her conditions, and whose mind guides every situation created by the conditions is happy"

(Seneca, 2020). According to Veenhoven (1991), a renowned researcher in the field of happiness, happiness is commonly described as the degree to which individuals positively view the overall quality of their lives. According to Lyubomirsky (2007), it is defined as a combination of feelings of joy, satisfaction, or well-being. Russell (2020) considers the concept of happiness along with its opposite, stating that individuals feel unhappy when they worry about competition, boredom, fatigue, jealousy, and the opinions of others; Russell also indicated that individuals engaged in love, family, pleasure, work, and hobbies are happy.

Individuals experience happiness and unhappiness as states of divine change, which manifest in their emotions at different times in daily life. Individuals can be both happy and unhappy temporarily. At this point, what matters is that happiness is permanent and continues without interruption. Research by Lyubomirsky et al. (2005) shows that living conditions impact happiness by 10%, life purpose by 40%, and genetic traits and personality by 50% for sustainable happiness. Various studies suggest that elements such as virtue, knowledge, consciousness, love, communication, empathy, respect for nature and people, and helpfulness can lead to happiness (Mobus, 2023; Smith, 2021). On the other hand, Kahneman, Diener and Schwarz (2003), who conducted studies on happiness, stated that happiness is closely related to factors such as love for others, hedonic pleasures, and the individual's insight into his inner world. The notion of happiness is a complex phenomenon that emerges from the combination of various experiences, emotional states, and external factors in an individual's life. Happiness refers to an individual's inner peace, contentment, and satisfaction with life, and is generally related to their level of enjoyment in various aspects of life. Happiness is a state in which an individual feels emotionally, mentally, socially, and physically satisfied. Researchers have repeatedly linked the notion of happiness to different factors.

Individual factors affecting happiness include personality traits, genetic structure, health status, financial income level, education level, job satisfaction, family relationships, and social connections. Several research has demonstrated that despite an improvement in living conditions compared to previous years, life satisfaction for those involved in social interactions may be decreased (Kubatko et al., 2022; Muhammad et al., 2022). The inverse relationship between economic growth and life satisfaction indicates that some factors are required to increase life satisfaction after a certain point in time; factors such as social trust, employment rates, and human resources in science and technology have a positive impact on life satisfaction. Furthermore, social interaction networks are the elements that affect individuals' life satisfaction and, consequently, happiness. Although happiness appears to be individually oriented, the social interaction dimension of social life in which individuals participate affects their understanding of happiness.

An individual's perception of happiness is affected by the cultural values and norms of society. While in some societies, individual success and material wealth are considered important determinants of happiness, in other societies, family relationships, social interactions, and a sense of belonging to mainstream society are of greater importance. Therefore, social norms have a significant impact on determining individuals' happiness levels. Social factors that affect happiness include factors such as inequality, social justice, safety, social support networks, cultural values, and political stability. Studies have shown that happiness levels are lower in societies with high-income inequality (Teeselink & Zauberman, 2023). Additionally, studies have found that the correlation between income and happiness tends to be higher in years with high-income inequality (Arslan, 2023). Social actors gain a strong sense of belonging to mainstream society through social support networks, enabling them to foster social relationships and ultimately boost their happiness levels.

Research on life satisfaction and happiness, which began in the 1940s, has continued to this day, and many research centres have used various methods to reveal the factors that affect the understanding of happiness of individuals, groups, and societies with various methods (Seker, 2009, p. 122). In life satisfaction research, the phenomenon of happiness is explained as a criterion that analyzes the general quality of individuals' current lives. In other words, it is considered a phenomenon that shows how satisfied individuals experience their lives. Individual happiness is now accepted as a measure of social well-being and an indicator of the level of economic development, which has led to an increase in the number of studies on happiness and its perceived value. Lawmakers have started utilizing statistical data from happiness research and established institutions at national and international levels to shape public policies.

The preeminent publication about global happiness is the "World Happiness Report," which has been published by the United Nations (UN) since 2012. According to this report's 2023 data, Finland ranks first in the country's overall ranking, followed by Denmark in second place, Iceland in third place, Israel in fourth place, and the Netherlands in fifth place. In the report, which includes more than one hundred and fifty countries, Turkey ranks one hundred and sixth. When we look at the least happy countries in the report, Afghanistan, where internal turmoil and social conflicts are most intense, comes first. Lebanon, Sierra Leone, Zimbabwe, and the Democratic Republic of the Congo follow Afghanistan. The United Nations World Happiness Report 2023 research found that although urban life offers a higher quality of life in terms of both employment opportunities and access to social opportunities and public services, individuals living in rural areas are happier than individuals living in cities.

When we look at the national level, "Life Satisfaction Research," which was started to be implemented by the Turkish Statistical Institute (TUIK) in 2023, shows the level of happiness in Turkey, which is ranked 106th in the World Happiness Report 2023 (Korkmaz et al., 2015, p. 79; Besel, 2015). Research in life satisfaction indicates that happiness stems from components that shape living conditions, including demographic, economic, physical, and social environments, as well as the country's situation (Guzel, 2018, p. 390). According to TUIK Life Satisfaction Survey 2023 data, the rate of individuals aged 18 and over who said that they were happy was 52.7%. The percentage of people who said that they were unhappy was 13.7%. First, reporting the happiness rate as a percentage is an important measure for understanding the general emotional state of society. A happiness rate of 52.7% could indicate that the majority are generally happy and enjoy life. However, a dissatisfaction rate of 13.7% indicates that certain segments of society remain dissatisfied, highlighting the need for addressing these issues.

Different descriptive theories addressing the concept of happiness (Set Point Theory and Comparison Theory) suggest that the value of happiness is limited and that it is difficult to increase happiness consistently, suggesting that striving for more happiness for greater happiness contradicts utilitarian principles (Veenhoven, 2009). Values that are sources of happiness, which are health, love, success, money, and work are examples of values that provide different degrees of happiness (Kerstetter et al., 2022). Furthermore, it has identified mental, emotional, and physical well-being, nurturing social relationships, and being in harmony with one's culture and environment have been identified as dominant factors for happiness (Singh et al., 2023). Research by Messner (2023) found that values such as conformity, tradition, helpfulness, self-determination, and hedonism have a positive effect on subjective well-being and increase happiness. However, some factors affect happiness itself rather than its source. These factors can be diverse and include psychological, sociological, economic, educational, cultural, and political (Yilmaz, 2018, p. 22). Trying to explain the phenomenon of happiness only with mental, emotional, and economic indicators and ignoring the social and cultural structure of societies and the physical environment by separating individuals from their social context will be incomplete in addressing the understanding of happiness in all its dimensions. For this reason, the social context, which constitutes the sociological aspect of happiness, is crucial.

3 Sociology of Happiness

Happiness has an important value in contemporary society. It is not only pursued by individuals for personal satisfaction but there is also increasing approval of the idea that the well-being of others is important and that governing bodies should strive to increase the happiness of the larger population (Bentham, 1789 cited in Veenhoven, 2009, p. 1). Individuals need to evaluate both their happiness and the happiness of other individuals within the social structure. Happiness studies have recently gained importance as an interdisciplinary research field that reflects the interaction between science and society (Delsignore et al., 2021). The subject of happiness studies in the social sciences is expanding and encourages study on the factors and outcomes of individuals' happiness.

The concept of happiness has always been complex and controversial, with different perspectives and definitions. While some argue that happiness is an enduring appreciation of life, others emphasise the subjective nature of happiness and its measurement with standardised questions (Ott, 2020). Researchers have empirically answered questions about happiness that were previously addressed more theoretically in the social sciences, religion, and philosophy using valid and reliable self-report happiness scales. Overall, the complexity and debates surrounding the definition and explanation of happiness demonstrate the concept's complexity.

The field of social sciences acknowledges the significance of social action within its social framework for the overall well-being of individuals and encourages greater collaboration between social scientists and policymakers (Helliwell & Aknin, 2018). The subject of happiness studies in the social sciences has grown and promoted studies on the factors and outcomes of individuals' happiness. The notion of happiness, understood as a state of well-being, entered the literature in the 1970s, and 'happiness', a relatively new concept, has also taken its place in studies in the field of sociology (Veenhoven, 2018). It was the Dutch sociologist Ruut Veenhoven who gave the concept such importance and popularity. Veenhoven is the author of pioneering work in the scientific study of happiness in the sense of subjective enjoyment of life. Through his work, he sought to understand and explain the social conditions for individual happiness, increasing interest in the concept of happiness as a goal of public policy. Veenhoven is considered a leading authority in happiness research (Vitterso, 2021).

According to Veenhoven (1991), social actors generally believe that if they improve their own situation, they will be happier by improving their situation

will make them happier. Veenhoven believes that improving social development will enhance the quality of life by upgrading housing, security, social
protection systems, and material conditions to develop the welfare state.
Happiness is the individual's attitude towards his or her life; therefore, happiness is based on subjective comparison and not objective utility (Veenhoven,
1991, p. 2). Indeed, happiness can sometimes be viewed as meaningless and
unimportant; happiness is seen as meaningless because a happy life does not
always mean a good life, and happiness is unimportant because living standards generally increase with economic power, success, and status, but this
does not mean people are happy because standards of comparison are arbi-
trary, and happiness is insensitive to the actual quality of life. While some
people can be subjectively happy even in objectively bad situations, other
people can be subjectively unhappy even if they are objectively doing well.
Individuals tend to be happier after difficult experiences because standards of
comparison decrease as a result (Rauch & Rothbaum, 2023). Happiness does
not arise by tolerating, because when standards change, the impact on happiness is usually only temporary.

Sociologists often neglect happiness in mainstream sociological studies,
viewing it as a problematic and subjective phenomenon linked to problems
of modernity such as consumerism and alienation (Cieslik, 2015). Veenhoven
(2014) pointed out that sociology remained insensitive to this issue.
Sociological approaches to friendship and happiness highlight the impact of
broader social and cultural conditions on well-being and emphasise the role of
friends in promoting happiness through social and emotional capital (Greco
et al., 2015). McKenzie (2016) proposes a sociological distinction between
happiness as positive affect and contentment as positive reflection, highlighting a lack of consistency in the use of terms such as happiness, contentment,
and well-being. Sociology covers happiness studies, with the latter extending
beyond traditional economic concerns (Jugureanu, 2016). Sociologists are
sceptical about the study of happiness, but an interdisciplinary approach has
been proposed that focuses on the processes and biographies of well-being
(Cieslik, 2017). Veenhoven (2007) states that sociology examines happiness at
two different levels, first at the macro level for international comparisons and
then at the micro level to identify differences within nations.

Sociology and the economics of happiness are two disciplines within the
social sciences that deal with happiness research, examining different aspects
and future directions (Hallberg & Kullenberg, 2019). In general, the study of
happiness in the social sciences aims to understand and improve well-being
through interdisciplinary collaboration, with a focus on social connection and
prosocial behaviour (Jugureanu, 2016). Considering that sociology is generally

interested in social problems, it seems that Veenhoven endeavoured to address happiness from a sociological perspective as the happiness of societies and nations. Veenhoven focuses on the concepts of "well-being" and "happiness," as well as the concept of "quality of life," which is interpreted as the degree of positive evaluation of life (Veenhoven, 2000, p. 264). Similar concepts are often used interchangeably but express fundamentally different values. When it comes to the term quality of life, the focus of evaluation is the 'life'. Although this concept typically pertains to individual life, it is occasionally applied at the social level.

In modern societies, the prevailing understanding is that most individuals are happy, and the average level of happiness in countries is increasing; however, inequalities in happiness still exist. According to the savanna happiness theory, the human brain is limited by evolutionary factors, causing situations and conditions that would have elevated the happiness of ancestors to also increase happiness today. Similarly, circumstances that would have decreased people's happiness in the past may still diminish in the present (Kanazawa, Li & Yong, 2022). Moreover, social pressure to be happy rather than sad is associated with lower well-being, particularly in countries with high levels of national happiness (Mert, 2022). In countries with high levels of happiness, there is a connection between decreased well-being and increased social pressure on individuals to be happy rather than sad. Therefore, although there is an overall increase in happiness, inequalities in happiness still exist (Dejonckheere et al., 2022).

Factors such as cultural dynamics, health status, working conditions, financial situation, and migration can affect individuals' understanding of happiness. For example, understanding and level of happiness play an important role in migration decisions; relatively unhappy people tend to change their place to happier places (Hendriks & Burger, 2021). Moreover, the mainstream social structure, cultural norms and values, expectations, health, safety, religious affiliation, material satisfaction, freedom of choice, and living in a democratic environment have been found to increase people's levels of happiness (Li et al., 2018). Acceptances shaped by collective consciousness in social life can cause existential crises of trust that impact the understanding of happiness. In this context, social actors' establishment of healthy relationships in social life—their relationships within the family, social environment, and relationships with society or community—can help individuals overcome crises by providing them with emotional support through social relations.

Researchers have found that young adults' understanding of happiness is influenced by factors like identity and belonging crises, job expectations, self-esteem, future anxiety, questioning the meaning of life, and feelings of

purposelessness (Handa, Pereira & Holmqvist, 2023). Young adults' understanding of happiness can be affected by the contradiction between the desire
for success and happiness, as well as the need to meet both material and spiri-
tual needs in an integrated manner (Righi & Masserini, 2023). In general, sociological factors shape young adults' understanding of happiness by influencing
their social relationships, values, attitudes, and overall well-being.

Happiness is based on meeting the needs of human nature, and it is not possible to achieve this satisfaction equally in all communities and societies today
(Veenhoven, 2007, p. 60). Different notions of happiness and well-being are
defined in terms of various needs, such as the need to have, to love, and to exist
(Sirgy, 2021). Studies in sociology have examined the relationship between
social position and happiness within communities and societies. Moreover, it
assessed the predictive effect of socioeconomic status and social capital on
happiness (Adedeji et al., 2023; Majeed & Samreen, 2021). Furthermore, social
capital serves as a protective factor against the negative effects of socioeconomic inequalities on happiness. Socioeconomic status, including income
level and education level, is associated with happiness; people with high socio-
economic status may be happier (Savadori & Kazemekaityte, 2021), but that
does not mean they are always happy.

The social interaction networks through which individuals participate in
their daily life practices have an impact on their understanding of happiness.
Various factors affect the relationship between social interaction and happiness. Nowadays, with the development of media and communication technologies, individuals continue most of their social interactions in their daily lives,
thanks to the development of communication technologies. Social interaction,
which can take place on a diverse and global scale thanks to mass communication and transportation technologies, also shapes individuals' understanding
of happiness. When people feel bad, they tend to engage in social relationships that increase their happiness level, and when they feel good, they tend to
engage in less social interaction (Kroencke et al., 2022).

From a sociological point of view, the concept of happiness is considered
not only as an internal resentment or as the individual's happiness but also
associating it with the social structure to which it belongs by its biological
birth. This approach emphasises that individuals' understanding of happiness should be assessed within the social context in which they find themselves. Understanding social actors' happiness is linked to various aspects of
communication, including the communication channels used, the type and
nature of communication, and the extent of social interaction. Today, the most
important determinant of individuals' perceptions of happiness is the type
and breadth of social interaction, which is experiencing rapid growth and can

take place on a global level. Social media platforms, whose number of users is increasing day by day and used for different purposes, allow instant global social interaction. The increased use of social media reduces face-to-face interaction while increasing virtual interaction.

Social media use can contribute to happiness by providing entertainment, filling gaps in relationships, and increasing life satisfaction (Hatamleh et al., 2023). Attan & Bolong (2022) found that social media motivations like social attraction, popularity, and extraversion positively impact happiness. Liking or disliking the content shared through multiple social media accounts significantly alters how individuals perceive and understand their happiness. The primary focus is on the concerns regarding the impact of increased usage of social media platforms on personal well-being and happiness. This is due to social actors frequently comparing their own lives with others on these platforms and being consistently exposed to selected and often idealised versions of other people's lives. This can foster feelings of inadequacy, jealousy, and social comparison, leading to a decline in overall happiness. Research shows that screen addiction and decreased face-to-face interactions due to excessive social media use heighten feelings of loneliness and isolation, which negatively impact happiness (Brooks, 2015). Increased social media use is associated with negative consequences for task accomplishment and holistic well-being and is linked to decreased performance in task completion, technology-induced stress, and decreased levels of satisfaction.

From a sociological point of view, the notion of happiness is the combination of relationships, cultural factors, social structures, social networks, and social interaction processes of which it is a part, according to the characteristics of the individual. Social norms, values, understandings, and attitudes affect the individual's understanding of happiness, from biological birth to sociological birth within the social whole of which the individual is a member. The social status and roles that people have within the social structure and the expectations of society from individuals shape the understanding of the happiness of social actors. Success, wealth, importance, individuality, or family ties within the social structure. These concepts cause individuals to focus more on these factors and shape their understanding of happiness.

There is a direct relationship between the level of happiness and the level of social participation. Social participation, increased health, and well-being, and decreased social isolation all contribute to life satisfaction and happiness (Wilding, 2023). Social participation and inclusion are extremely significant for individuals to take part in society and feel valued. Participating in social activities and decision-making processes that affect their destiny during socialisation processes affects individuals' understanding of happiness by strengthening their social and community ties. Culture determines individuals' values, beliefs, lifestyles, and daily life practices. All societies create a different cultural structure and pass it on to future generations through socialisation processes. As part of social life, the culture of social actors determines their understanding of happiness and cultural norms directly from the daily lives of individuals. Understanding happiness as an emotion, a value, or the idea of a good life, as well as the interdisciplinary development of the sociology of happiness and well-being, has recently made a significant contribution to the sociology of happiness studies (Kanasz, 2013).

4   Conclusion

The concept of happiness has been discussed with different dimensions in various disciplines (psychology, philosophy, economics, and politics), and the concept of its place in the lives of individuals has been continuously explored and studied to understand how it affects individuals, societies, and communities with its different dimensions. Most of the happiness research conducted from a social science perspective focuses on how to achieve greater happiness for a wider audience using rational solutions such as science-based social policy and, in this context, how to increase happiness for a wider audience.

While happiness is a psychological concept for individuals, it transforms into a sociological concept for society. Happiness is generally defined as a state in which individuals feel generally well-being, and emotionally, mentally, and physically satisfied. However, the understanding of happiness may differ depending on individuals, cultures, societies, values, and life experiences. Furthermore, happiness can take on a different meaning over time through various life events, experiences, and periods. The concept of happiness, which expresses the importance of human existence, is a comprehensive assessment of the satisfaction and vitality that individuals obtain from their entire lives.

Happiness has a main place in sociology studies because it affects attitudes and behaviours and has political consequences. In this respect, the sociology of happiness, as a part of the social sciences, systematically analyses the factors that affect individuals' understanding of happiness. Traditional sociology expressed scepticism about the study of happiness, often defining it narrowly and treating happiness as a critique of capitalism and consumerism. This approach focused on social problems rather than recognising that people can thrive in modern society. Happiness research must acknowledge and incorporate its results to better understand human well-being and experiences.

Sociologists can consider the social context of happiness and the negative consequences of happiness-related policies and discourses. Moreover, sociology contributes to the sociogenesis of happiness by analysing the social processes through which the concept of happiness is adopted by various communities. Sociogenesis offers an important perspective on the process of development, human happiness, and the self-realisation of individuals. Sociologists are actively involved in happiness research by establishing systematic connections between well-being and scientific research, thereby offering a different perspective on the subject. In general, the sociology of happiness aims to understand the social, cultural, and economic factors that influence individuals' understanding of happiness, to generate scientific knowledge, and to create happier societies with this scientific knowledge.

References

Adedeji, A., Olonisakin, T. T., Buchcik, J., and Idemudia, E. S. (2023). Socioeconomic Status and Social Capital as Predictors of Happiness: Evidence and Gender Differences. *Humanities and Social Sciences Communications*, *10*(1), 1–8.

Arslan, H. (2023). Happiness Inequality in Post-Socialist Countries during Neoliberal Transition. *Comparative Sociology*, *22*(1), 30–73.

Attan, S. A., and Bolong, J. (2022). Factors Influencing Facebook Usage for Life Happiness Enhancement. International *Journal of Academic Research in Business & Social Sciences*, *12*(14), 89–108.

Besel, F. (2015). Economic, Social and Political Analysis of Life Satisfaction Research Results by Provinces. *Journal of Karabük University Social Sciences Institute*, *5*(2), 227–236.

Brooks, S. (2015). Does Personal Social Media Usage Affect Efficiency and Well-being? *Computers in Human Behaviour*, *46*, 26–37.

Cengiz, E. (2010). Aristotle's Doctrine of Virtue and Happiness. *The Philosophy World*, *52*, 43–51.

Cieslik, M. (2015). 'Not Smiling but Frowning': Sociology and the 'Problem of Happiness'. *Sociology*, *49*(3), 422–437.

Cieslik, M. (2017). Sociological Approaches to Happiness. In: *The Happiness Riddle and the Quest for a Good Life* (p. 67–91). London: Palgrave Macmillan.

Dejonckheere, E., Rhee, J. J., Baguma, P. K., Barry, O., Becker, M., Bilewicz, M., ... and Bastian, B. (2022). Perceiving Societal Pressure to be Happy is Linked to Poor Well-Being, Especially in Happy Nations. *Scientific Reports*, *12*(1), 1514.

Delsignore, G., Aguilar-Latorre, A., and Olivan-Blazquez, B. (2021). Measuring Happiness in the Social Sciences: An Overview. *Journal of Sociology*, *57*(4), 1044–1067.

Diener, E., and Biswas-Diener, R. (2008). *Happiness: Unlocking the Mysteries of Psychological Wealth*. New Jersey: John Wiley & Sons.

Greco, S., Holmes, M., and McKenzie, J. (2015). Friendship and Happiness from a Sociological Perspective. In: M. Demir (Eds.), *Friendship and Happiness: Across the Lifespan and Cultures* (p. 19–35). Basingstoke: Springer.

Guzel, S. (2018). Income inequality, prosperity, and happiness. *Anemon Mus Alparslan University Journal of Social Sciences*, 6(3), 389–394.

Hallberg, M., and Kullenberg, C. (2019). Happiness Studies: Co-production of Social Science and Social Order. *Nordic Journal of Science and Technology Studies*, 7(1), 42–50.

Hamzaoglu, N. M. (2022). Beyond Money: A Social Analysis of Happiness. *Journal of Beykoz Academy*, 10(2), 374–389.

Handa, S., Pereira, A., and Holmqvist, G. (2023). The Rapid Decline of Happiness: Exploring Life Satisfaction among Young People across the World. *Applied Research in Quality of Life*, 18(3), 1549–1579.

Hatamleh, I. H. M., Safori, A. O., Ahmad, A. K., and Al-Etoum, N. M. D. I. (2023). Exploring the Interplay of Cultural Restraint: The Relationship between Social Media Motivation and Subjective Happiness. *Social Sciences*, 12(4), 228.

Helliwell, J. F., and Aknin, L. B. (2018). Expanding the Social Science of Happiness. *Nature Human Behaviour*, 2(4), 248–252.

Helliwell, J. F., Huang, H., Norton, M., Goff, L., and Wang, S. (2023). World Happiness, Trust And Social Connections In Times Of Crisis. In: *World Happiness Report* (pp. 29–76). Retrieved from: https://happiness-report.s3.amazonaws.com/2023/WHR+23.pdf.

Hendriks, M., and Burger, M. J. (2021). Happiness and Migration. In: K. F. Zimmermann (Eds.), *Handbook of Labour, Human Resources and Population Economics* (pp. 1–23). Cham: Springer International Publishing.

Jugureanu, A. (2016). A Short Introduction to Happiness in Social Sciences. *Belvedere Meridionale*, 28(1), 55–70.

Kahneman, D., Diener, E., and Schwarz, N. (2003). *Well-being: The Foundations of Hedonic Psychology*. New York: Russell Sage Foundation.

Kanasz, T. (2013). Emotion and Value Perspectives in Sociological Investigation of Happiness. *European Journal of Humanities and Social Sciences*, 1, 80–92.

Kanazawa, S., Li, N. P., and Yong, J. C. (2022). Sunshine on My Shoulders Makes Me Happy ... Especially If I'm Less Intelligent: How Sunlight and Intelligence Affect Happiness in Modern Society. *Cognition and Emotion*, 36(4), 722–730.

Kerstetter, D., Shen, X., Yi, X., Pan, B., Zhang, G., Li, R., ... and Li, G. (2022). Sources of Happiness: A Mixed Methods Phenomenological Study of Factors Affecting Residents' Subjective Wellbeing in Shenzhen, China. *Psychological Reports*, 125(1), 167–199.

Korkmaz, M., Germir, H. N., Yucel, A. S., and Gurkan, A. (2015). An Analysis on Sociodemographic Components Affecting Life Satisfaction. *Journal of Psychiatry and Psychology Research*, *3*(2), 78–111.

Kroencke, L., Harari, G. M., Back, M. D., and Wagner, J. (2023). Well-Being In Social Interactions: Examining Personality-Situation Dynamics in Face-To-Face and Computer-Mediated Communication. *Journal of Personality and Social Psychology*, *124*(2), 437–460.

Kubatko, O., Roubik, H., Kubatko, V., Odewole, O., Stepanenko, Y., Kovalov, B., and Kozmenko, S. (2022). Life Satisfaction and Digital Transformation of Society Evidence From European Economies. *International Journal of Global Environmental Issues*, *21*(2/3/4), 245–245.

Li, T. C., Chu, C. C., Meng, F. C., Li, Q., Mo, D., Li, B., and Tsai, S. B. (2018). Will Happiness Improve the Psychological Integration of Migrant Workers? *International Journal of Environmental Research and Public Health*, *15*(5), 1–22.

Lomas, T. (2023). *Happiness*. Cambridge: MIT Press.

Lyubomirsky, S. (2007). *The How of Happiness: A Scientific Approach to Getting the Life You Want*. New York: Penguin Press.

Lyubomirsky, S., Sheldon, K. M., and Schkade, D. (2005). Pursuing Happiness: The Architecture of Sustainable Change. *Review of General Psychology*, *9*(2), 111–131.

Majeed, M. T., and Samreen, I. (2021). Social capital as a source of happiness: evidence from a cross-country analysis. *International Journal of Social Economics*, *48*(1), 159–179.

McKenzie, J. (2016). Happiness vs Contentment? A Case for a Sociology of the Good Life. *Journal For the Theory of Social Behaviour*, *46*(3), 252–267.

Mert, A. E. (2022). Happiness at the Macro Level: A Critical Discussion on the Compatibility of Different Indicators. *Istanbul University Journal of Sociology*, *42*(2), 309–323.

Messner, W. (2023). Being happy. The Role Of Personal Value Priorities In Subjective Well-Being Across European Countries. *International Journal of Cross-Cultural Management*, *23*(2), 389–421.

Mobus, F. (2023). Socrates on Self-Improvement: Knowledge, Virtue, and Happiness. By Nicholas D. Smith. *Ancient Philosophy*, *43*(1), 277–282.

Muhammad, T., Paul, R., Meher, T., Rashmi, R., and Srivastava, S. (2022). Decomposition of Caste Differential in Life Satisfaction Among Older Adults in India. *BMC Geriatrics*, *22*(1), 832–846.

Omarova, A., and Kenzhakimov, G. (2023). Sociological Measurement of the Happiness Index In Central Asian Countries. *Journal of Community Positive Practices*, *1*, 17–28.

Ott, J. (2020). The Concept and the Nature of Happiness as Subjective Well-Being. In: J. Ott (Eds), *Beyond Economics: Happiness as A Standard In Our Personal Life And Politics* (pp. 17–33). London: Palgrave Macmillan.

Rauch, S. A. M., & Rothbaum, B. O. (2023). *Making Meaning of Difficult Experiences*. Oxford: Oxford University Press.

Righi, A., and Masserini, L. (2023). Measuring Relational Factors Underlying Subjective Happiness. *Current Psychology, 42*(11), 9225–9236.

Russell, B. (2020). *The Art of Being Happy* (Y. Saglamturk, Trans.). Istanbul: Say Publications.

Savadori, L., and Kazemekaityte, A. (2021). Socioeconomic Status and Consumer Happiness. In: T. Dutta & M. K. Mandal (Eds.), *Consumer Happiness: Multiple Perspectives* (pp. 69–85). Singapore: Springer.

Seker, M. (2009). The Economy of Happiness. *The Istanbul Journal of Sociological Studies, 39,* 115–140.

Seneca, L. A. (2020). *On Happy Living* (C. Cevik, Trans.). İstanbul: Türkiye İs Bankası Publications.

Singh, S., Kshtriya, S., and Valk, R. (2023). Health, Hope, and Harmony: A Systematic Review of the Determinants of Happiness Across Cultures and Countries. *International Journal Of Environmental Research And Public Health, 20*(4), 3306.

Sirgy, M. J. (2021). Effects of Needs and Need Satisfaction on Wellbeing. In: M. Joseph (Eds.), *The Psychology of Quality of Life: Wellbeing and Positive Mental Health* (pp. 263–281). Cham: Springer International Publishing.

Smith, N. D. (2021). *Socrates on Self-Improvement: Knowledge, Virtue, and Happiness*. Cambridge: Cambridge University Press.

Teeselink, B. K., and Zauberman, G. (2023). The Anna Karenina Income Effect: Well-Being Inequality Decreases with Income. *Journal of Economic Behavior & Organization, 212,* 501–513.

Turkish Statistical Institute. (2023). *Life Satisfaction Survey, 2023*. Retrieved from: https://data.tuik.gov.tr/Bulten/Index?p=Yasam-Memnuniyeti-Arastirmasi-2023-49692&dil=1.

Veenhoven, R. (1991). Is Happiness Relative? *Social Indicators Research, 24,* 1–34.

Veenhoven, R. (2000). The Four Qualities of Life: Ordering Concepts and Measures of the Good Life. *Journal of Happiness Studies, 1,* 1–39.

Veenhoven, R. (2014). Sociology's Blind Eye for Happiness. *Comparative Sociology, 13*(5), 537–555.

Veenhoven, R. (2007). Quality of Life Research. In: C. D. Bryan & D. L. Peck (Eds.), *21st Century Sociology: A Reference Handbook* (pp. 54–62). California: Sage.

Veenhoven, R. (2009). Wellbeing in Nations and Well Being of Nations is there a Conflict Between Individual and Society. *Social Indicators Research, 91,* 5–21.

Veenhoven, R. (2018). The Sociology of Happiness: Topic in Social Indicators Research. *Frontiers of Global Sociology, 243,* 243–251.

Vitterso, J. (2021). A Passion for Happiness: Ruut Veenhoven, Eudaimonia and the Good Life. In: A. C. Michalos (Eds.), *The Pope of Happiness: A Festschrift for Ruut Veenhoven* (pp. 261–275). Cham: Springer International Publishing.

Wilding, A., Munford, L., and Sutton, M. (2023). Estimating the Heterogeneous Health and Well-Being Returns to Social Participation. *Health Economics*, *32*(9), 1921–1940.

Yilmaz, E. (2018). The Relationship Between Income and Happiness in Behavioural Economics and an Application: The Example of Samsun Province (Unpublished Master's Thesis). KTO Karatay University, Institute of Social Sciences, Türkiye.

CHAPTER 12

Happiness in Working Life: the Role of Psychological Capital

Ulviye Tüfekçi Yaman

Considering that working individuals spend a significant part of their day and life in working life, it is inevitable that working and experiences in working life affect the individual's state of happiness. Individuals who are happy in their working life will have a sense of satisfaction and this situation will have positive reflections on the area outside of working life. It is possible to say that individuals can concentrate better on work, achieve their goals more easily, experience a higher sense of appreciation, and with this, their general happiness levels will increase, and they will experience less stress and anxiety. Since the beginning of the 2000s, the concept of positive psychology has come to the forefront. Positive psychology states that instead of correcting the wrong points in human nature, positive characteristics should be emphasized and in this way, the satisfaction and happiness levels of individuals in different areas of life can be increased. Psychological capital, which is defined in the context of positive psychology, plays a role in revealing the intrinsic, positive, and strong aspects of the individual and developing these aspects. In this context, this study will try to explain the contribution of positive psychological capital to individuals being happier in their working lives.

1 Introduction

The concept of happiness is generally the degree to which a person evaluates his or her life as a whole positively (Veenhoven, 2009). In other words, it is the feeling of a general sense of satisfaction with life along with more frequent positive affect and less frequent negative affect (Myers and Diener, 1995). Happiness is a situation related to how individuals perceive and evaluate their life experiences as a whole. Such an assessment would take into account, among other factors, the work, the work environment, economic conditions, and working life. For this reason, it can be said that one of the factors that has an impact on the happiness of the individual is the phenomenon of work (Turan, 2018).

It is quite complex to understand the concept of happiness, which can be expressed as "how the individual perceives and evaluates his life experiences as a whole", as well as the well-being of the individual in working life and its outcomes. In his studies, the American psychologist Csikszentmihalyi states that individuals experience a strange internal conflict in their relationships with the work they do to earn a living. So much so that people generally prefer not working to working, even when they feel good in their work environment. Individuals become happier, stronger, more creative, and satisfied because they are challenged while working and can feel that they are using their skills; in their free time, they become sadder, weaker, senseless, and unsatisfied because they feel that there is not much to do and that they are not using their skills sufficiently. Despite these findings from the research, people want to work less and have more free time (Csikszentmihalyi, 2005).

Although the meaning of work varies for individuals, the activity of work had a central role in the lives of individuals until the last quarter of the 20th century. The change in individuals' perspectives on work and the developments affecting working life have led to an intensification of research on the meaning of work. Increases in welfare and educational attainment in recent years have also brought about some changes in expectations regarding work. In addition to wages, security, and good working conditions have become important for employees (Keser and Kümbül Güler, 2021). Although there are some changes in the expectations of employees, it would not be wrong to say that one of the basic expectations is to be satisfied with working life and activities. The concept of happiness, which emerges as a reflection of the positive emotional state of the individual, is expressed with names such as workplace happiness, working happiness, or happiness at work (Erer, 2021). Warr (2007) states that working individuals are happier if their jobs contain the characteristics they generally desire and if their own characteristics and mental processes encourage the existence of happiness.

Employee happiness is the feeling of being pleased and satisfied with one's job, having a positive attitude towards the organization one works for, being able to establish good relationships in the work environment, and being able to exhibit positive behaviour voluntarily (Turan, 2018). In other words, employee happiness is the state of remembering positive emotions more than negative ones, which is nourished by the general happiness levels of individuals, and a state of optimism, especially hope, associated with this positive perspective, enjoying the moment regardless of the conditions, and a permanent state of satisfaction with their work with the transfer of positive emotions (Erhan, 2021).

When considered from the perspective of the working individual, inevitably, the working life in which he/she spends most of his/her time affects the general level of happiness and well-being of the individual. An individual who is happy in business life will have a feeling of satisfaction and this will have positive reflections on areas outside of business life. Accordingly, a person's working and non-working private lives are closely related, and the happiness of employees has also a positive impact on their life outside of work. In many respects, it is important for both the individual and the organization that the individual is in a positive state of mind. From the employee's point of view, the results may include higher levels of happiness at home, less stress and anxiety, increased concentration and enjoyment of work, easier achievement of goals, and a higher sense of appreciation. In terms of the organization, there may be a working environment in which more productive, more loyal, more efficient, and more optimistic employees tend to solve problems instead of complaining, in cooperation and mutualization, away from conflict (Turan, 2018).

The science of positive psychology uses the concept of happiness to explain positive experiences and thus contributes to the increasing interest in the subject of happiness (Keser, 2018). Especially in recent years, with the development of positive psychology, it is seen that this perspective manifests itself in the context of positive organizational behaviour at the organizational level and is discussed in the examination of employee behaviour. It can be said that happiness or positive emotional experiences are increasingly emphasized in the work environment, and in this context, the emphasis on pleasant judgments (positive attitudes) or pleasant experiences (positive emotions, moods, feelings, flow states) in working life is increasing (Fisher, 2010).

Some studies suggest that positive psychological capital can be a precursor to increasing employee happiness (Joo and Lee, 2017; Taştan et al., 2020). It can be said that the happiness of working individuals can be increased by improving the positive psychological capital levels of employees. Therefore, it would first be meaningful to explain the concept of positive psychology, which can be considered the starting point of the concept of positive psychological capital, and its organizational reflections.

2 Definition of Positive Psychology

It is possible to say that the concept of positive psychology has come to the fore in the last twenty-five years. Before World War II, three tasks of psychology were the subject point: (1) treating mental illnesses; (2) making the lives of all people more productive and satisfactory; (3) identifying and development high talents. Since World War II, psychology has become a science related to healing and focused on damage repairment within a disease model (Seligman and Csikszentmihalyi, 2000), has almost lost its other two functions.

After World War II, the field of psychology has exhibited an almost entirely negative approach; clinical psychologists have devoted almost all their attention to the diagnosis and treatment of pathologies. Social psychologists, on the other hand, have been preoccupied with the prejudices, delusions, deficits, and dysfunctions of individual behaviour (Luthans, 2002a). During this period, psychology has turned into a science largely devoted to healing, and the utilization mainly of the disease model on behalf of repairing the resulting damage has become the subject point. The state of being focused specifically on pathology has led to ignoring the fact that strengths are one of the most important tools in therapy (Gündüz, 2016). Since the beginning of the 2000s, it has been seen that the science of psychology is incomplete in this aspect, and the concept of "positive psychology" has come to the fore at the point that the positive aspects of individuals should also be developed.

The founder of positive psychology is considered to be Martin Seligman, a professor at Pennsylvania University. As a result of his successful work, Seligman was appointed president of the American Psychological Association in 1998, and in 1999, at the 107th APA Annual Congress, he stated that his agenda was to change the pathological perspective of psychology. Since his position as president, he has become the symbolic leader of positive psychology (Hefferon & Boniwell, 2018).

Seligman states that a memory he had with his daughter, Nikki, influenced his interested in positive psychology. While cleaning the weeds in her garden, Nikki sings and dances while scattering the weeds that her father has collected. Seligman shouts at his daughter getting angry at this situation and Nikki first walks away, then comes back and says to her father: "Dad, do you remember the times before my fifth birthday? From the age of three to five, I was always a whining child. I whined every day. When I reached the age of five, I decided not to whine anymore. This was the most difficult thing I've ever done. If I have stopped whining, you can also stop grumbling." From now on, Seligman began to think that, rather than fixing what was wrong, it should be focused on the topics of identifying, and nurturing the best qualities being possessed and developing those strong aspects (Seligman and Csikszentmihalyi, 2000).

Positive psychology has shown rapid progress thanks to the original research performed by Seligman and his colleagues, by way of examining the strong aspects of the individuals, dealing with tracking the measurement of their well-being, and mental development and positive health development (Leimon and McMahon, 2018). Although Seligman is considered to be the founder of positive psychology, it is also seen that some philosophers and scientists dealt with the study areas of positive psychology before.

Before Seligman, Abraham Maslow first used the concept of "positive psychology" in his book titled "Motivation and Personality" which he wrote in 1954 (Maslow, 1954). Hefferon and Boniwell (2018) evaluate those who studied the "good life" before positive psychology was considered a discipline into four groups;

(1) Aristotle, who lived between BC 384 and 322, performed studies on the subjects of morality, virtue, and good life, and stated that the most important well-being for humanity was happiness (Hefferon and Boniwell, 2018).

(2) The idea of pragmatism, put forward by Jeremy Bentham and continued by John Stuart, argued that the right actions or policies made by the state are those that provide the greatest well-being, and they called this the "greatest happiness principle" or "principle of utility". Unlike the previous philosophers, the pragmatists claimed that it was possible to measure happiness and worked on it (Hefferon and Boniwell, 2018).

(3) The evaluations of William James (1890) in which he intertwined physiology, psychology, and philosophy in the 'emotions' section of his highly popular article published with the title "Principles of Psychology" are very important (Hefferon and Boniwell, 2018). Again, the articles of James (1902) on "healthy-mindedness" and the manifesto of Franklin (1959) on the search for meaning can also be considered important steps for positive psychology (Alparslan *et al.*, 2019).

(4) It can be said that humanist psychology and positive psychology, which emerged in the late 1950s and early 1960s, have common interests. The main motivation in humanistic psychology is focused on positive qualities such as mental health, happiness, contentment, kindness, sharing, generosity, and compassion. The humanist thinkers state that individuals have responsibilities for their destinies. For individuals who are aware of their innate motivations to realize their development and potential, this mentioned perspective considers life as a process (Hefferon and Boniwell, 2018). It is seen that both humanistic psychology and positive psychology emphasize the works of fully functional individuals and healthy individuals and their self-actualization. Maslow, one of the psychologists who popularized humanistic psychology, complained that psychology was too preoccupied with disorder and dysfunction, saying little about the potentials, virtues, attainable desires, and full psychological satisfaction of the individual; he stated that it rather reveals more of their deficiencies, diseases or sins (Linley *et al.*, 2006).

Positive psychology can be defined as the study of the conditions and processes that contribute to the development or optimal functioning of individuals, groups, and institutions (Gable and Haidt, 2005). In other words, positive psychology is a subfield of general psychology in which the scientific method is used to investigate and explain the positive aspects of life, and the clinical interventions promoting well-being are developed based on this research, Positive psychology is concerned with understanding and facilitating (1) happiness and well-being, (2) positive traits and engagement in interesting activities, and (3) the development of meaningful positive relationships, social systems, and institutions (Carr, 2014).

The aim of positive psychology is expressed by a core group composed of well-known research-oriented positive psychologists such as Seligman and Diener (2000), Christopher Peterson (2000), and Rick Snyder (2000), as to shift the emphasis on the wrong ones in the individuals to right ones, to the strong aspects as opposed to weaknesses, dealing with resistance rather than resilience and dealing with the improvement and development of health and well-being as opposed to the cure of pathologies. According to (Luthans, 2002a) Sheldon and King (2001), Positive psychology is nothing more than the scientific study of the strengths and virtues of ordinary people. Positive psychology is concerned with finding out what works, what is right, and what thrives in the "average person."

Positive psychology, which is a clinical endeavour, aims to increase the well-being and happiness level of the individual rather than correcting the deficiencies, and in this context, it plays a complementary role rather than replacing traditional clinical psychology (Carr, 2016). Along with positive psychology, the mission of the science of psychology, which focuses on curing mental illnesses in general, initially adopted but later neglected, to enable the individual to realize his or her potential and thus have a more productive and happier life, has come to the fore again. In addition, the science of psychology has gained a feature striving to develop those strong aspects to have the individuals to reach a more productive, happier, and healthier life by focusing on the strong aspects of the individual, such as positive individual characteristics, competencies, virtues, and values (Kümbül Güler, 2018).

3   Organizational Dimension of the Positive Psychology

Positive psychology has made significant progress in the organizational field, as in many other fields. Since the Hawthorne Studies, it has been known that there is an obvious relationship between the positive emotions and performances of the employees. However, the field of organizational behaviour has also paid more attention to managerial and employee disorders and problems in the workplace. It is generally interested in issues such as motivating and directing ineffective employees, correcting insufficient skills and abilities, developing dysfunctional attitudes and behaviors such as resistance to change, managing conflicts more effectively, and coping with stress and burnout (Luthans, 2002b).

Besides, it is possible to mention a consensus in the world and organizations that there is a need for a more balanced approach both focusing on correcting the weaknesses, taking the negative aspects into account, and trying to develop the strong aspects by handling the positive aspects (Luthans and Youssef, 2007).

Because of the increasing demands in the workplace and a greater need for information activities and innovation, organizations need to find ways to identify what their employees can do and enable them to be the best. Positive psychology will have a high contribution to ensuring success in work life due to its significant focus on development and its ability to transform into many factors contributing to organizational performance. Positive psychology can be beneficial within the point of showing the management how human capital can be developed and used, in guiding the organizational policy, or in enabling the employees to make their best contribution (Davis, 2010).

Positive organizational psychology, which evaluates organizations from a positive psychology perspective, is defined as the scientific examination of the positive subjective experiences and characteristics in the work environments and organizations and their application for increasing the effectiveness and quality of life in the organizations (Donaldson and Ko, 2010).

The reflection of positive psychology on the work and the organizational environment has manifested itself with two sub-currents: (1) "Positive Organizational Scholarship ", conducted by researchers from the University of Michigan; (2) "Positive Organizational Behavior" conducted by researchers from the University of Nebraska" (Kümbül Güler, 2018).

3.1   Positive Organizational Scholarship

The studies on positive organizational scholarship as an identifiable field of study began at the University of Michigan in the early 2000s. Positive organizational scholarship is considered to be an umbrella concept used to unify various approaches in organizational studies, each of which includes the concept of "positive". When the definitions for the concept are examined, it is seen that they all contain similar emphasis describing the processes, dynamics, perspectives, and results that are considered to be positive (Cameron and Spreitzer, 2011).

Positive organizational scholarship endeavors to investigate the organizations expressed in appreciation, cooperation, virtuousness, liveliness, and meaningfulness, which are the key indicators of success in achieving prosperity and human well-being. Investigating traits such as reliability, resilience, humility, originality, respect, and forgiveness among employees, and handling the issues of excellence, transcendence, positive deviance, and extraordinary performance are to be considered. It can be said that organizational science has so far paid little attention to such phenomena (Bernstein, 2003).

This field is primarily concerned with particularly the positive attributes, processes, and outcomes of the organizations and their members. It deals with the concepts typically described with words such as excellence, successfulness, improvement, prosperity, flexibility, or virtue. While representing an expanded perspective, it places greater emphasis on the ideas of "kindness" and "positive human potential". It draws attention to the facilitators (processes, skills, structures, methods, etc.), the motivations (unselfish, self-sacrificing, selfless contributor, etc.), and the results or effects (vitality, meaningfulness, joy, high quality, etc.) (Cameron *et al.*, 2003).

In essence, positive organizational scholarship represents a particular way of thinking, a value orientation, and a stance toward organizational research. It deals with the factors in organizations that enable the development of manpower, promote vitality and improvement in the employees, realize possible flexibility and renewal, and improve individual and organizational performance. It examines the positive aspect of organizational performance and investigates the positive deviance or how the organizations and their members develop in extraordinary forms (Bernstein, 2003).

3.2   *Positive Organizational Behavior*

Positive organizational behaviour is a concept introduced as a result of the studies of researchers at the University of Nebraska Gallup Leadership Institute (Luthans *et al.*, 2007a). In his psychology literature research, while finding approximately 375,000 articles about "negatives" (disease, depression, anxiety, fear, anger, etc.), Luthans (2002a) found only about 1,000 articles about various "positive" concepts and abilities of individuals, demonstrating that the positive organizational behavior approach was an important need (Wright, 2003).

Just as positive psychology does not claim to have discovered positivity towards individuals, positive organizational behaviour also acknowledges that positive reinforcement, process justice, job satisfaction and commitment, social and organizational citizenship behaviours, and many other positive structures have been found in the organizational research of the previous years. Accordingly, positive organizational behaviour tries to re-emphasize the importance of a positive approach rather than a change of paradigm (Youssef and Luthans, 2007). Positive organizational behaviour is considered an

approach that has the potential to transform the research and practice of organizational behaviour and human resources management, without denying the
importance of examining the negatively oriented structures and approaches
(Luthans *et al.*, 2007a).

Positive organizational behaviour which handles the organizational dimension of positive psychology, is defined as "the research and application of the
strengths and psychological capacities of positively oriented human resources
that can be measured, developed, and effectively managed." (Luthans, 2002a;
Luthans, 2002b). In this context, for a psychological power or capacity to be
included in the understanding of positive organizational behaviour, there must
be a capacity that is open to development and manageable in terms of improving performance (Luthans and Youssef, 2007). Luthans and Avolio (2009) summarize the specific criteria for positive organizational behaviour as follows:

1)   It should be based on theories, research, and valid measurements.
2)   It must be situational and therefore be open to development.
3)   It must have an impact on performance.

Positive organizational behaviour capacities are situational and therefore
open to learning, development, change, and management in the workplace.
These capacities are of the characteristic that can be developed through training programs, managed on the job, or self-improved (Luthans, 2002a).

Focusing on the positive aspects of the individuals within the organization
can also have important outcomes. The individuals make positive choices in
work-related decisions or the challenges related to a new task, make more and
more challenging motivational efforts in tasks with positive effects, and are
determined to be more resilient instead of giving up when faced with problems and failure might be considered. Additionally, it is supported by research
that these individuals can be successful in overcoming problems and resisting
stressful situations by developing positive thought patterns (Luthans, 2002b).

It is argued that there are some points where positive organizational behavior and positive organizational scholarship differ. Firstly, it can be said that
research topics vary. While positive organizational scholarship mostly considers positive situations and characteristics at the organizational level, positive
organizational behavior examines the positive characteristics at the individual
level and the impact of these characteristics on performance development. It
can be seen that the importance given to performance development is greater
in positive organizational behaviour (Kutanis and Oruç, 2014). Although
the concepts that both approaches deal with are very close to each other,
the positive organizational behavior scholarship focuses on virtue, compassion, employee empowerment, and similar issues; the positive organizational

behavior focuses on issues such as hope, optimism, flexibility, resilience, and positive capital (Narcıkara, 2017).

Based on the premise of positive psychology, the positive organizational behaviour proposed by Luthans and his colleagues handles the strong and psychological capacities with positively focused human resources that can be measured, developed, and managed for performance improvement in workplaces. These positive organizational behaviour capacities, which are called positive psychological capital, include self-sufficiency, hope, optimism, and resilience (Peterson and Spiker, 2005). At this point, it will be useful to explain the positive psychological capital and its basic components.

3.3   *Positive Psychological Capital*

It is seen that the types of capital that provide a competitive advantage for organizations have also changed along with the changes realized in working life (Figure 12.1). The capitals such as financial, physical, and technological, which are traditional types of capital, are no longer considered sufficient and ideal resources to sustain the competitive environment. As the human factor becomes effective in the competitive equation, the importance of traditional types of capital that can be easily evaluated has begun to decrease. The human, social, and positive psychological capital, which prioritizes the human factor, emerges as types of capital that gain importance in this context (Kümbül Güler, 2018).

Human capital is generally referred to as competencies obtained from knowledge, skills, ability or education, experience and certain identifiable skills. Social capital also includes interpersonal, intergroup and inter-organizational relationships, networks and connections; besides the basic group and community resources, social structure, and cultural dynamics (Luthans and Youssef, 2004).

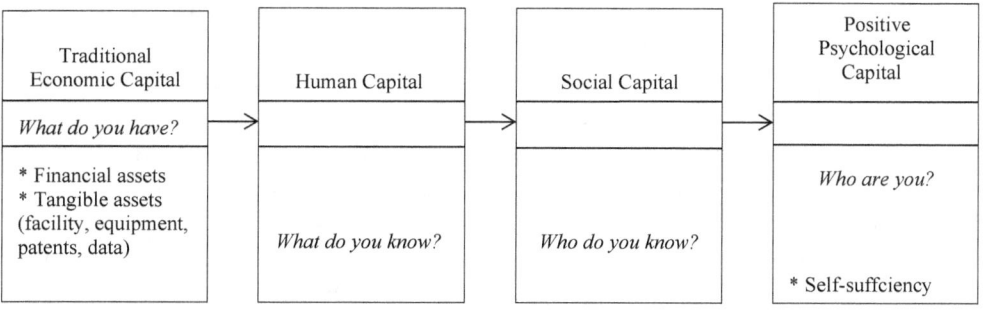

FIGURE 12.1   Expanding the capital for competitive advantage
SOURCE: LUTHANS *ET AL.*, 2004

However, positive psychological capital is expressed as a concept that is considered in the context of positive organizational behaviour and that represents its characteristics in the best way. Psychological capital plays a role in revealing the internal, positive and strong aspects of the individual and developing these mentioned aspects. Along with the achievement of this, it is desired to teach individuals that they can be happier, increase their success and psychologically be better. On the other hand, it can be said that individuals who are positively oriented and have a high level of happiness will make significant contributions to the establishment of successful and productive organizations (Alparslan *et al.*, 2019).

The psychological capital is a concept that goes beyond the human capital. It does not imply explicit knowledge, skills and abilities that can only be built through educational programs or even on-the-job experience. It is not equivalent to the organization-specific implicit knowledge that managers and employees develop over time during their socialization processes. In other words, psychological capital refers to more than just the things to be known or one's expertise. Psychological capital goes beyond social capital. It offers new and exciting opportunities on the opportunities provided by social relationships and networks between individuals, departments and organizations. In this respect, it means more than an effective contact group or people in a beneficial and functional relationship (Luthans *et al.*, 2007a).

The positive psychological capital which means the positive psychological state of the individual, consists of the components of self-sufficiency, hope, optimism and resilience. These components that make up the positive psychological capital (self-sufficiency, optimism, hope and resilience) have different structures and characteristics. However, although they are conceptually different and independent from each other, the positive psychological capital formed by the combination of these structures, as the main factor, is more effective than the sum of the effects of the individual structures (Kümbül Güler, 2018). Psychological capital is expressed as a higher-level core structure that synergically combines the effect levels of these components. Therefore, in general, the impact of investing, developing, and managing the psychological capital of the employees on their performance and attitudinal results is expected to be greater than the individual capacities that constitute it (Luthans *et al.*, 2007a).

Each component of psychological capital is meaningful by itself, based on theory, validated by empirical research data, and has a positive impact on attitudes, behaviours, and performance. Additionally, each one is considered a psychological state (not a trait) and therefore can be developed. When all of these four different elements exist in a situation with appropriate organizational antecedents, the motivational tendency of the individual towards accomplishing the tasks and goals increases significantly. Briefly, the thing that allows psychological capital to be considered as a higher structure is that the simultaneous presence of these elements provides greater benefit (Levene, 2015).

Many examples can be given regarding the interaction between the components of the psychological capital. It will be the point of argument that the hopeful people who have ways to achieve their goals will be more motivated, be able to overcome difficulties and thus be more resilient. Confident people will be able to transfer and apply their hope, optimism, and resilience to specific tasks in specific areas of their lives. A resilient person will be skillful at the issue of using the adaptation mechanisms necessary for realistic and flexible optimism. These examples demonstrate the many positive outcomes that can result from communication between the conditions of psychological capitalism (Luthans *et al.*, 2007a). Since it is thought that it would be useful to know what these components that make up positive psychological capital mean in a more detailed way, they will be examined one by one below.

4   The Basic Components of Positive Psychological Capital

4.1   *Self-efficacy*
Self-efficacy is defined as the perception of the individual about how well the ways of action required to cope with possible situations can be carried out (Bandura, 1982) In other words, self-efficacy is not about the number of skills that the individuals have, but about the things that they believe they can do with what they have under various circumstances (Bandura, 1997). Their beliefs in self-sufficiency determine how individuals feel, think, motivate, and the way they behave (Bandura, 1994).

A strong sense of self-sufficiency increases the success and individual well-being of a person in many ways. Individuals with high beliefs about their abilities approach difficult tasks as challenges to be overcome, rather than threats to be avoided. These individuals increase and sustain their efforts in the face of failure and quickly regain their sense of competence after failures and setbacks. When threatening situations arise, they approach them with confidence that they can exercise control over them. Such an effective outlook also enables personal achievements to be produced, stress to be reduced and defenses against depression to be developed (Bandura, 1994).

The beliefs of the individuals about self-sufficiency will be able to help determine how much effort they will expend on an activity, how long they will endure when faced with obstacles, and how resilient they are in the face of negative situations. The higher their sense of self-sufficiency is, the higher their effort, determination, and flexibility will be. As a result of these effects, the self-efficacy beliefs of the persons may be strong determinants and predictors of the level of success ultimately achieved (Pajares, 1996).

4.2   *Optimism*

It is seen that the concept of optimism is conceptualized in two different ways. While, on one hand, optimism is considered as a comprehensive personality trait, on the other hand, it is interpreted as an explanatory style (Carr, 2016). Optimism, which is considered a personality trait, is defined as a generalized positive perspective or expectation (Youssef-Morgan and Luthans, 2015). In other words, it is expressed as a general expectation that better things, rather than negative things will happen in the future. Scheier, Carver, and their colleagues argue that people with optimistic traits pursue valuable goals when faced with difficulties, can regulate their personal situations with effective coping strategies, and can achieve their goals accordingly (Carr, 2016).

Seligman, Peterson, and their colleagues interpret optimism as a style of explanation. Accordingly, optimistic individuals use a style of attribution that explains the positive events with personal, permanent, and widespread reasons; and the negative events as external, temporary, and situation-specific (Youssef-Morgan and Luthans, 2015). In other words, when an optimistic individual encounters a negative situation, he/she will use an explanation style such as "This event occurred due to some reasons or people outside of me, it will last for a short time, not for a long time, and its effect will be at small scale.". A pessimistic individual, on the other hand, will interpret the current negative event as: This event happened because of me, it always happens this way, this situation will continue and will have an impact on other situations (Hefferon and Boniwell, 2018).

Studies are showing that optimistic individuals have better social connections because they work harder. They report that the optimists have more social support than pessimists. They may also have characteristics such as more constructive problem-solving, better relationships with spouses and children, and greater resilience against loneliness during the later periods of life. On the other hand, it is also stated that having strong social networks increases optimism (Carver and Scheier, 2014).

4.3   *Hope*

Hope is considered by some theorists as a concept with emotional content, and by others as a two-dimensional concept that includes a cognitive dimension as well as an emotional dimension. While the first dimension is evaluated as the individual feels strong in achieving the goals, the second dimension is considered as the ability to find ways to achieve the goals (Usta, 2019).

Snyder and his colleagues, who have important studies on the concept of hope, defined this concept as a thinking process that includes action and ways toward the goals of the individual (Snyder and Sympson, 1997). Here, activeness means that a person takes action and continues in a certain way toward a goal. The process of thinking about ways refers to the perceived competence of the individual in determining the ways to achieve the goals. In other words, hope is expressed as the energy of struggling to achieve important and attainable goals (Hefferon and Boniwell, 2018).

Hope theory refers to both the ability to generate plans to achieve goals and the need for energy to implement those plans (Bailey *et al.*, 2007). Goals are considered as the support of hope theory. A goal must be achievable but involve some degree of uncertainty about its achievement. If the gain is certainly perceived, the accompanying motivation will generally be low. Additionally, individuals must believe that they can create applicable ways to their goals. Even though the individual generally focuses on a route, he or she should be able to identify alternative paths to maintain hopeful thinking in case of encountering an obstacle (Snyder *et al.*, 2000).

Hope is considered an important factor in individuals taking action toward the goals they set and coping with the obstacles they encounter. Here, beyond just hoping and waiting, seeking alternative solutions, evaluating and updating the current situation, and then starting over is also desired to be expressed (Gündüz, 2016). Individuals with high levels of hope are expected to grasp their goals more clearly, have more confidence in their abilities to cope with stress, and have higher motivation to actively apply coping strategies to achieve their goals. People with high levels of hope may also evaluate stressful conditions as a struggle rather than a threat (Usta, 2019).

4.4   *Resilience*

Although resilience was previously considered a rare personality trait related to adaptability and coping, it was conceptualized as a "state" with research conducted in the 1970s. Many studies conducted over the years have also confirmed that resilience is not a rare phenomenon (Luthans *et al.*, 2006b) and can be developed.

Resilience is a dynamic process by which individuals exhibit positive adaptation despite the experiences of significant adversity or trauma (Luthar and Cicchetti, 2000). In other words, it is defined as the capacity to gather strength again in the face of positive but seemingly overwhelming changes such as difficulties, uncertainties, failure, and even increased responsibilities (Luthans and

Youssef, 2004). Here, resilience means not only being able to cope with negative situations but also going beyond normal in very positive and challenging events (Luthans *et al.*, 2007a).

Performed researches suggest that resilient people can thrive and grow through failures and challenges. Even after failure, they can reach not only their previous situation but also higher performance levels and find meaning and value in their lives in this process (Luthans and Youssef, 2004). The three components of such resilience are expressed as follows: resolute acceptance of reality; Deep belief that life is meaningful, often reinforced by strong values; An extraordinary ability to adapt and improvise to significant changes (Larson, 2004).

It is also thought that resilience will make important contributions to the working environment. In particular, the improvement of performance, job satisfaction, and organizational commitment in organizations is expected to bring potential positive results with enriched social capital (Luthans *et al.*, 2007a).

With practices aimed at improving psychological capital components, organizations will be able to ensure that employees improve themselves and thus create the desired working environment. The individuals with improved psychological capital levels will both feel better in their business life and reflect the positive outcomes of this on their work performance and will be in a more positive emotional state in their non-work lives as a result of this situation. At this point, how psychological capital levels can be improved becomes an important issue.

5   Development of Psychological Capital

Positive psychology is concerned with emphasizing and developing positive characteristics instead of correcting the wrong points in human nature. Individuals with developed positive aspects can lead a happy life with a high level of satisfaction and can benefit those around them. Developing positive psychological capital, which focuses on who the individual is and how to be better in the future, will be the best investment for the individual. For organizations, working with individuals with developed psychological capital can provide many important advantages (Luthans *et al.*, 2007b).

Theoretical and practical studies have shown that positive psychological capital is related to performance, job satisfaction, and other work attitudes. Each of the components of psychological capital is a long-term, rare,

TABLE 12.1   Management of psychological capital

Management of psychological capital

Development Through Self-Efficacy	* Mastery experiences
	* Representative learning/modeling
	* Social persuasion
	* Positive feedback
	* Physiological and psychological arousal
Development Through Hope	* Goal setting
	* Participating initiatives
	* Demonstrating trust
	* Attendance
	* Contingency planning
	* Mental rehearsals
	* Re-targeting
Development Through Optimism	* Optimism towards the past
	* Appreciation for the present
	* Seeking opportunities for the future
	* Realistic perspectives
	* Flexible perspectives
Development Through Resilience	* Profit-orientated strategies
	* Risk orientated strategies
	* Process orientated strategies

SOURCE: (LUTHANS AND YOUSSEF, 2004)

synergistic effect when combined with others, and can be measured, renewed, and developed (Luthans *et al.*, 2006a). By developing each of the components of self-efficacy, hope, optimism, and resilience, it will be possible to increase the levels of psychological capital and thus contribute to the happiness levels of employees (Table 12.1).

Self-efficacy is defined as the belief that an individual can perform a job or task. It is stated that basically, four factors are effective in the development of self-efficacy beliefs; mastery/success experiences, representative learning/modelling, social persuasion and positive feedback, and physiological and psychological stimulation opportunities (Bandura, 1997; Luthans and Youssef, 2004; Luthans *et al.*, 2007a). To form strong beliefs about self-efficacy, previous achievements, and mastery experiences through the interpretation of these achievements are the most important sources (Tarhan, 2016). In a simulation or real working environment specially prepared for employees or managers, the positive effect of achieving success in a task of gradually increasing difficulty may increase the self-confidence of employees. In addition, a trainer or manager can break down a complex task into its sub-components and teach employees simple sub-skills one by one. This may contribute to the increase of psychological capital by allowing employees to experience small successes more frequently. These simple tasks and skills can be gradually integrated into more complex tasks and provide opportunities for mastery (Luthans *et al.*, 2007a).

Individuals can also develop their self-efficacy beliefs through indirect learning by modelling the behaviours of other individuals. This method can be used in cases where mastery experiences are not possible, the work environment is risky, or the preparation of simulations is very costly (Kümbül Güler, 2018). In such cases, watching a successful manager or employee or dealing with a similar situation with a successful employee helps the observer to develop self-efficacy. In addition, even in the absence of real role models, "imaginary experiences" in which the employee imagines that he/she has managed to cope effectively with difficult situations are also successful (Luthans and Youssef, 2004).

Realistic and positive verbal/social persuasion can also encourage the individual, motivate him/her to succeed, improve his/her skills, and increase his/her sense of individual competence (Tarhan, 2016). Monitoring the performance of the employee and giving him/her accurate and realistic feedback can be an effective method as a part of social persuasion (Kümbül Güler, 2018). Appreciation almost magically encourages people to realize their potential. When a behaviour is appreciated, it will be more likely to be repeated, become more permanent, and start to make the person feel self-sufficient (Mutlu, 2023).

The physiological and psychological stimulation that individuals receive from their bodies during their performances may also be important in the construction of self-efficacy. Individuals usually rely on how they feel physically and emotionally to evaluate their abilities. If these feelings are negative, such as fatigue, illness, anxiety, depression, or stress, self-efficacy will be greatly reduced. On the contrary, if the physical and emotional mood of the individual is positive, it may be a good starting point, although it may not have a great contribution to self-efficacy (Luthans *et al.*, 2004). In this respect, ensuring that the employee is physically and psychologically alert at the point of directing the employee to certain behaviors can be considered a precondition for the development of self-efficacy (Kümbül Güler, 2018).

An important component for the development of psychological capital is hope. Although hope is seen by some as a characteristic that cannot be easily changed, some approaches show a developmental characteristic. Some specific approaches have been successful in developing hope. One of these approaches is related to effective goal setting. Goals set in a participatory manner or presented using a reasonable framework can increase the level of hope. This also affects the desire and ability to develop creative ways to achieve one's goals (Luthans et al., 2007a).

The goals should be difficult enough to stimulate excitement and exploration but still perceived as achievable. It would also be useful to divide difficult, long-term, and challenging goals into smaller, near-term, and more manageable parts (Luthans et al., 2007a). In the training to be given to increase the level of hope, it will be effective to apply a combination of result-oriented, cognitive-behavioural, and verbal expression methods that enable individuals to set clearer goals, to produce several different ways to achieve success, to gather mental energy to achieve the goal, and to see difficult obstacles as a struggle to be achieved (Kümbül Güler, 2018).

In addition, managers and employees should be encouraged to develop their hopes and enjoy the process of achieving their goals, rather than focusing only on the ultimate gains. It is also important that they learn when and how to re-set goals when faced with absolute goal barriers so that they do not fall into the trap of false hope (Luthans and Yousef, 2004).

Another component that should be considered in the development of psychological capital is optimism. Individuals with a pessimistic explanation style usually attribute positive events in their lives to luck, the help of others, or situational factors. These individuals rarely learn from successes and failures or grow from the challenges they face (Luthans and Yousef, 2004). It is possible to train managers and employees to adopt a more optimistic explanation style. Schneider (2001) suggests three particularly applicable perspectives for developing realistic optimism in the workplace (Luthans et al., 2007a): (1) tolerance for the past; (2) appreciation of the present; (3) seeking opportunities for the future. The first approach, "tolerance for the past", means that managers and employees learn to accept their past failures and forgive themselves for their mistakes because they cannot reverse them. The second approach is "appreciation of the present", which means being satisfied with the positive aspects of their present life, including what they can or cannot control. The final approach is "seeking opportunities for the future". It means that the future and its uncertainties are seen as opportunities for growth and progress and are embraced with a positive, welcoming, and confident attitude (Luthans and Yousef, 2004).

Seligman states that learned optimism is possible by changing people's explanation styles. Identifying negative comments about events, evaluating their accuracy, producing more accurate comments, and preventing the tendency to imagine the worst possible outcomes can be beneficial (Mutlu, 2023). Organizations, whether large or small, need optimistic, talented, and motivated individuals. Although some individuals are lucky enough to be born optimistic, other individuals can benefit by learning optimism through the efforts of the organization (Seligman, 2006).

It is also important to develop the resilience component in employees and organizations, which is defined as the ability of individuals to return to their previous level and recover in case of failure, conflict, or difficulties. Resilient individuals exhibit more emotional stability when faced with difficulties, are more flexible to changing demands, and are open to new experiences. It is thought that human resource departments can use expanding sources of knowledge to create a multifaceted approach to developing a more resilient workforce. These approaches are categorized into two main groups: proactive and reactive (Luthans *et al.*, 2006b).

In the proactive approach, three strategies that can be adapted to the workplace are mentioned.

(*1*) *Asset-oriented strategies* focus on increasing the perceived and actual level of assets and resources that can increase the probability of positive outcomes (Luthans *et al.*, 2006a). Developing the human, social, and psychological capital of managers and employees can enable them to better cope with personal and organizational problems (Luthans and Yousef, 2004). What is important here is to contribute to the employability of the organization's employees by organizing workshops for continuous training and development (Kümbül Güler, 2018).

(*2*) *Risk-orientated strategies* refer to the management rather than prevention of risk factors associated with challenges and developmental opportunities from a positive perspective. A favorable development can be overwhelming and perceived as a high-risk situation, along with the opportunity for growth and increased responsibility. In this case, an appropriate alternative risk management strategy may present a developmental opportunity. This development will include coaching/mentoring and frequent constructive feedback. It is also necessary to directly avoid psychologically or physically destructive and unnecessary risk factors (Luthans *et al.*, 2007a).

(*3*) *Process-oriented strategies* include using the strength of the necessary adaptive systems to utilize the individual's asset inventory to manage emerging risk factors. Through strategic planning and organizational learning, organizations can make effective use of financial and human resources to respond flexibly and quickly to new developments and make the organization better prepared to deal with emerging crises (Luthans and Yousef, 2004).

In the reactive approach proposed in the development of resilience, it is suggested that four different personality dimensions will be effective in the development of individual resilience. Bonnano (2004) states that the dimensions of positive emotion, self-enhancement, attribution or locus of control, and hardiness can contribute to creating pathways for individual resilience. Although this approach comes from the clinical field, it can also be effective in building resilience in employees, leaders, and organizations (Luthans *et al.*, 2006b).

(*1*) *Strategies for using positive emotions:* According to the "expand and build" theory of positive emotions developed by Fredrickson (2004), positive emotions expand individuals' repertoire of thoughts and actions and help them to build their permanent resources. Positive emotions specifically trigger a variety of thoughts and actions, while negative emotions lead to narrowing the mind. Positive emotions contribute to a store of personal resources that can be called upon when resilience is needed (Luthans *et al.*, 2006b).

(*2*) *Strategies using self-development/enhancement:* This approach is a tendency similar to the individual trait towards overly positive or unrealistic self-serving judgments. However, it is stated that people with this biased thinking tendency are also more adaptable and better at coping with stressful situations. In this respect, it can be considered as a trait that increases the resilience of the individual (Luthans *et al.*, 2006b).

(*3*) *Strategies using attribution or locus of control:* Another strategy may be that individuals use optimistic attributions to get rid of the impact of a negative situation. Attribution can be expressed as the perception of the cause of an event. While internal attributions (explaining the situation with reasons originating from oneself) may increase the frustration of failure, an external locus of control (explaining the situation with reasons originating from the environment) may be useful to increase resilience. It may be possible to train employees to learn optimistic attribution styles and contribute to resilience (Luthans *et al.*, 2006b).

(*4*) *Strategies using hardiness:* Bonnano (2004) states that hardiness consists of three dimensions. These are being determined to find a meaningful purpose in life, the belief that individuals can influence their environment and the outcomes of events, and learning and growing from positive or negative life experiences. Hardiness can be a situational characteristic and can be developed and used as a reactive strategy to develop resilience. For example, in work environments, leaders can help their followers to become more conscious and introspective, developing self-awareness and finding meaning in their work. Employees who interact with and model their leaders can become more resilient by learning how their leaders grow from experiences such as success and failure (Luthans *et al.*, 2006b).

While significant changes are taking place in working life, the meaning that individuals attribute to work is also changing. The gains that individuals want to obtain in return for the act of working can be quite different. However, being happy in working life can be considered as an expectation that applies to almost all employees. One of the factors that may have an impact on ensuring happiness in working life is the development of positive psychological capital of employees. Positive psychological capital, which has emerged along with the positive organizational behavior approach, states that the strengths of employees, which organizations see as their most valuable assets, can be developed. Managing and developing employees' psychological capital, which consists of self-efficacy, hope, optimism, and resilience components, will have positive results for both employees and organizations. It can be said that individuals with developed psychological capital will increase their well-being in working life.

References

Alparslan, A. M., Yastıoğlu, S., and Taş, M. A. (2019). Mutlu Eden Yöneticiler: Pozitif Psikoloji Bağlamında Araştırmalar ve Öneriler. Ankara: Nobel Akademik Yayıncılık.

Bailey, T. C., Eng, W., Frisch, M. B., and Snyder, C. R. (2007). Hope and optimism as related to life satisfaction. The Journal of Positive Psychology. 2(3): 168–175.

Bandura, A. (1982). Self-efficacy mechanism in human agency. American Psychologist. 37(2): 122–147.

Bandura, A. (1994). Self-efficacy. In: V. S. Ramachandran (Ed.), Encyclopedia of human behaviour. New York: Academic Press. pp. 71–81.

Bandura, A. (1997). Self-Efficacy: the exercise of control. New York: W. H. Freeman and Company.

Bernstein, S. D. (2003). Positive organizational scholarship: Meet the movement: An interview with Kim Cameron, Jane Dutton, and Robert Quinn. Journal of Management Inquiry, 12(3): 266–271.

Bonanno, G. A. (2004). Loss, Trauma, and Human Resilience: Have We Underestimated the Human Capacity to Thrive After Extremely Aversive Events?. American Psychologist. 59 (1): 20–28.

Cameron, K. S., and Spreitzer, G. M. (2011). Introduction: What is Positive About Positive Organizational Scholarship? In: K. S. Cameron, & G. M. Spreitzer (Eds.) The Oxford Handbook of Positive Organizational Scholarship. New York: Oxford University Press. pp. 1–14.

Cameron, K. S., Dutton, J. E., and Quinn, R. E. (2003). An introduction to positive organizational scholarship. In: K. S. Cameron, J. E. Dutton, and R. E. Quinn (Eds.) Positive Organizational Scholarship. San Francisco: Berrett-Koehler. pp. 3–13.

Carr, A. (2014). Positive psychology. In: A. Michalos, Encylopedia of Quality of Life. New York: Springer. pp. 1–13.

Carr, A. (2016). Pozitif Psikoloji. (Ü. Şendilek, Ed.) İstanbul: Kaknüs Yayınları.

Carver, C. S., and Scheier, M. F. (2014). Dispositional optimism. Trends in Cognitive Sciences. 18(6): 293–299.

Csikszentmihalyi, M. (2005). Akış Mutluluk Bilimi. (S. K. Akbaş, Ed.) Ankara: HYB Yayıncılık.

Davis, O. (2010). Why the workplace needs positive psychology. https://www.research gate.net/publication/260146068_Why_the_Workplace_Needs_Positive_Psychology, accessed 10 February 2024.

Donaldson, S. I., and Ko, I. (2010). Positive organizational psychology, behaviour, and scholarship: A review of the. Journal of Positive Psychology. 1–50.

Erer, B. (2021). İşyeri mutluluğunun öncülleri ve sonuçları üzerine nitel bir çalışma. Pamukkale University Journal of Business Research. 8(1): 215–229.

Erhan, T. (2021). İşyeri mutluluğu: Bir kavram incelemesi. International Journal of Society Researches. 17(38): 5686–5712.

Fisher, C. D. (2010). Happiness at work. International Journal of Management Reviews. 12: 384–412.

Fredrickson, B. L. (2004). The broaden-and-build theory of positive emotions. The Royal Society. 359: 1367–1377.

Gable, S. L., and Haidt, J. (2005). What (and why) is positive psychology?. Review of General Psychology. 9(2): 103–110.

Gündüz, H. Ç. (2016.) 21. yüzyılda pozitif psikolojinin parçası olarak umut ve Türkiye'deki yeri. In: A. D. Yıldız (ed.) Pozitif Psikoloji Bağlamında Umut. Ankara: Nobel Akademik Yayıncılık. pp. 41–72.

Hefferon, K., and Boniwell, I. (2018). Pozitif Psikoloji Kuram, Araştırma ve Uygulamalar. (T. Doğan, ed.) Ankara: Nobel Akademik Yayıncılık.

Joo, B. K. and Lee, I. (2017). Workplace happiness: work engagement, career satisfaction, and subjective well-being. Evidence-based HRM: a Global Forum for Empirical Scholarship. 5(2): 206–221.

Keser, A. and Kümbül Güler, B. (2021). Çalışma Psikolojisi. Kocaeli: Umuttepe Yayınları.

Kutanis, R. Ö., and Oruç, E. (2014). Pozitif örgütsel davranış ve pozitif psikolojik sermaye üzerine kavramsal bir inceleme. The Journal of Happiness & Well-Being. 2(2): 145–159.

Kümbül Güler, B. (2018). Pozitif psikolojik sermaye: Tanımı, bileşenleri ve yönetimi. In: A. Keser, G. Yılmaz, and S. Yürür (eds) Çalışma Yaşamında Davranış Güncel Yaklaşımlar. Kocaeli: Umuttepe Yayınları. pp. 15–37.

Larson, M. D. (2004). Positive Psychological Capital: A Comparison With Human and Social Capital And An Analysis of a Training Intervention. Lincoln, NE: University of Nebraska.

Leimon, A. and McMahon, G. (2018). Pozitif Psikoloji for Dummies. (E. Tanıl, Ed.) Ankara: Nobel Akademik Yayıncılık.

Levene, R. A. (2015). Positive Psychology At Work: Psychological Capital and Thriving as Pathways to Employee Engagement. Master of Applied Positive Psychology (MAPP) Capstone Projects, University of Pennsylvania, Pennsylvania.

Linley, P. A., Joseph, S., Harrington, S., and Wood, A. M. (2006). Positive Psychology: Past, Present, and (Possible) Future. The Journal of Positive Psychology, 1(1): 3–16.

Luthans, F. (2002a). The need for and meaning of positive organizational behaviour. Journal of Organizational Behavior. 695–706.

Luthans, F. (2002b). Positive organizational behaviour: Developing and managing psychological strengths. Academy of Management Executive, 16(1), 57–75.

Luthans, F., and Avolio, B. (2009). The "point" of positive organizational behaviour. Journal of Organizational Behavior. 30: 291–307.

Luthans, F., and Youssef, C. M. (2004). Human, social, and now positive psychological capital management: investing in people for competitive advantage. Organizational Dynamics, 33(2): 143–160.

Luthans, F., Luthans, K. W., and Luthans, B. C. (2004). Positive psychological capital: Beyond human and social capital. Business Horizons. 47(1): 45–50.

Luthans, F., Avey, J. B., Avolio, B. J., Norman, S. M., and Combs, G. M. (2006a). Psychological capital development: toward a micro-intervention. Journal of Organizational Behaviour. 27: 387–393.

Luthans, F., Vogelgesang, G. R., and Lester, P. B. (2006b). Developing the psychological capital of resiliency. Human Resource Development Review. 5(1): 25–44.

Luthans, F., and Youssef, C. M. (2007). Emerging positive organizational behaviour. Journal of Management, 33(3): 321–349.

Luthans, F., Youssef, C. M., and Avolio, B. J. (2007a). Psychological Capital: Developing the Human Competitive Edge. New York: Oxford University Press.

Luthans, F., Avolio, B. J., Avey, J. B., and Norman, S. M. (2007b). Positive psychological capital: measurement and relationship with performance and satisfaction. Personnel Psychology, 60: 541–572.

Luthar, S., and Cicchetti, D. (2000). The construct of resilience: Implications for interventions and. Dev Psychopathol, 12(4): 857–885.

Maslow, A. H. (1954). Motivation and Personality. New York: Harper & Row.

Mutlu, H. (2023). Bu Bir Yatırım Tavsiyesidir Psikolojik Sermaye. İstanbul: Doğan Yayınları.

Myers, D. G. and Diener, E. (1995). Who is happy?. Psychological Science. 6(1): 10–19.

Narcıkara, E. (2017). Örgüt ortamında artarak yükselen olumluluk: pozitif örgüt okulu perspektifi. İş'te Davranış Dergisi. 2(1): 20–33.

Pajares, F. (1996). Self-efficacy beliefs in academic settings. Review of Educational Research, 66(4): 543–578.

Peterson, S. J., and Spiker, B. K. (2005). Establishing the positive contributory value of older workers: a positive psychology perspective. Organizational Dynamics. 34(2): 153–167.

Seligman, M. E. (2006). Learned Optimism: How to Change Your Mind and Your Life. New York: Vintage Books.

Seligman, M. E., and Csikszentmihalyi, M. (2000). Positive psychology: an introduction. American Psychologist. 55(1): 5–14.

Snyder, C. R., Ilardi, S. S., Cheavens, J., Michael, S. T., Yamhure, L., and Sympson, S. (2000). The role of hope in cognitive-behavior therapies. Cognitive Therapy and Research. 24(6): 747–762.

Snyder, J. C., and Sympson, S. C. (1997). Hope: An individual motive for social commerce. Group Dynamics: Theory, Research, and Practice. 1(2): 107–118.

Tarhan, S. (2016). Özyeterlik, Kişilik Özellikleri ve Umut. In: A. D. Yıldız (Ed.) Pozitif Psikoloji Bağlamında Umut. Ankara: Nobel Akademik Yayıncılık. pp. 175–200.

Taştan, S., Küçük, B. A. and İşiaçık, S. (2020). Towards Enhancing Happiness at Work with the Lenses of Positive Organizational Behavior: The Roles of Psychological Capital, Social Capital and Organizational Trust. Postmodern Openings. 11(2): 192–225.

Turan, N. (2018). Çalışma mutluluğu: Kavram ve kapsam. Uludağ Journal of Economy and Society, 37(1), 169–212.

Usta, F. (2019). Umut. In: A. Akın, & Ü. Akın (Eds.) Psikolojide Güncel Kavramlar 1: Pozitif Psikoloji. Ankara: Nobel Akademik Yayıncılık. Pp. 73–82.

Veenhoven, R. (2009). How do we assess how happy we are? Tenets, implications and tenability of three theories. In: A. K Dutt and B. Radcliff (eds.) 'Happiness, Economics and Politics: Towards a multi-disciplinary approach', Edward Elger Publishers, Cheltenham UK, pp. 45–69.

Wright, T. A. (2003). Positive Organizational behaviour: an idea whose time has truly come. Journal of Organizational Behavior. 24(4): 437–442.

Youssef-Morgan, C. M., and Luthans, F. (2015). Psychological capital and well-being. Stress and Health, 31: 180–188.

CHAPTER 13

Harmony in Motion: Examining the Relationship between Happiness, Flow Theory, and Physical Activity

Gözde Ersöz

The literature has extensively shown the connection between physical activity and mental health. Exercise promotes better mental health by reducing the symptoms of stress, anxiety, and sadness. This is probably because exercise causes endorphins and other feel-good neurochemicals to be released. Exercise programs' social and structural components may also provide people with a sense of routine and community, both of which are very good for mental health. But as pointed out, it could be difficult for people with poor psychological health—like those who are depressed or under stress—to start or maintain an exercise program. This difficulty is consistent with Muraven and Baumeister's (2000) theory of the depletion of self-regulatory resources, which holds that mental stress can sap the energy needed for self-improvement activities like exercise. This may further erode self-efficacy and self-confidence, resulting in a vicious cycle whereby poor mental health impedes physical activity, hence reducing the psychological advantages of exercise. This ongoing chapter emphasises the value of customised interventions to help people with low psychological well-being get over obstacles to exercising, which will eventually create a positive feedback loop between mental health and physical activity.

1 Introduction

Happiness is an important concept that human beings strive to achieve at all times, and generally describes the positive psychological state of the individual. Discussions on this subject have continued from the past to the present, starting with important Greek philosophers such as Plato and Aristotle. Today, in psychology, especially in the tradition that started with humanistic psychology and continued with positive psychology, the psychology of happiness exists as an important field of discussion (Arvas, 2017). Happiness is generally understood as the state of being in a positive mood. Within the subject of happiness, researchers have addressed subjective well-being, psychological well-being, life satisfaction and quality of life. In general, the concepts of "subjective well-being" and "psychological well-being" are defined as positive mental health and are used more comprehensively and synonymously with the concept of happiness, including subjective well-being and life satisfaction (Camfield & Skevington, 2008). Since happiness includes general life satisfaction, the concept of "life satisfaction" has also come to the fore. Life satisfaction is a general evaluation of one's quality of life according to one's criteria (Diener et al., 1985). In other words, whether individuals are satisfied with their lives is revealed by a comparison of their standards and their current situation. The issue of happiness is also addressed within the framework of "quality of life". The World Health Organization's definition of the concept of "quality of life", which is also used concerning biological health, comes to the fore. According to this definition, quality of life is people's perception of their position in life in the context of the culture and value systems they live in and about their own goals, hopes, standards and interests (Camfield & Skevington, 2008).

The issue of happiness has taken place extensively in the history of philosophical thought. In this context, hedonism, utilitarianism and the Aristotelian approach have examined the issue of happiness throughout history. The approach that defines happiness as the sum of a person's pleasure-based activities (Nettle, 2005; Ryan & Deci, 2001) and the concept of happiness defined by individual and social interests are referred to as utilitarianism. The approach that defines happiness as a state related to virtues is known as the Aristotelian approach (Ulaş, 2002; Aristotle, 2009).

After the Enlightenment, the sciences diverged and the concept of "happiness", which was one of the important topics of philosophy, has become one of the important topics of psychology. With the increasing interest in happiness in the psychology literature in recent years, the use of the concept of well-being has also increased considerably. As a concept that includes topics such as health, happiness and quality of life, the concept of well-being is an ever-expanding area of research. In addition, the concepts of well-being and happiness are often used interchangeably (Deci & Ryan, 2008).

Depending on the approaches to happiness in philosophical thought, two different approaches to well-being have emerged in the psychology literature as *Hedonist and Evdemonist Approach* (Ryan & Deci, 2001). In research on well-being, the *hedonist approach* focuses on happiness and defines well-being as obtaining pleasure and avoiding pain, while the *eudemonic approach*, which developed based on Aristotle's views, is defined by the degree to which the individual fully fulfils his/her potentials by focusing on understanding and self-realization (Wills, 2009). In addition, researchers have argued that the concept of subjective well-being, which they use about happiness, reflects the hedonic approach to happiness and the concept of psychological well-being reflects the hedonic approach (Deci & Ryan, 2008). Humanistic psychologists were the first to be interested in happiness. Maslow's concept of self-actualization, developed as one of the important concepts of humanistic psychology, describes the coming together of human powers with an efficient and intense pleasure. While Maslow states that feelings such as life satisfaction, happiness, euphoria and peace, and the ability to cope with problems are subjective states that emerge with self-actualization, a relationship between self-actualization and happiness is established based on the Aristotelian tradition (Maslow, 2001).

Erich Fromm, one of the important names of humanist psychology, defines happiness in his work "Virtue and Happiness" as an increase in vitality, sharpness of emotion and thought, and creativity, while he argues that unhappiness is related to the weakness of these abilities and functions (Fromm, 1999).

According to *Csikszentmihalyi*, another important figure in the positive psychology movement, happiness can be achieved through flow, which he defines as people immersing themselves in an activity to the extent that they do not care about anything else. Csikszentmihalyi put forward his "flow theory", which he also calls the theory of high-level experience, based on the data he obtained by examining the times when people are most enjoyable and investigating the reasons why these people feel this way. For this, he started by examining people who immerse themselves in their work such as painters, athletes, musicians and surgeons (Csikszentmihalyi, 2005). According to the results he obtained, these people work as if there is no issue, no problem other than the work they are doing. In other words, they feel that they are lost in the activity, that is, they work in the flow (Myers & Diener, 1995). Csikszentmihalyi claims that when people give themselves to an activity that is compatible with their abilities within this flow experience, they feel much happier than when they are not doing anything meaningful (Diener, Lucas & Oishi, 2002). According to Csikszentmihalyi, the flow experience is much more than a passive feeling of comfort. Although television, as one of the most important tools in human life in postmodern times, functions as a consolation for loneliness and unhappiness, it does not have the potential to create positive emotions since it is a passive activity (Csikszentmihalyi, 2005). To summarize; the individual's getting lost in the task, feeling that he/she has cognitive competence and control over the task, and the intrinsic pleasure and enjoyment he/she derives from the activity he/she is doing is the "flow state" (Csikszentmihalyi, 2005). (Csikszentmihalyi, 1990). In this part of the book, the flow experience, which deals with the concept of happiness from the perspective of positive psychology, the Flow Theory will be explained in detail and the reasons for the feeling of happiness in physical activity, exercise and sports activities, which have a mediating role in making people feel happy, will be explained and the flow experience experienced in these activities will be discussed concerning the concept of motivation.

2   Flow State

The flow experience is defined as the internal pleasure experienced by the individual when he/she concentrates fully on the activity gives all his/her attention to the activity and feels that he/she has a sufficient level of skill according to the perceived difficulty in the activity (Jackson, Thomas, Marsh, & Smethurst, 2001). Moneta (2004) defined flow experience as the individual's focus on the task, the internal pleasure he/she derives from the activity when he/she feels cognitive competence and control over the task, and feeling integrated with the activity. Asakawa (2004), on the other hand, defined flow experience as "an optimal state of mind that occurs when the individual thinks that he/she is competent during the activity he/she is doing and when he/she focuses on the task and is highly motivated and enjoys it". In another definition, this concept is described as a process of consciousness complexity and reintegration experienced at "equal" and "high" levels of both the difficulties required by any activity (perceived difficulties) and the skills required to overcome these difficulties (perceived skills or competencies) (Csikszentmihalyi, 1990).

Kimiecik and Harris (1996) suggested that the flow experience is accompanied by having fun and positive affect. With this view, they conceptualized the sense of flow, which includes various cognitive components such as individuals' perception of balance between clear goals, intense concentration, task difficulty, and skill (Vlachopoulos, Karageorghis, & Terry, 2000).

Csikszentmihalyi conceptualized the flow experience in nine dimensions (Csikszentmihalyi, 2002; Jackson & Csikszentmihalyi, 1999). Three dimensions are proposed as the conditions under which flow occurs (Nakamura & Csikszentmihalyi, 2002):

1. Task Difficulty/Skill Balance: It is the perception of the balance between the challenge of the task and the person's ability to accomplish the task (e.g.: I am challenged, but I believe that my skills will overcome the challenge).

2. Clear goals: Feeling that he/she knows the requirements of the action, feeling that he/she knows the goals for the action (e.g.: I know very well what I want to do)

3. Specific Feedback: The state of feeling how one is performing in line with the requirements and goals of the movement and the individual's ability to get feedback/information from the performance (e.g. I have a clear idea of my performance).

The other six dimensions are suggested to be characteristics of the flow experience (Csikszentmihalyi, 2002; Nakamura & Csikszentmihalyi, 2002):

4. Task Focus: Complete focus on the task (e.g. I focus my attention completely on what I am doing).

5. Sense of Control: Feeling that they have control over their activity (e.g. I have control over what I do).

6. Decreased Self-Awareness: Not caring about others' evaluations of my activity (e.g. I am not interested in what others might think of me).

7. Action-Awareness Combination: Feeling and perceiving that he/she can do the requirements of the task automatically, without thinking, in a compliant manner (e.g. I make the right movements without thinking).

8. Transformation of Time: Immersing oneself in time during the activity, getting lost in the activity, not feeling the passage of time, being fully involved in the activity (e.g. I feel that time is differentiated).

9. Goal Attainment Experience: The intrinsic satisfaction or reward that an individual receives from an activity (e.g. I enjoy trying something).

An individual can lead a good life if he/she gives his/her full attention to the activities he/she does (Nakamura & Csikszentmihalyi, 2002) and this is realized by experiencing flow in the activities that people do. Moreover, since experiencing a sense of flow results in personal development (Seligman, & Csikszentmihalyi, 2000), it is important to understand and examine this concept. Csikszentmihalyi (1990) developed the Flow Theory to better understand this concept. This model will be explained below.

3   Flow Theory

The concept of "flow experience" was first developed by Mihaly Csikszentmihalyi in 1965 in his doctoral dissertation on the subjective experiences of artists. Based on this concept, later studies have been conducted with hundreds of individuals who seem to spend their time with activities of their own choice, such as chess players, games and leisure activities, alienation and purposelessness, intercultural differences, working women, low and high

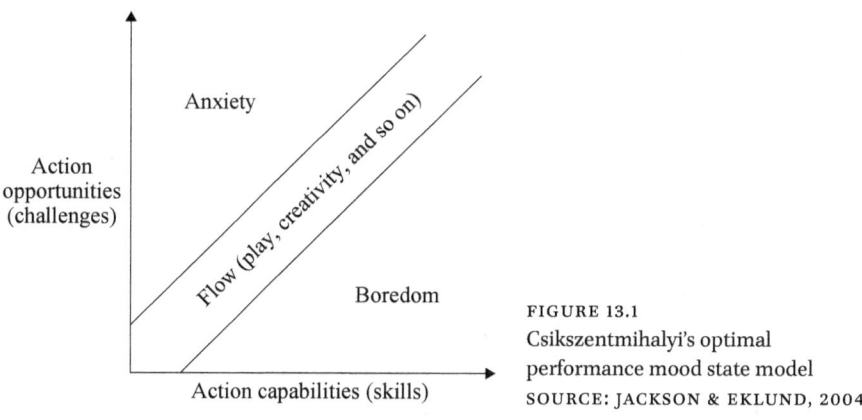

FIGURE 13.1
Csikszentmihalyi's optimal
performance mood state model
SOURCE: JACKSON & EKLUND, 2004

achieving English and Mathematics students, ocean travellers, people who
have suffered great hardships alone (Aydın, 2005). The model proposed by
Csikszentmihalyi, which was developed to reveal the formation of the flow
experience, is presented in Figure 13.1.

According to this model, flow experience occurs when an individual can
accomplish activities that require a high level of challenge and difficulty and
gain control over these tasks. According to the model, the individual experiences feelings of anxiety if he/she does not have the skills to accomplish
high-challenge tasks, boredom and distress if his/her skills are higher than the
requirements of the task, and apathy if his/her skills are low and the task is
not challenging (Jackson & Eklund, 2004). According to the model, the dual
combination of the difficulty level of the activity or goal and the low and high
levels of skills results in four distinct conditions. These are:

1.   High level of challenge – High level of skill = Flow
2.   Low level of difficulty – High level of skill = Boredom
3.   Low level of difficulty – Low level of skill = Emotional blunting (apatheia)
4.   High level of difficulty – Low level of skill = Anxiety (Csikszentmihalyi,
     1990).

Csikszentmihalyi's flow theory model explains why the activities experienced
in the flow experience lead to growth and exploration. A person cannot enjoy
doing the same thing at the same level for a long time and either get bored
or frustrated. After such an experience, the desire to enjoy it again pushes
the person to develop their skills or discover new opportunities to use them
(Aydın, 2005).

In 1975, Csikszentmihalyi used this model in his book "Beyond Boredom
and Anxiety" to explain the reasons that drive individuals to leisure activities
(Aşçı, Çağlar, Eklund, Altıntaş, & Jackson, 2007), while other researchers have

developed this model to describe different types of motivation and to under-stand what the flow experience is (Csikszentmihalyi & Nakamura, 1989).

The Flow Experience Model, which can reveal the reasons for the activity performed by individuals, is one of the few models related to the concept of motivation that puts forward hypotheses about the relationships between affect, motivation and cognition (Csikszentmihalyi & Nakamura, 1989). The flow experience mentioned in this theory is a holistic sensitivity experienced in moments when the person is completely absorbed in the activity and inter-twined with it (Aydın, 2005).

The concept of flow experience has tried to combine motivation, person-ality and subjective experience in a holistic framework, and studies on this concept are of great importance as it is related to concepts such as positive emotional states and life satisfaction (Aşçı, Çağlar, Eklund, Altıntaş, & Jackson, 2007). There are many studies on this concept, which has been addressed by different disciplines and its relationship with various psychological phenom-ena has been investigated. The studies on this subject are summarized below.

4   Studies on Flow Experience

The concept of flow experience has been studied in different fields such as cross-cultural psychology, shopping and marketing, hobbies and leisure activities, leisure studies including web and computer use (Rettie), informat-ics and neuropsychology, religion and value studies. It has also been studied in fields related to education. For example, music, dance and art education, foreign language education (Egbert), special education (Jonson), counsellor education (Whitmire), educational technology and teaching, and educational administration are some of the fields in which this concept is addressed about education (Sahranç, 2007). In studies conducted in the field of education, it has been stated that students seek activities that they find enjoyable and that they can associate with positive emotions (Boekaerts, 1993; Csikszentmihalyi & Rathunde, 1993; Schultz & Pekrun, 2007). Bassi and DelleFave (2004) and DelleFave and Bassi (2003) confirmed that adolescents experience higher lev-els of flow in home study and structured leisure activities than in other activi-ties (Bassi & DelleFave, 2004).

Apart from these disciplines, the concept of flow experience has been used in several studies including life satisfaction (Han, 1988), stress (Donner, & Csikszentmihalyi, 1992), anxiety (Jackson, Kimiecik, Ford, & Marsh, 1998), perceived competence (Basom & Frase, 2004), goal orientation (Jackson & Roberts, 1992), self-perception (Jackson, Thomas, Marsh, & Smethurst, 2001) and motivation (Jackson, Kimiecik, Ford, & Marsh, 1998; Kowal & Fortier, 2000). The flow experience, which is related to many psychological phenomena, has also been investigated in sports and exercise environments.

5   Flow Experience in Sport and Exercise

Flow state, also known as optimal emotional state, is one of the important concepts in terms of reflecting the mental and psychological state that occurs with the optimal performance experience in a sport and exercise environment. Optimal emotional experience and related behaviours in athletes and exercisers have been the focus of attention of researchers in the field of sport and exercise psychology in recent years (Aşçı, Çağlar, Eklund, Altıntaş, & Jackson, 2007).

The flow experience, which can be experienced during many activities such as sports, art and work (Kivikangas, 2006), has the following characteristics: Fusion of movement and awareness, focusing attention on a limited stimulus area, temporary loss of self-awareness, cognitive sufficiency and a sense of control, having clear goals, receiving immediate feedback and intrinsic motivation (Csikszentmihalyi, 1990).

For a child, the experience of flow is building a tower bigger than any tower he has ever built before, trying to put the last piece of the tower with trembling fingers. For a swimmer, the experience of flow is the moment when he tries to break his record. For a violinist, it is mastering a very complex musical passage. There are thousands of opportunities and challenges for each individual to improve. Such experiences need not necessarily be pleasurable in the moment. A swimmer's muscles may become extremely tired during a race that he or she will never forget, he or she may feel that his or her lungs are about to burst at that moment, and he or she may be overwhelmed with exhaustion; yet, looking back, these moments were the best moments of life for that swimmer (Özşahin, 2003).

Similar to these examples, during the flow experience, individuals who exercise do not realize how time passes during the activity, they are fully focused on the task they are doing, they are internally motivated, they enjoy the task they are doing, they feel that they are doing the task without difficulty, they feel that they are integrated with the activity and that they have control over all movements. When the individual reaches this experience, he/she does his/her best with a feeling of automatization and a high level of self-confidence (Aşçı, Çağlar, Eklund, Altıntaş, & Jackson, 2007).

The concept of flow experience has been mostly addressed in sport and physical activity settings (Stein, Kimiecik, Daniels, & Jackson, 1995; Vlachopoulos,

Karageorghıs, Terry, 2000). Studies in this field are mostly on athletes. However, in the context of physical activity, the line between sport and exercise has been blurred from time to time as non-elite and hobby athletes' sports are also a type of exercise (Phillips, 2005).

Csikszentmihalyi (2000) examined the flow experience in rock climbing athletes. In investigating this concept, Csikszentmihalyi (2000) adopted a qualitative approach in the context of physical activity, along with other studies examining elite athletes (Jackson, 1992; Jackson, 1995; 281).

Jackson (1992), in his research examining the factors associated with elite ice skaters experiencing flow during performance, stated that the factors that seem to be associated with experiencing this concept include positive mental attitude, positive affect before and during the competition, maintaining appropriate focus, physical readiness, and harmony with the partner in pairs; while the factors that disrupt or prevent optimal performance mood are physical problems and mistakes, inability to focus, negative mental attitude, and lack of spectator support (Jackson, 1992).

In another qualitative study conducted by Jackson (1996), Csikszentmihalyi's (1990) conceptual model was taken as a basis and it was stated that elite athletes in seven different sports experienced flow within the framework of the model described by Csikszentmihalyi (1990) (Jackson, 1996).

Russell (2001) interviewed 42 collegiate athletes from different sports and investigated which factors facilitate, which factors hinder and which factors disrupt the state flow experience. The results were in line with previous qualitative research in this field and revealed that athletes experienced similar emotions in the flow experience regardless of sport type and gender (Russell, 2001).

In a study by Jackson et al. (2001) that examined the relationship between flow experience and some psychological skills and self-concept in athletes from three different sports, it was concluded that these two concepts were related to flow experience. In addition, absence of negative thinking, goal setting, emotional control, and relaxation were found to be moderately and highly related to different degrees of flow experience (Jackson, Thomas, Marsh, & Smethurst, 2001).

Jackson (1995) asked athletes in athletics, rowing, swimming, cycling, triathlon, American football, and ice hockey about what facilitates, disrupts, and hinders the flow experience, and found that preparation (physical and mental), self-confidence, focus, how the performance feels and progresses, and the highest level of motivation and arousal are among the most important factors affecting whether the flow experience is experienced.

There are few studies in the literature on the flow experience of exercisers (Grove & Lewis, 1996; Phillips, 2005; Vlachopoulos, Karageorghis, & Terry,

2000). Grove and Lewis (1996) conducted flow and hypnotic susceptibility measurements twice during each class of an exercise class that met twice a week for six weeks and found that the flow experience increased from the beginning to the end of the classes and that this experience was greater in individuals who were susceptible to hypnosis than in those who were not. When participants who exercised for more than 6 months were compared with those who exercised for less than 6 months, it was found that the duration of exercise was significantly related to the flow experience.

In the studies investigating whether the flow experience differs according to the gender variable, there are studies indicating that this concept does not differ between male and female participants (Jackson, Thomas, Marsh, & Smethurst, 2001; Koehn, 2007; Russell, 2001), Murcia et al. (2009) found that the continuous flow experience was higher in men than in women. Murcia, Gimeno, and Coll (2008) stated that men had higher mean scores than women in the "sense of control" sub-dimension. In addition to the different findings of gender variables on flow experience, there is a consensus in the literature that flow experience and motivation (especially intrinsic motivation) are consistently positively related to each other. However, it is not clear how this is established. It is clear that intrinsic motivation and Csikszentmihalyi's (1990) concept of the experience of goal attainment are similar constructs, and thus it is predicted that there is a positive relationship between flow experience and intrinsic motivation (Phillips, 2005).

In physical activity, exercise and sports environments, there is an experience of flow and this experience makes individuals happy. On the other hand, adopting physically active living habits, exercising and doing sports also make individuals happy. Different views on the relationship between active living and happiness are found in the literature. We will now discuss the studies describing this relationship.

6   Exercise and Happiness

In addition to the positive physiological effects of regular physical exercise, there are also many psychological benefits. Researchers have explained the mechanisms and benefits of exercise on psychological health as follows: Aerobic exercise increases the release of noradrenaline and dopamine, induces euphoria due to the increase in plasma beta-endorphin levels and changes positive mood (Bruggman and Ferguson 2002, Challagan 2004; Daley 2002). According to Mutrie (2002), Fox examined 36 randomized controlled trials and found a positive relationship between physical activity and mood. It is emphasized that regular exercise lowers blood pressure, slows down pulse rate, facilitates breathing, reduces stress and anxiety symptoms, reduces negative emotions such as anger and aggression, provides emotional control, and improves sleep quality (Artal and Sherman 1998; Landers 2004; O'Brien 2004). In a study investigating the relationship between physical exercise and sleep in Finland, 1600 individuals were asked how they perceived the effects of exercise on sleep. 39% of the men and 30% of the women stated that exercise had a significant effect on improving sleep (O'Conner & Youngstedt, 1995).

The relationship between exercise and psychological health is mostly focused on depression. Depression is an emotional condition that negatively affects the quality of life of millions of people worldwide (Gelenberg, 2010). Although pharmacotherapy and psychological interventions are primarily used in the treatment of depression, recent studies have shown that exercise reduces depression symptoms in support of traditional treatments (Antunes et al., 2005; Blumenthal et al., 1999; Chu et al., 2011; Callaghan et al., 2011). Previous studies have indicated that exercise has the same effect as medication (Brenes et al., 2007; Blumenthal et al., 2007) or psychological interventions (Fremont & Craighead, 1987) in the treatment of depression. According to Landers (2004), exercise shows antidepressant effects from the earliest period of depression treatment, regulates the changes in daily life due to depression and increases the interaction of the individual with the environment. Artal and Sherman (1998) applied 8-week walking, running and recreational therapies to clinically hospitalized depressed patients and found that depression levels were low only in walking and running groups. Many studies have shown that exercise 3–4 times a week can reduce depression symptoms like standard antidepressant drug treatments (Daley, 2002; Landers, 2004; Matthew & Wattles, 2001). The National Service Framework for Mental Health (NICE) recommends that people receiving treatment for depression should be directed to exercise and support their treatment in this way. According to the NICE depression guideline, counselor-led, structured, three times a week (45 minutes hour) mild to moderate exercise for more than 10–14 weeks regulates depression symptoms (NICE, 2009). In the guideline published by the Scottish Intercollegiate Guidelines Network (SIGN), it was stated that depression can be managed by exercise without the use of medication in adults. In the UK, an exercise referral system was established (DOH, 2001) and those who wanted to get help with exercise were supported by preparing a physical activity program, but after general evaluations, it was not understood whether the desired results were achieved in terms of the effectiveness of this system and recommendations could not be made for future studies (Sorensen, 2006).

Physical exercise has been reported to have positive effects on many clinical diseases such as anxiety disorders, somatoform disorders, and substance abuse among mental problems. Experimental studies show that exercise is also very effective in reducing anxiety. In a study involving 36 patients with anxiety disorders, it was reported that at the end of an 8-week aerobic exercise program, there was a significant decrease in anxiety levels in other subcategories defined except social phobia. In these patients who were followed up for one year, it was observed that improvements in general anxiety disorder and agoraphobia without panic attacks continued and the recurrence rate of panic attacks and agoraphobia decreased (Thachuk and Martin, 1999).

One of the issues affecting the psychological state of individuals is the concept of "self-efficacy", which is defined as the belief that a person can initiate a behaviour that can have an impact on what is happening around him/her and sustain it until the result is obtained. Self-efficacy was defined by Bandura as the belief in one's abilities to manage the situations expected of him/her (Luszczynska, Urte, & Ralf, 2005). According to Bandura, self-efficacy is shaped by environmental, behavioural and cognitive factors (Bandura, 1977) and is defined as an individual's ability to control his/her emotional performance in difficult situations (Schunk, 1991). Research has shown that the concept of self-efficacy is effective in exercise participation (McAuley, 1992), weight control (Bernier & Avard, 1986) and the development of health-related behaviours (O'Leary, 1992). Self-efficacy is also associated with depression. Having a low level of self-efficacy is one of the factors that cause depression (Bandura, 1986). In general, individuals may become depressed if they begin to doubt their ability to perform an action that is important to them (Ahrens, 1987). In some long-term studies in adults, self-efficacy beliefs in parenting (Olioff & Aboud, 1991), work (Pomaki, ter Doest, & Maes, 2006), and other important personal goals (Olioff, Bryson, & Wadden, 1989) have been found to predict depression.

One of the emotional states that exercise positively affects is psychological well-being. The fact that exercise participants have low levels of stress, anxiety and depression problems may be beneficial for participating in an exercise program. Likewise, low levels of psychological well-being of individuals may also be effective in exercise participation. For example, Muraven and Baumeister (2000) argued that people have limited energy to change themselves and that mental stress can reduce this energy. In addition, low levels of psychological well-being may be related to self-confidence and self-efficacy. Individuals who are depressed or stressed may have problems completing an exercise program and this naturally negatively affects the psychological well-being of the person (Jones, Harris, Waller, & Coggins, 2005). Previous research supports the relationship between psychological well-being and physical activity (Fox, 1999). Current studies in this field now focus on understanding physical activity behaviour and increasing this behaviour to contribute positively to psychological well-being (Sebire, Standage, & Vansteenkiste, 2009).

7   Conclusion

The problem of happiness is an important issue that has been thought and discussed from past to present and different opinions have been put forward about what it is. Happiness, which is generally identified with the presence of a positive emotional state and the absence of a negative emotional state, can have many sources, many reasons, as well as many factors that prevent it.

In the history of philosophical thought and the science of psychology, many explanations have been offered on the subject of happiness. In general, two currents have come to the fore regarding the nature of happiness and how it can be achieved. While hedonism says that happiness is a state of mind that arises in situations that give pleasure to the individual, a significant number of people have argued that this is not a real and lasting happiness, but a state of momentary contentment, and have tried to explain happiness with more profound reasons. Here, the relationship between happiness and virtue emerged. Especially today, with the influence of the Positive Psychology movement, the relationship between happiness and virtue has been addressed by many researchers and it is seen that the interest in this subject is increasing.

Mihaly Csikszentmihalyi, one of the pioneering scientists in the field of positive psychology, has tried to understand the topic of "happiness" through studies on how people experience inner satisfaction from their pursuits and creativity. He interviewed artists, writers, athletes, chess masters and surgeons who did their work for the sheer joy of it, even without the rewards of money or fame, and found that joy came not from moments of stress and relaxation, but from moments of concentration, when their attention was completely focused on something else. He called this the "flow experience". The reason for the definition of "flow" was that the people he interviewed described this intense experience as being like a river flowing, being carried by the current, flowing.

When an individual experiences a sense of flow, they experience the following states:
– At that moment in time, one has a state of concentration in which one's attention is intense and completely focused on one point.

- It is the merging of one's behavior and awareness.
- Self-awareness (self-consciousness) is lost.
- The person feels that they have control over the situation or activity.
- Temporal experience is distorted; one's subjective experience of time changes.
- The experience of the activity becomes intrinsically rewarding, an autotelic (self-purposeful) experience.
- The person receives immediate feedback during the activity.
- The person feels that they have the potential to succeed.
- One's other needs become unimportant to him and he becomes absorbed in the activity.

Csikszentmihalyi developed "Flow Theory" as a result of his research. In Flow Theory, there are two dimensions: "difficulties" and "skills". According to this theory, if the difficulty level of the activity we do is much higher than our existing skills, the individual experiences disappointment in the activity. On the contrary, if the activity is very easy and we have no difficulty in doing this activity, we experience the feeling of boredom. Let's say a person wants to do a physical activity but does not feel competent to do that activity, it is likely to experience anxiety at that moment and exit the flow channel. Likewise, if one wants to do a physical activity but the activity is extremely simple and below one's skill level, one will experience boredom and will have difficulty being motivated and will again exit the flow channel. Therefore, the prerequisite for achieving flow, that is, for the person to be able to continue exercising and feel pleasure, is a balance between the skills and ability level of the person and the difficulty of the action.

It has been demonstrated for many years that participation in exercise and sports brings joy and happiness to people. Sports and physical activity positively affect individuals' life satisfaction by increasing social interaction, self-confidence and self-esteem and reducing anxiety and depression. Despite this, most people are still not physically active, that is, they do not make efforts to increase their daily active time. Studies have shown that regular exercise increases subjective well-being and happiness and reduces depression in largely healthy people (Ertürk, 2021).

Living a physically active life and exercising regularly make individuals happy for physiological and psychophysiological reasons and can also put people in a state of emotional flow. In order to continue exercising and maintain active living habits, it is important for individuals to be happy in their physical activities. Experiencing happiness seems to be more possible by going into a state of flow. When individuals experience the 9 dimensions of the flow

experience mentioned below, they will experience the feeling of flow and will be able to show continuity in these activities.
- Challenge-Skill Balance,
- Action-Awareness Merging,
- Clear Goals,
- Unambiguous Feedback,
- Total concentration on the task at hand,
- Sense of Control,
- Loss of Self-consciousness,
- Transformation of Time,
- Autotelic Experience

References

Aristotle (2009). Nicomachean Ethics, trans. Saffet Babür, Ankara: Bilgesu Publications.

Ahrens, A. H. (1987). Theories of depression: The role of goals and the self-evaluation process. Cognitive Therapy and Research.11: (6): 665–680.

Antunes, H. K.; Stella, S. G.; Santos, R. F.; Bueno, O. F.; de Mello, M. T. (2005). Depression, anxiety and quality of life scores in seniors after an endurance exercise program. Rev. Bras. Psiquiatr. 27, 266–271.

Artal, M. and Sherman, C. (1998). Exercise Against Depression. The Physician and Sports Medicine, 26: (10): 57–61.

Arvas, F. B. (2017). The Concept of Happiness in Psychology and Islamic Religious Thought Tradition: A Comparative Study. Journal of Human and Social Sciences Research, 6(4), 109–128.

Asakawa, K. (2004). Flow experience and autotelic personality in Japanese college students: How do they experience challenges in daily life? Journal of Happiness Studies, 5(2): 123–154.

Aşçı, F. H., Çağlar, E., Eklund, R. C., Altıntaş, A., and Jackson, S. (2007). Adaptation Study of State and Trait Optimal Performance Emotion State-2 Scales, Journal of Sport Sciences Hacettepe J. of Sport Sciences, 18 (4): 182–196.

Aydın, K. B. (2005). The Effect of Stresle Coping Group Program Based on Akış Kuramına on Stresle Coping Strategies of Ergenlerin Stresle Coping Strategies, Doctoral Dissertation, Ankara.

Bandura, A. (1977). Self-efficacy: toward a unifying theory of behavioural change. Psychological Review, 84: (2), 191.

Bandura, A. (1986). The explanatory and predictive scope of self-efficacy theory. Journal of social and clinical psychology, 4 (3): 359–373.

Basom, M. R. and Frase, L. (2004). Creating optimal work environments: Exploring teacher flow experiences, Mentoring and Tutoring, 12: 241–258.

Bassi M. and Delle Fave A. (2004). Adolescence and the changing context of optimal experience in time: Italy 1986–2000. Journal of Happiness Studies, 5:155–179.

Blumenthal, J. A.; Babyak, M. A.; Doraiswamy, P. M.; Watkins, L.; Hoffman, B. M.; Barbour, K. A. et al. (2007). Exercise and pharmacotherapy in the treatment of major depressive disorder. Psychosomatic Medicine. 69: (7), 587.

Boekaerts, M. (1993). Being concerned with well-being and with learning. Educational Psychologist, 28(2): 149–167.

Brenes, G. A.; Williamson, J. D.; Messier, S. P.; Rejeski, W. J.; Pahor, M.; IP, E.; and Penninx, B. W. (2007). Treatment of minor depression in older adults: a pilot study comparing sertraline and exercise. Ageing and Mental Health. 11: 61–68.

Brugman T. & Ferguson S. (2002). Physical Exercise and Improvements In Mental Health. Journal of Psychosocial Nursing. 40: (8), 24–31.

Callaghan, P.; Khalil, E.; Morris, I., and Carter, T. (2011). Pragmatic randomized controlled trial of preferred intensity exercise in women living with depression. BMC Public Health 11, 465. doi: 10.1186/1471-2458-11-465.

Camfield, L., & S. M. Skevington (2008). "On Subjective Well-Being and Quality of Life", Journal of Health Psychology, 13 (6): 764–775.

Challagan, P. (2004). Exercise: A Neglected Intervention in Mental Health Care? Journal of Psychiatric & Mental Health Nursing. 11: (4), 476–483.

Chu, C.; Ni, Y.; Tan, G.; Saunders, C. J. and Ashburner, J. (2011). Kernel regression for fMRI pattern prediction. Neuroimage 56: 662–673.

Csikszentmihalyi, M. (1990). Flow: The Psychology of Optimal Experience. New York: Harper & Row Publishers, Inc.

Csikszentmihalyi, M. and Nakamura, J. (1989). The Dynamics of intrinsic motivation: A study of adolescents. In R. Ames & C. Ames (Eds.), Research on motivation in education: Goals and cognitions, New York: Academic Press., p. 45–71.

Csikszentmihalyi, M. (2002). Flow: The classic work on how to achieve happiness. Random House.

Csikszentmihalyi, M. (2005). Flow: The Science of Happiness, trans. Semra Kunt Akbaş, Ankara: HYB publications.

Csikszentmihalyi, M. and Rathunde, R. (1993). The measurement of flow in everyday life toward a theory of emergent motivation. In R. Dienstbier (Ed.), Nebraska symposium on motivation: Vol. 38. Perspectives on motivation (pp. 57–97). Lincoln: University of Nebraska Press.

Daley, A. J. (2002). Exercise Therapy and Mental Health In Clinical Populations: Is Exercise Therapy A Worthwhile Intervention?. Advances In Psychiatric Treatment. 8, 262–270.

Deci, E. L., and R. M. Ryan (2008). "Hedonia, Eudaimonia and Well-Being: An Introduction", Journal of Happiness Studies, 9: 1–11.

Department of Health. The NHS plan. London: DoH, 2001.

Diener, Ed; R. A. Emmons; R. J. Larsen and S. Griffin (1985). The Satisfaction With Life Scale, Journal of Personality Assessment, 49: 71–75.

Diener, Ed; R. E. Lucas and S. Oishi (2002). "Subjective Well-Being: The Science of Happiness and Life Satisfaction", Handbook of Positive Psychology, edt. C. R. Snyder & S. J. Lopez, pp. 63–73, New York: Oxford University Press.

Donner, E., and Csikszentmihalyi, M. (1992). Transforming stress to flow. Executive Excellence, 9, 16–17.

Fox, K. R. (1999). The influence of physical activity on mental well-being. Public Health and Nutrition, 2, 411–418.

Fremont, J., & Craighead, L. W. (1987). Aerobic exercise and cognitive therapy in the treatment of dysphoric moods. Cognitive therapy and Research, 11: (2), 241–251.

Fromm, Erich (1999). Virtue and Happiness, trans. Ayda Yörükan, 5th edition, Istanbul: TIB Culture Publications.

Gelenberg, A. J. (2010). The prevalence and impact of depression. The Journal of Clinical Psychiatry, 71: (3), 1–478.

Grove, J. R. and Lewis, M. A. E. (1996). Hypnotic susceptibility and the attainment of flowlike states during exercise. Journal of Sport & Exercise Psychology, 18: 380–391.

Han, S. (1988). The relationship between life satisfaction and flow in elderly Korean immigrants. In M. Csikszentmihalyi, & I. S. Csikszentmihalyi (Eds.), Optimal experience: Psychological studies of flow in consciousness, New York: Cambridge University Press., pp. 138–149.

Jackson, S. A. and Roberts, G. C. (1992). Positive performance states of athletes: Toward a conceptual understanding of peak performance. The Sport Psychologist, 6: 156–171.

Jackson, S. A. (1992). Athletes in flow: A qualitative investigation of flow states in elite figure skaters. Journal of Applied Sport Psychology, 4: 161–180.

Jackson, S. A. (1995). Factors influencing the occurrence of flow state in elite athletes. Journal of Applied Sport Psychology, 7: 138–166.

Jackson, S. A. (1996). Towards a conceptual understanding of the flow experience in elite athletes. Research Quarterly for Exercise and Sport, 1: 76–90.

Jackson, S. A., and Csikszentmihalyi, M. (1999). Flow in sports. Human Kinetics.

Jackson, S. A., Kimiecik, J. C., Ford, S. K. and Marsh, H. W. (1998). Psychological correlates of flow in sport. Journal of Sport and Exercise Psychology, 20: 358–378.

Jackson, S. A. & Eklund, R. C. (2004). The Flow Scales Manual. Morgantown, WV: Fitness Information Technology, Inc.

Jackson, S. A., Thomas, P. R., Marsh, H. W., and Smethurst, C. S. (2001). Relationships between Flow, Self-Concept, Psychological Skills, and Performance, Journal Of Applied Sport Psychology, 13: 129–153.

Jones, F.; Harris, P.; Waller, H. and Coggins, A. (2005). Adherence to an Exercise Prescription Scheme: The Role of Expectations, Self-Efficacy, Stage of Change and Psychological Well-Being. British Journal of Health Psychology. 10, 359–378.

Kivikangas, J. M. (2006). Psychophysiology of flow experience: An explorative study, Department of Psychology, University of Helsinki, Master's thesis.

Koehn, S. (2007). Opensity And Attainment Of Flow State, Victoria University, School Of Human Movement, Recreation And Performance, Faculty Of Human Development, Doctorate Thesis.

Kowal, J. and Fortier, M. S. (2000). Testing relationships from the hierarchical model of intrinsic and extrinsic motivation using flow as a motivational consequence, Research Quarterly for Exercise and Sport (RQES), 71(2): 171–181.

Kowal, J. and Fortier, M. S. (1999). Motivational Determinants of Flow: Contributions From Self-Determination Theory, The Journal of Social Psychology, 139 (3): 355–368.

Landers, D. M. (2004). The Influence of Exercise On Mental Health. Retrieved November 20, from http:// www.fitness.gov/ mentalhealth.htm.

Luszczynska, A.; Urte, S. and Ralf S. (2005). "The General Self-Efficacy Scale: Multicultural Validation Studies", The Journal of Psychology, 139: (5), 439–457.

Maslow, A. (2001). Psychology of Being Human, trans. Okhan Gündüz, Istanbul: Kuraldışı Publications.

Matthew, G. and Wattles, M. S. (2001). Professionalization of Exercise Physiology. Journal of Sport & Exercise Psychology. 4: (4), 246–258.

McAuley, E. (1992). The role of efficacy cognitions in the prediction of exercise behavior in middle-aged adults. Journal of Behavioral Medicine. 15, 65–88.

Moneta, G. B. (2004). The Flow Experience Across Cultures, Journal Of Happiness Studies 5: 115–121.

Muraven, M. and Baumeister, R. F. (2000). Self-regulation and depletion of limited resources: Does self-control resemble a muscle? Psychological Bulletin. 126, 247–259.

Murcia, J. A. M., Gimeno, E. C. and Coll, D. G. (2008). Relationships among Goal Orientations, Motivational Climate and Flow in Adolescent Athletes: Differences by Gender, The Spanish Journal of Psychology, Vol. 11, No. 1: 181–191.

Murcia, J. A. M., Noguera, F. C., Coll, D. G., Gimeno, E. C., and Pérez, L. M. R. (2009). Flow Disposicional en salvamento Deportivo: Una Aproximacion Desde La Teoria De La Autodeterminacion, Revista de Psicología del Deporte, Vol. 18, num: 23–35.

Mutrie, N. (2002). Healthy Body, Healthy Mind. The Psychologist, 15: (8), 412–413.

Myers, D. G., and Ed Diener (1995). "Who is Happy", American Psychological Society, 6 (1): 10–17.

Nakamura, J., and Csikszentmihalyi, M. (2002). The concept of flow. Handbook of positive psychology, 89, 105.

National Institute for Health and Clinical Excellence. Advanced breast cancer: diagnosis and treatment. (Clinical guideline 81.) London: NICE, 2009. www.nice.org.uk/CG81.

Nettle, D. (2005). Happiness: The Science Behind Your Smile, New York: Oxford University Press.

O'Brien, K. (2004). Exercise For Mental Health. Retrieved November 8, 2004, from http://www.thinkmuscle.com/articles/obrien/exercise-for-mental-health.htm.

O'Conner, P. J. and Youngstedt, S. H. (1995). Influence of Exercise on Human Sleep. Exercise and Sport Sciences Review. 23:105–134.

O'Leary, A. (1992). Self-efficacy and health: Behavioral and stress-physiological mediation. Cognitive Therapy and Research. 16, 229–245.

Olioff, M. and Aboud, F. E. (1991). Predicting postpartum dysphoria in primiparous mothers: Roles of perceived parenting self-efficacy and self-esteem. Journal of Cognitive Psychotherapy. 5: 3–14.

Olioff, M.; Bryson, S. E. and Wadden, N. P. (1989). Predictive relation of automatic thoughts and student efficacy to depressive symptoms in undergraduates. Canadian Journal of Behavioral Science. 21:353–363.

Özşahin, N. (2003). Lise Öğrencilerinin Günlük Yaşamdaki Akış deneyimilarının İncelenmesi, Ankara University, Institute of Educational Sciences, Department of Educational Sciences, Educational Psychology Program, Master's Thesis, Ankara.

Phillips, L. L. (2005). Examining Flow States And Motivational Perspectives Of Ashtanga Yoga Practitioners, the University of Kentucky, Doctorate Thesis.

Pomaki, G.; ter Doest, L. & Maes, S. (2006). Goals and depressive symptoms: Cross-lagged effects of cognitive versus emotional goal appraisals. Cognitive Therapy and Research, 30, 499–513.

Russell, W. D. (2001). An examination of flow state occurrence in college athletes. Journal of Sport Behavior, 24: 83–107.

Ryan, R. M, and E. L. Deci (2001). On Happiness and Human Potentials: A Review Of Research on Hedonic and Eudaimonic Well-Being, Annu. Rev. Psychology, 52: 141–166.

Sahrançı, Ü. (2007). Stress Kontrolü, Genel Öz-Yeterlilik, Durumluk Kaygı ve Yaşam Doyumuyla İlişkili bir Akış Model, Gazi University, Institute of Educational Sciences, Department of Educational Sciences, Division of Psychological Counseling and Guidance, PhD Thesis, Ankara.

Schultz, P. A., and Pekrun, R. (Eds.). (2007). Emotions in education. New York: Academic Press/Elsevier.

Sebire, S. J.; Standage, M. and Vansteenkiste, M. (2009). Examining intrinsic versus extrinsic exercise goals: Cognitive, affective, and behavioural outcomes. Journal of Sport & Exercise Psychology. 31, 189–210.

Seligman, M. E. P., and Csikszentmihalyi, M. (2000). Positive psychology: An introduction. American Psychologist, 55: 5–14.

Sørensen, M. (2006). Motivation for physical activity of psychiatric patients when physical activity was offered as part of treatment. Scandinavian Journal of Medicine & Science in Sports, 16: (6), 391–398.

Stein, G. L., Kimiecik, J. C., Daniels, J. and Jackson, S. A. (1995). Psychological antecedents of flow in recreational sport, Personality & Social Psychology Bulletin, 21(2):
125–135.

Tkachuk, G. A., and Martin, G. L. (1999). Exercise therapy for patients with psychiatric disorders: Research and clinical implications. Professional Psychology: Research
and Practice, 30: (3), 275.

Ulaş, S. E. (2002). Philosophy Dictionary, Ankara: Bilim ve Sanat Publications.

Vlachopoulos, S. P., Karageorghis, C. I., and Terry, P. C. (2000). Hierarchical Confirmatory
Factor Analysis Of The Flow State Scale In Exercise, Journal Of Sports Sciences, 18:
815–823.

Wills, E. (2009). Spirituality and Subjective Well-Being: Evidence for New Domain in
the Personal Well-Being Index, Journal of Happiness Studies, 10: 49–69.

CHAPTER 14

Behind the Global Crises: Ways out of Pandemic and Environmental Disasters for a Sustainable Future

Hakan Yıldırım

The type of work and production volume typically influence the choice of production technique. Workshop, batch, repetitive, continuous and project processes are the five main categories. In particular, there are numerous aspects to consider when choosing a procedure because each type has its pros and cons. This paper aims to describe the five main types of processes by comparing them with examples. It concludes that repetitive and continuous processes first emerged during the Industrial Revolution, while workshops and batch processes were initially managed by humans. It can be said that this procedure allows for a wide variety of operations and requires highly skilled workers and equipment that is very flexible, while workshops focus on small-scale production of a wide range of goods. However, it is noticeable that this type has disadvantages such as complex scheduling and high cost per unit. A jewellery repair shop or a veterinary clinic are obvious examples of job shops. Batches may need to be used for moderate output and moderate product variety. In this context, services for large groups, such as bakeries and air travel, are excellent examples. High flexibility is seen as an advantage of this type, while scheduling complexity and a modest cost per unit can be disadvantages. Pencil, TV and car production lines are examples of products with repetitive processes. While this type has the advantage of allowing large volumes, it is also known to have disadvantages such as minimal flexibility expensive equipment and downtime. The continuous process is known to use low-skilled workers, rigid equipment and the largest output numbers. Examples of continuous processes are steel, sugar, grain, oil, electricity and internet production. High quantities and efficiency are the advantages of this type, while rigidity and lack of variety are the disadvantages. It is noticeable that project work scenarios such as making a movie, publishing a book or building a dam are typically selected for the project process type. Since projects are so diverse, they can have characteristics of all types. In this context, this study uses examples to compare and contrast the five main process types and their respective benefits and drawbacks. Batches are used for medium quantities and task variety, while job shops are often used when small quantities of unique products need to be produced. It is noticeable that repetitive and continuous types emerged after the Industrial Revolution, which now serve as high-volume production types for the general public.

1   Introduction

2020 could take its place as a turning point in modern history due to a severe, unheard-of crisis that exposed the vulnerability of countries to major shocks and the weakness of global systems. The global disruption to economies, cultures and health systems caused by the COVID-19 pandemic can be considered a key case in revealing structural flaws lurking beneath the façade of stability. This crisis has unfolded at a time when environmental degradation and climate change are becoming evident, with catastrophic droughts and devastating wildfires affecting ecosystems and populations across Europe and the world.

The trend of increasing environmental degradation is causing natural disasters to occur more frequently, which could push humanity towards a sixth mass extinction (Johnson, 2023). The destabilisation of entire ecosystems that support the survival of living things can be expressed as a component of biodiversity loss that goes beyond the extinction of individual species. Humanity's dependence on the stability of nature is becoming painfully evident as the "survival system" appears to be collapsing at an alarming rate (Mines, 2023).

The interdependence of environmental health and human well-being can come to light when these crises (health, climate change and biodiversity loss) come together. The pandemic has highlighted the close link between ecosystem health and disease emergence, shedding light on how biodiversity loss, human interference with natural ecosystems and illegal wildlife trade increase the risk of zoonotic diseases (Brema et al. 2022; Chen et al., 2024). As vulnerable people are often the most affected by environmental and health crises, this reality can exacerbate existing socioeconomic inequalities, poverty, exclusion and gender inequality. These cascading effects highlight the urgent need for comprehensive and system-wide change that addresses social inequality and climate and environmental concerns (Kapucu et al., 2024).

This is a crucial time for European policymakers. While there is an ideological commitment to a "green recovery", real progress will require long-term, revolutionary steps in the coming periods. To "build back better" by embracing a climate-neutral, sustainable and equitable future, policymakers must choose between returning to pre-pandemic economic models that caused environmental degradation and social inequality. Wildlife Conservation Foundation

(WWF) believes that post-COVID recovery offers an opportunity to fix social injustice, biodiversity loss and climate change simultaneously. The EU and its member states appear to have a one-time chance to align economic stimulus measures and post-COVID-19 recovery policies with the UN Sustainable Development Goals (SDGs) to achieve an economy that promotes lasting, equitable prosperity alongside planetary boundaries (WWF, 2020; WWF, 2021).

This means that the EU needs to adopt new decision-making paradigms that consider social and environmental impacts in an integrated way so that when the time comes to assess the effectiveness of this recovery, it will not only be through traditional economic metrics. Indicators of progress in Europe towards recovery from COVID-19 and the interlinked challenges of climate change and biodiversity loss should focus on sustainability, well-being and quality of life. To ensure an inclusive, resilient and sustainable recovery, there is a clear need for a full-fledged "prosperity economy" that properly links the economic, social and environmental pillars of sustainable development in line with the SDGs and the European Green Deal (Grossi et al., 2024).

This vision can be realized through the 2030 Agenda and the 17 Sustainable Development Goals. Recognized as a comprehensive and universal framework, the Sustainable Development Goals (SDGs) were established in 2015 to address the interconnected challenges of poverty, inequality, environmental degradation and conflict to leave no one behind. The 2030 Agenda focuses equally on social inclusion, environmental stewardship and economic stability to chart a path towards a thriving economy and a socially just, inclusive recovery that honours the world's borders (Fallah Shayan et al., 2022). This paradigm, besides being aspirational, is necessary for humanity to secure a future where both people and the planet thrive.

2   Economic Theory of Doughnuts and Related Concepts

From the German point of view, the techniques of the doughnut economy are part of a family of methodologies, especially when it comes to comprehensive, impact-oriented claims. Particularly relevant tools in this context are the 'municipal management model', derived from the 'new management model' produced by the Municipal Joint Office for Administrative Management in the early 1990s. As a result, cities have started to think much more strategically and impact-oriented. These concepts are expanded and refined in the study "Pathways to a Common Municipal Strategy", especially as these policy initiatives focus on impact (Korhonen and D'Amato, 2021).

It emphasizes the importance of an impact-oriented, holistic approach, recommends involving municipal departments in the formulation of the plan, calls for linking the strategy to the municipal budget and regular monitoring of its results. This goal is best served by grassroots approaches, such as the city government strategy, which aims to effectively reshape the entire city, especially by involving civil society. As such, they give municipal strategists the chance to consolidate what has already been established. It also encourages even broader impact thinking by highlighting the conflicts of interest between local and global perspectives, especially when viewed from a global perspective.

In this context, doughnut economics enables municipal planners to incorporate current strategic methods and, if required, give them new life. Sustainability has long been a problem for many cities. This conversation has been fuelled by the climate issue and movements like Fridays for Future, which have drawn interest from a sizable portion of the population. Many cities have been managing their sustainability for a while now by using the Sustainable Development Goals (Salguero et al., 2024).

The idea of achieving sustainable economic activity while adhering to ecological constraints was first discussed in the study of Raworth (2017), and it is understood that the idea was put forward together with the doughnut economy method. In addition, some strategies emphasize the "Economy for the Common Good", climate neutrality, circular economy, the United Nations' 2030 Agenda and related SDGs, and a method known as the "precautionary post-growth position" to operationalize sustainability for communities and other stakeholders (Cator, 2024).

The main question that decision-makers in German cities must answer in light of this conceptual diversity is: What is the added value that doughnut economics offers in comparison to other approaches, and how can it help realise the overarching paradigm of "sustainable development," specifically in terms of delivering integrated urban and economic development? The concept of doughnut economics, like other ideas about sustainability, has not been established exclusively at the local level. For municipalities, this necessitates transformation and adaptation measures that can be implemented and whose effectiveness can be assessed.

This primarily depends on the required division of administrative domains of expertise, a reasoning that fails to adequately address numerous social and environmental issues. Therefore, implementing doughnut economics in municipalities brings up important issues such as: Where does the relevant municipal authority start and stop? What are some ways to bring global issues down to the local level? Could ideas like the doughnut make disparities between different urban neighbourhoods worse rather than better?

Doughnut Economics presents a hopeful picture of humanity's shared destiny: a global economy that, through its distributive and regenerative architecture, achieves a thriving equilibrium. Given the interconnected challenges of climate change, violent war, forced migration, rising inequality, xenophobia and ongoing financial instability, such a goal may seem naïve, even naive. Watching or reading the daily news makes it clear that the risk of social, ecological, economic and political collapse is very real. It can be easy to see that the glass is half empty for humanity. In pursuing these concerns, human beings may soon find themselves looking at the economics of survival and collapse, which, like all powerful frameworks, can contribute to the self-fulfilment of the same outcomes (Heidemann, 2023).

However, enough individuals still believe in the future and remain committed to making it a reality. As a generation, we probably have the opportunity to take significant steps to reverse the damage done to the planet, and it is important to fully grasp this. Globally, there is also the realization that if it is decided to do so, there are the financial resources, technological know-how and technological capabilities to eradicate extreme poverty in all its manifestations.

3   Happiness Economics and Instant Gratification

Doughnuts can be described as the pinnacle of "instant gratification"—food that appeals to the senses and provides instant gratification. After buying and eating a doughnut, we may experience a quick surge of happiness, a temporary mood boost brought on by indulging in flavour and decadence. According to happiness economics, these temporary pleasures increase satisfaction in the here and now but may not always contribute to long-term happiness. This is because, from a broader perspective, such delicacies are temporary pleasures and can provide pleasure while they are being experienced. Overindulgence in foods that provide instant gratification can reduce pleasure over time, especially if these foods jeopardize health or financial stability.

However these "quick pleasures" are used in contrast to sustainable sources of satisfaction according to happiness economics, which examines what causes and sustains happiness. Research in this field points to meaningful life activities, strong social ties and physical health as more important factors for true well-being. For example, doughnuts may improve your mood momentarily, but they fail to help with the long-term, typically more complex and subtle aspects of happiness. From a happiness economics perspective, it is clear that a healthy and moderate diet will sustain well-being over time, whereas a diet heavy in confectionery will not (Alvarez-Monzoncillo, 2022).

Moreover, behavioural economics can explain why people gravitate towards doughnuts when they understand the cognitive consequences of overdoing it. The term "present bias" refers to the tendency to favour short-term gains over long-term goals. This is because when a doughnut is readily available, for example, the desire for instant gratification can override concerns about the long-term health effects of consuming excessive amounts of sugar or processed foods. This present bias can lead to self-gratifying choices at the expense of future well-being. Happiness economists are trying to better understand this behaviour to encourage people to make more decisions that lead to long-term happiness.

In the field of happiness economics, the allure of "fast pleasure" foods such as doughnuts draws attention to the trade-off between immediate gratification and sustained satisfaction. A hunger for doughnuts could be initially satiated, but if they develop into a habit, they may cause health problems that eventually reduce happiness. It is in line with more general economic debates about how to effectively strike a balance between short-term expenditure and long-term growth. If people prioritise fleeting pleasures over stability and health, their well-being may be at risk, much like an economy cannot survive forever on disintegrating stocks.

From a policy perspective, the happiness economy has several important questions about how society can incentivize decisions that will improve long-term well-being. Public health campaigns aim to encourage healthier lifestyles and less consumption of processed and sugary foods to increase happiness over time. Through understanding the factors that contribute to current bias and instant gratification, policymakers can create interventions that encourage people to make decisions that balance their current pleasure with their future happiness and health. This could include educating the public about good eating habits or enforcing laws prohibiting the promotion of high-sugar foods to encourage more health-conscious choices (Krousel-Wood et al., 2022).

As the economics of happiness suggests, the good life is more complex than a single doughnut. While sometimes eating a doughnut can enhance the pleasures of life, a truly happy existence requires a combination of rational decisions, valued relationships and meaningful pursuits. Understanding the limits of instant gratification, the happiness economy can offer a holistic approach to well-being that values balance. It is well known that choosing long-term pleasures that support one's health, relationships and personal development is often more important than choosing the temporary satisfaction of a quick treat.

4   The Future of Doughnut Economics through 21st-Century Economic Design

The concept of Doughnut Economics is a radical transformation of existing economic systems, in the sense that they are more sustainable and socially acceptable to the extent that they take into account people and the environment in which they live. This model, detailed in Kate Raworth's Doughnut Economics, proposes constrained economic growth within the so-called safe and just space, which has an ecological ceiling and a social foundation. However, this respectable growth model only allows for economic activity that does not exceed certain social or environmental limits, so-called 'planetary boundaries', thus ensuring that all the basic conditions for existence are met without degrading the environment. As for the 21st century, with its many opportunities and challenges, such as climate change, social justice issues and so on, the Doughnut model offers an approach that helps reconcile the desire for economic growth with the need for a sustainable framework (Michaelsen and Esch, 2023).

In essence, Doughnut Economics offers a paradigm shift. The main reason for this is the addition of indicators of economic success that do not focus only on growth, as traditional models do with GDP by focusing only on growth. The premise is that an economy should not only grow but also advance social and environmental goals, shifting the focus from the mere increase of goods and services to the overall health of the population. In this context, the Model allows variables such as social justice, the state of the environment and the standard of living to be included in ex-ante economic assessments. This shift necessitates a restatement of existing concepts of economics to return to productivity growth as well as human capital development, so that new indicators, including non-monetary figures such as social welfare and ecological health as well as financial indicators, can be accepted by policymakers and institutions (Ludwig et al., 2020; Esch, 2022).

Adapting the principles of the Doughnut Economy to the national and municipal levels of the economy could be a catalyst for sustaining sustainable development and building resilience in such economies as they face the challenges of the 21st century. Cities such as Amsterdam and Copenhagen have begun to apply the Doughnut model to solve urban problems such as eviction, overconsumption and pollution without exceeding the limits set by the planet. These pilot projects can offer an encouraging view that the Doughnut model can provide real solutions to many cities' real problems and that these solutions can be shaped to become solutions to the problems faced by other cities. When such models are applied at the local level, it will be possible for the government to very effectively build the evidence supporting the effectiveness of the Doughnut Economy to build resilient urban economies step by step (Lazard, 2022).

Doughnut economics can only work at a very small scale if institutional inertia is overcome because traditional economic systems are so polarized in the growth paradigm. Switching to Doughnut Economics calls for basic institutional revolutions, for example, reorganizing policies and transforming the financial systems that now exist which are based on profit maximization only, leaving out social and ecological factors. Changes in the institutional frameworks require both political will and public support as well as a campaign to educate various stakeholders on the advantages of Doughnut Economics (Khmara and Kronenberg, 2023). This will help mobilise support for carrying out its message that Doughnut Economics as a new economic model is possible and realistic to achieve.

Doughnut Economics can make tangible the social and environmental equity that they argue should be at the heart of being strong economies of the twenty-first century. It promotes redistributive policies that give people access to basic needs such as energy, clean water, health care and education. These policies should translate into actual policies, such as laws against systemic injustices, especially tax cuts, social security and the financing of public goods. The Donut Economy focuses on the equitable distribution of resources across groups to bridge the gap between dominant and vulnerable populations, thereby creating a fairer economic system for more effective public good (Constantini, 2024).

Doughnut Economics is also based on environmental sustainability, arguing that all economic endeavours must remain within ecological limits to prevent the destruction of the biosphere. Such a paradigm can enable a transition to a circular economy that minimises waste and conserves resources, aligning production and consumption patterns with nature's regenerative potential. Doughnut's goals are fundamentally ecological and cannot be realised without policies that encourage sustainable behaviour: carbon pricing, renewable energy investments, and sustainable exchange policies. Doughnut Economics aims to create a circular economy for long-term environmental sustainability, addressing pressing issues such as climate change, biodiversity loss and resource scarcity (Patwa et al., 2021; Khan, 2024).

The use of doughnut economics also provides opportunities for cross-sectoral collaboration and innovation. This paradigm encourages cooperation across disciplines and stakeholders, such as academia, industry, civil society and politics, to create systematic plans for sustainable development. For example, the private sector, which plays a critical role in production and resource consumption, needs to adopt sustainable practices. Working with the business sector can help mitigate the doughnut philosophy by encouraging investment in environmentally sound production processes, sustainable value chains and green technologies. By encouraging cross-sectoral collaboration (Raworth, 2017), the doughnut economy paves the way for a piecemeal and harmonised approach to achieving sustainability goals.

Time will tell if Doughnut Economics ends up with a bright future: but the fate of this new economic story ultimately lies in the emergence of a narrative that resonates with diverse global actors and societies. A compelling narrative that reorients Doughnut Economics from musing about a desirable future to catalysing action towards achieving one is the first step for broad uptake of these ideas as means to many urgent ends (Khan, 2024). Supporters of Doughnut Economics can also promote a wider understanding of its benefits and practical applications using public campaigns, education, and clear communication about the policy. This narrative can provide backing for the structural transformations needed to build twenty-first-century economies, one that promotes development in which human well-being and planet health go hand-in-hand.

5   Conclusion

2020 stands out as an important turning point in terms of the COVID-19 pandemic revealing important fault lines in the health and economic system. On the other hand, the vulnerability of economies unprepared for such large-scale shocks will be exposed. The loss of biodiversity and degradation of ecosystems, together with rapid environmental degradation, may signal the onset of the sixth mass extinction, one of the most critical problems facing humanity soon. The key lesson is that to make global systems more resilient, the focus should be on long-term sustainability rather than short-term returns. Economic, environmental and public health crises highlight the urgent need for fundamental policy reforms that place equity, sustainability and health at the centre of society. These systemic challenges are likely to exacerbate social inequalities, however, it is becoming increasingly clear that a more holistic and cross-cutting response to these challenges is needed.

Previously neglected problems of environmental degradation are now emerging as a consequence of ecological threats that not only endanger bio-diversity but also contribute to deepening socio-economic inequalities, as it is always the most vulnerable communities that are most affected. It is therefore important to promote resilience-building policies that ensure the protection of all sectors of society as well as the environment, to avoid distorted growth in the future. In this context, the European Union is at a critical crossroads: it can return to a pre-COVID economic order that generates inequality and worsening environmental impacts, or it can follow a more optimistic and ambitious path towards a climate-neutral, green, equitable and sustainable economy. The COVID recovery phase is perhaps the best time to reorient economic policy towards the UNSDGs and ensure that social and environmental needs are addressed in the process. To achieve this shift in perspective, it will be necessary to focus on sustainability, well-being and quality of life—the most sought-after success factors in recent history—rather than on more traditional economic considerations such as GDP, which have been so prevalent in recent times. To seize such a golden opportunity for Europe, it is necessary to redefine the criteria for success from the traditional business-first mindset to broader determinants of social justice and ecological health.

Comprehending the development in a more advanced manner along with the relationship between economic security, environment and society would be considering a long-term mindset. This paradigm shift is characterized by the idea upheld by the well-being economy principle, where the economy, society and environment are interlinked to the SDGs and the European Green Deal.

More specifically, the 2030 Agenda aims to address the interlinked problems of social exclusion, environmental degradation and economic pressures with a single overarching strategy for sustainable development. Achieving the 12 Sustainable Development Goals of a balanced relationship between humanity and the earth is not a goal to be celebrated, but a prerequisite for human existence. As the doughnut economy model illustrates this global paradigm shift, an economy fosters inclusive development while operating within ecological limits. This expands the scope for change in terms of sustainability, resilience and emerging challenges such as social inequalities, global warming and economic turbulence. While this challenge may seem daunting, it can be met through creative and competitive ideas and processes. The development of a fair and equitable global economy is crucial at a time when cooperation is needed to achieve such a state of affairs.

References

Alvarez-Monzoncillo, J. M. (2022). The Dynamics of Influencers Marketing, Routledge, ISBN: 978-0-367-67890-6.

Brema, J.; Gautam, S. and Singh, D. (2022). Global implications of biodiversity loss on pandemic disease: COVID-19. COVID-19 and the Sustainable Development Goals. 305–22. doi: 10.1016/B978-0-323-91307-2.00006-7.

Cator, C. (2024). Transforming the City for Sustainable Futures? Contestation and Alternatives in Amsterdam. Copenhagen Business School. PhD Series No. 24.

Chen, F.; Jiang, F.; Ma, J.; Alghamdi, M. A.; Zhu, Y. and Hong Yong, J. W. (2024). Intersecting planetary health: Exploring the impacts of environmental stressors on wildlife and human health, Ecotoxicology and Environmental Safety, 283: 116848.

Constantini, A. (2024). Applying the Doughnut Model as Compass to Maximize the Social Contribution to the Twin Transition. Retrieved from: https://www.diesis .coop/wp-content/uploads/2024/03/DOUGHNUT_MODEL_DIESIS_2024.

Esch, T. (2022). The ABC model of happiness-neurobiological aspects of motivation and positive mood, and their dynamic changes through practice, the course of life. *Biology* 11:843. doi: 10.3390/biology11060843.

Fallah Shayan, N.; Mohabbati-Kalejahi, N.; Alavi, S. and Zahed, M. A. (2022). Sustainable Development Goals (SDGs) as a Framework for Corporate Social Responsibility (CSR). *Sustainability*, *14*, 1222.

Grossi, T.; Rayner, L., Brandy, D. and Dervish, X. (2024). The Social Pillar and The Future of the EU Social Agenda, Policy Study, ISBN: 9782931233696.

Heidemann, K. (2023). Combating Crises From Below: Social responses to polycrisis in Europe. Maastricht University Press.

Johnson, C. N. (2023). "Past and Future Decline and Extinction of Species." The Royal Society. https://royalsociety.org/news-resources/projects/biodiversity/decline-and -extinction/.

Kapucu, N.; Ge, Y.; Rott, E. and Isgandar, Ha. (2024). Urban resilience: Multidimensional perspectives, challenges and prospects for future research, Urban Governance, 4(3): 162–179.

Khan, T. (2024). Circular-ESG Model for Regenerative Transition. *Sustainability*, *16*, 7549.

Khmara, Y. and Kronenberg, J. (2023). On the road to urban degrowth economics? Learning from the experience of C40 cities, doughnut cities, Transition Towns, and shrinking cities, Cities, 136(9):104259.

Korhonen, J. and D'Amato, D. (2021). Integrating the green economy, circular economy and bioeconomy in a strategic sustainability framework, Ecological Economics, 188: 107143.

Krousel-Wood, M.; Peacock, E.; Bradford, W. D.; Mohundro, B.; Craig, L. S.; O'Connell, S.; Bazzano, L.; Shi, L. and Ford, M. (2022). Time Preference for Immediate Gratification: Associations With Low Medication Adherence and Uncontrolled Blood Pressure. Am J Hypertens, 35(3):256–263.

Lazard, O. (2022). Can Cities Use the Doughnut Model to Hack Liberal Democracy?, Retrieved from: https://carnegieendowment.org/research/2022/02/can-cities-use -the-doughnut-model-to-hack-liberal-democracy?lang=en&center=europe.

Ludwig, V. U., Brown, K. W., and Brewer, J. A. (2020). Self-regulation without force: Can awareness leverage reward to drive behaviour change? *Perspect. Psychol. Sci.* 15, 1382–1399.

Michaelsen, M. M. and Esch, T. (2023). Understanding health behaviour change by motivation and reward mechanisms: a review of the literature. *Front. Behav. Neurosci.* 17:1151918.

Mines, K. (2023). There Is a Path Forward in Haiti—but It's Not the One We Are On. United States Institute of Peace. https://www.usip.org/publications/2023/06/there -path-forward-haiti-its-not-one-we-are.

Patwa, N.; Sivarajah, U.; Seetharaman, A.; Sarkar, S.; Maiti, K. and Hingorani, K. (2021). Towards a circular economy: An emerging economies context, Journal of Business Research, 122: 725–735.

Raworth, K. (2017). Why it's time for Doughnut Economics, IPPR Progressive Review 24(3):216–222.

Salguero, R. B., Bogueva, D. and Marinova, D. (2024). Australia's university Generation Z and its concerns about climate change. *Sustain Earth Reviews* 7(8).

WWF (2020). Nature-based solutions and the post-COVID recovery. Retrieved from: https://wwf.panda.org/wwf_news/?364346/Nature-based-solutions-post-COVID-19 -recovery.

WWF (2021). Once-in-a-decade opportunity to reverse biodiversity loss. Retrieved from: https://www.wwf.eu/?4770416/Once-in-a-decade-opportunity-to-reverse-biodiver sity-loss.

Index

9 7 9 8 8 8 8 9 0 8 0 0 6